About the Author

Patricia Jolly was born in West Ham in 1946 into a family of greengrocers. She recalls her early childhood through the 40s and 50s to being a teenager during the 60s with Mods and Rockers and the years beyond to 2008. The stories she shares are of tragedy, humour and sadness.

Dedication

In memory of my mum and dad, Billy and Bette Jolly, my
inspiration.

Patricia Jolly

A JOLLY TIME IN CANNING TOWN

AUSTIN MACAULEY
PUBLISHERS LTD.

A CIP catalogue record for this title is available from the British Library.

ISBN 9781785543821 (Paperback)
ISBN 9781785543838 (Hardback)

www.austinmacauley.com

Published (2015)
Austin Macauley Publishers Ltd.
25 Canada Square
Canary Wharf
London
E14 5LQ

Printed and bound in Great Britain

Acknowledgments

Thanks to John Calloway who suggested the title for this book.

To Theresa, Barbara, Diane, Jackie, Kay and our dear friend Denny for all your love and support over many many years.

AN INTERESTING INSIGHT INTO THE SOCIAL HISTORY OF THREE GENERATIONS OF COCKNEY COSTERMONGERS LIVING AND TRADING IN CANNING TOWN IN THE EAST END OF LONDON 1870-2008

THE AUTHOR

1946 was the year I was born. The Prime Minister at that time was Clement Atlee. Britain had not long come through a war that had left it almost broke. The country was going through a tough time of austerity and rationing. They were truly anxious times.

My mother and father had anxious times of another kind. Mum was pregnant and having a difficult time of her own bringing me into the world. As I grew up I realised that I must have been a blessing in disguise. Watching me grow must have helped my parents in taking their minds off the dreariness of living through those austere times. I grew up to be a happy child and always thought that my surname of Jolly was appropriate to my nature. I became curious and inquisitive about my name and my forebears who bore it, so I set out to discover more about them and how they eked out an existence as costermongers. And that is how I came to writing this book, which is my cue for the first chapter.

The Jollys

George Jolley — ???

William Walter Jolley — Ellen Miller

Willie Jolley | Mary Jolley | John Jolley | Letitia Jolley | Jane Jolley | Joseph Jolley — Elizabeth Watson

Mary

Joseph Jolley | Jean Jolley | William Jolley — Bette Taylor | Iris Jolley | John Jolly | Alice Jolley

Patricia Jolly | Elizabeth Jolly

Richard Jolly | Lynda Jolly | Lisa Jolly | John Jolly | Julie Jolly — Jesse Reeder

The Watsons

George Watson — Annie Spicer

Alec Watson — Liley Romain | Jessie Watson | Joseph Watson | Henry Watson — Ellen Marison | George Watson — Emma Romain | Maud Watson — John Murray | Elizabeth Watson — Joseph Jolley

Alec Watson

Doreen Watson | Iris Watson | Peter Watson | David Watson

Joan Watson

John Murray | Annie Murray | June Murray

Willie | Mary | John | Letitia | Jane | Joseph

3

Chapter 1

I have been trying to trace my family tree on and off, for a number of years. At the start I thought it was going to be easy. I felt I knew a lot about my maternal and paternal families, having grown up with lots of aunts and uncles and also great-aunts and uncles and cousins.

Because of my mother originating from Newcastle I thought that my mum's side of the family would be hard to trace. She had a bad memory for dates and family events. For example, my mum, born in 1922 said she was 14 when her mother, Isabella Rosina Ladysmith Taylor (I love that name) died, making the year 1936. I later found that her mum actually died in 1940 and my mum was 18 years old.

I knew my maternal grandfather, John Taylor had remarried in 1948 and lived in Wallsend, near Newcastle. I saw little of him, so I didn't get to know him very well. But, from the little I did see of him I knew him to be a nice man and I did love him. I will mention more of him later on in this book.

Mum had three brothers and two sisters, Ernie, Freddy, Ethel, Lilla and Eddy. They had scattered themselves around the country after the war. I did get to meet all of them, some more regular than others. Sadly they all died fairly young in their 50s 60s and early 70s. So it was for these reasons that I thought it would be easier to trace my father's side of the family first, as I still had a few aunts and uncles left on the Jolley side of the family. How wrong I was about that! But I decided to go ahead with the little I did find. I thought it would be interesting to see it set down on paper.

When I was younger, I was happy to listen to the stories that were told. Some questions were asked, but we never had the foresight then to dig deeper into the history of these tales. One day we would be very interested to know where we came from, who were these people, and what were they like? Were they different to those we actually knew? I wish I had dug a lot deeper because I might have found out a lot more. But I found out enough to relate the following stories of my foreparents, one of which is my great-grandfather, William Walter Jolley. He turned out to be a slippery little character and a bit of a mystery. The only thing I am sure about at this time is that our family surname was originally spelt with the letter 'e', Jolley.

I think I have pinned down that my great-grandfather William Walter was born around 1870, in Hundon in Suffolk The earliest story that everybody knows and seems to agree on is that William Walter Jolley made his way to London with a friend called Charles Webb (nicknamed Jinksy), and that they came from a farming agricultural background. William Walter's father was called George and he was a butcher. Which makes sense since Suffolk was known for breeding pigs.

London beckoned these two young men trying to make their way in the world. They did odd jobs along the way for farmers in order to gain bed and board. One of the jobs they took was to act as scarecrows in a field, to frighten the crows away. (One would do anything for a crust.) Once they arrived in East London, William W took board and lodgings with a family in Canning Town who were costermongers. This is most likely where he decided this was the business he eventually would become involved with. The costermonger trade was one in which the Jolly family were to stay in for three generations.

William had a bit of an eye for the ladies, and quickly set up home with a very young girl from Shadwell called Letitia Miller. No one seems to know how he or she met. He was

5

about 20 and she was about 17. She had fallen pregnant and had a baby that they named Willie who was born 11 October 1894. William and Letitia didn't marry until 16 December 1895. At this time William was working as a stoker at Beckton Gas Works. With so much fuel on hand he would steal some of the coal and then go around the streets with a cart selling it on. With this side-line he was able to start saving money to start his dream job as a greengrocer and become his own boss.

By 1900 William and Letitia had three more children Mary, John, and baby Letitia. They were now living in Rathbone Street, Canning Town, above the Home and Colonial grocers shop. He was now the fruiterer and greengrocer that he had aspired to be, with a stall in Rathbone Street Market, and also a horse and cart.

Whilst living above the Home and Colonial, William and his wife Letitia suffered a terrible tragedy. Baby Letitia, just seven months old, was accidentally suffocated between her parents in bed. It must have been a terrible time for the family to lose a child that way and so young. Subsequently, Letitia went on to have two more children, Joseph and Jane. Then in 1907 Letitia died, aged 31.

It emerged that William, as well as being a ladies' man was also a bit of a wife beater. The story is told that as he walked behind his wife Letitia's coffin, people started to throw stones at him, he quickly scooped up his youngest child Jane and carried her, thus putting a stop to the stone throwing for fear they might hit the child.

By 1911 aged 41, William had found himself another woman, aged 28, with several children of her own, and proceeded to have a couple more with her, a boy and a girl. Not much is known about the boy, but the girl was called Alice; she became known as Franny. There is a story about how she came to be called Franny. She was quite a small child, and the smallest denomination in the coinage of the time was a Farthing; the cockneys called it a Fard'n. So that became Alice's nickname, eventually it evolved into Franny.

William's eldest daughter, Mary, didn't want to have anything to do with this new woman. As soon as she was able, she took her brothers and sister and set up home in Hallsville Road and looked after them herself. She was just 17 so she was taking on quite a responsibility for one so young. But Mary and young Willie still carried on working on their father's stall in Rathbone Street Market. Their father was a hard taskmaster, very strict in business. But this didn't stop young Mary stealing money here and there to help look after her siblings. When her father found out about her stealing he beat her with a horsewhip. Mary was a strong woman who went on to become a good businesswoman herself with a shop in Pretoria Road, Canning Town.

In time Mary's own daughter, whom she called Letitia after her mother, later became known as Jenny. Jenny along with her husband Billy Crick had a greengrocers shop in Hermit Road and traded under the name of Jen Jolly for many years.

William Walter Jolley was what you would call a dapper man; he would strut along like a cock wearing his bowler hat and fancy suit, as he approached his stalls and those working on them he would call 'Heads up!' meaning for everyone to stand up to attention. By all accounts he was a bit of a taskmaster.

My granddad Joseph Jolley was born above the Home and Colonial shop in 1898, not a lot is known about his childhood apart from being taken off to live with Mary when he was just 13 years old, he probably helped out on the stall when he wasn't at school and learnt the trade he was to follow in.

In 1916 Joe was about 18 and joined the Merchant Navy, Obviously the Great War, as it came to be known, was taking place having started in 1914, but whether Joe saw any of the action is not known. His older brother John was in the Great War and was wounded. He was brought back to England but later died of his wounds. Joe was listed as a Ship's Fireman. I know he sailed to the Americas and the Orient from the many souvenirs he brought back from his travels.

Joe was a good-looking young man with black hair and an easy smile. As he entered his twenties he started courting a beautiful looking young girl called Elizabeth Watson. Liz as she was known lived just a stone's throw from Joe's family. The Watson family were also in business as general dealers; they also had a stall in Rathbone Street Market. These two people would have known each other from very young teenagers.

Liz Watson was born in 1898 to George and Annie Watson. Following her were Jessie, who died in her teens, Then Alec, Maud, Henry, George and John. This was a very formidable family, hardworking, very strict with high principles, probably due to their Catholic upbringing. Liz was about 17 when she went to work in the munitions factory at Woolwich Arsenal. At its peak, during World War I, the Royal Arsenal extended over some 1,300 acres and employed around 80,000 people. The Royal Arsenal by then had the Royal Gun Factory, the Royal Shell Filling Factory (which closed in 1940), the Research and Development Department and the Chief Chemical Inspector, Woolwich (the successor to the War Department Chemist).

In addition to both the massive expansion of the Royal Arsenal and private munitions companies, other UK government-owned National Explosives Factories and National Filling Factories were built during World War I. All the National Factories closed at the end of the War; with only the three Royal (munitions) Factories (at Woolwich, Enfield and Waltham Abbey Royal Gunpowder Mills) remaining open through to World War II.

During the quiet period after the end of World War I, the Royal Arsenal built steam railway locomotives. The Royal Arsenal also cast the memorial plaques given to the next-of-kin of deceased servicemen and servicewomen from the Great War. Liz was a real grafter and wanted to do 'her bit'. While her young man Joe Jolley was away at sea.

Joe wooed Liz for a long time, but she was having none of it. Joe would get dressed up in his Sunday best with his high starched collar to go calling on Liz. The more she spurned Joe's advances the keener he got. Joe persevered and finally won the girl he wanted, and they were married in 1919 in St Margaret's Catholic Church in Barking Road, Canning Town. He was 22 and she was 21. The marriage of two people from costermonger backgrounds would have meant no expense spared and so it would be a very large wedding. (Sadly, no photographs survive of this event, but we know that it was usual for costermongers to have a large group photos taken with the horse carts in the background with the shafts raised).

Joe and Liz took up residence in 27 Brunel Street, Canning Town, close to where they were both living previously because according to the 1911 census the Watson's had been living in 49 Brunel Street. (Brunel St is named after the Victorian engineer Isambard Kingdom Brunel. Canning Town Ironworks supplied the ironwork for the Royal Albert Bridge over the Tamar at Saltash, which Brunel designed and built. Incidentally this is also where West Ham FC originated, they had crossed hammers as their insignia hence the name 'The Hammers'.) There was living accommodation above the shop; it had a large yard with room to stable a horse and cart as well as the stall. It wasn't long before Joe and Liz started a family and first to come along was Joseph junior, then William (Billy named after his grandfather William Walter) followed by Jean (known as Jinny).

Liz and Joe worked very hard and as they had a good living they were able to pay for someone to look after the kids. Her name was Mrs Hawkins. She was a friend of Liz's, but she was Nanny Hawkins to the children, and the kids idolised her, especially Billy.

Nanny Hawkins liked a beer and she liked to take snuff. She would sometimes take the kids to the Queens Theatre in Poplar. When the call of nature came upon her and she wanted to do a wee, she would just lift her skirt a little and put one foot on the pavement and one in the road and just relieve herself. Billy didn't like her doing this and found it embarrassing, but it didn't stop him loving his Nanny Hawkins.

Joe Jolly used to lend money to people. Many people didn't have much in those days. It seemed however, that a lot of them possessed a musical instrument of some kind. Very often it was their musical instruments that they gave Joe to hold on to till they could afford to get them back from him. More often than not the instrument remained his property and he learned to play most of them including the harmonica, but not a lot of people knew this, especially his own children, as Billy was to find out in later life.

27 Brunel Street suffered a few tragedies in its past history and many ghostly stories could be told about it. In 1929, Liz's own mother, Annie Watson, fell down a steep flight of stairs at the wedding of her own daughter, Maud. She broke her back and died a few days later in Whipps Cross Hospital. In early 1948 her brother John (known as Jack) suffocated by turning his face into a pillow during one of his many fits.

Liz liked to relate spooky stories about 27 Brunel Street. One is about the night everyone was in bed and she could hear someone playing the piano in the parlour. She crept downstairs and sure enough the piano was being played but no one was sitting at it; the keys were moving by themselves. On another occasion a funny noise woke them up and again creeping downstairs they found all the cups, which were on the hooks on a dresser, were swinging to and fro.

This prompted them one summer evening to have an ouija board séance. There was Liz and a few of her friends, and also Nanny Hawkins. They were all very serious about what they were doing but a little scared. The ouija board is made up of letters of the alphabet laid out in a circle, with two more words 'yes' and 'no'. The people lightly put their index fingers on an upturned glass placed on the board and wait for the glass to move.

Usually someone will ask a few times, "Is there anyone there?" and the glass gradually starts to move and picks up a bit of speed.

Then one of the people in the circle will start to ask questions like, "Who are you?" Then the spirit should spell out their name by making the glass move to each letter in turn.

Well, in Liz's séance the glass started to move around the board and Liz asked the question, "Was anyone there?" The glass slowly started to move towards the letters and as it did so they were trying to work out what name was being spelled out.

Suddenly, the curtains in the kitchen they were sitting in parted and a large head shoved its way in through the window and made a loud noise. The women jumped up screaming and falling over each other as they tried to get away from this ghostly creature. They found out soon after that it was one of the horses that had walked out of its stable and was being a bit too inquisitive. The experience frightened the life out of all of them, and they stayed away from séance's for a long time after that.

In those days a lot of yards were like farmyards and in the Jolley yard, besides the horse, were chickens, goats, and a donkey. Any of which would cause havoc from time to time. Nanny Hawkins was down on her hands and knees cleaning the front step one day when the donkey barged over her followed by the goat and went running off up the street to be caught luckily by a few local children before the animals did any more damage. My granddad, Joe, brought home some ducklings to join the rest of the fowl roaming around the yard. My nan decided that because they were ducks they must need water to swim in, and so she put them in a high sided tank with plenty of water. But there was no means for them to get out. She was surprised when she came down the next morning to find they had all drowned.

Joe and Liz liked to go out together to the races or other events. Young Billy didn't like to see his mum and dad going out and leaving him. For some reason every time they went out he asked, "Can you bring me back a monkey?" I think the logic there was that if he asked for something to be brought back, it meant that his mummy and daddy would have to come back!

Chapter 2

All the kids attended St Margaret's Catholic School in Canning Town. In those days nuns were the teachers. (They were very strict.) But the Jolley kids were good kids and didn't get into too much trouble. This was borne out by Billy's lovely testimonial from his teacher, which I have transcribed here as follows:

St Margaret's Boys School in Canning Town. July 22nd 1936

Wm George Jolly attended this school from infancy and left in STD VII. Whilst here his conduct was exemplary; his attendance perfect and his conduct excellent. He was intelligent, and industrious, working with success in all subjects. Personally, he was neat, honest, generous, obedient and courteous. He was scrupulous in his attendance to duty. I consider him thoroughly loyal and reliable and can with confidence recommend him

Signed Richard H Sutcliffe (Headmaster)

Joe junior was an easy-going chap just like his dad. Usually it was expected that the eldest boy would follow in his dad's footsteps and go into the family business. Therefore Joe began learning the trade from an early age. Billy also was an easy-going boy with probably the best sense of humour out of all his family and a kind young lad as well; he too was learning the trade of the family business. Jean was very independent and liked fashion and clothes, and did her bit in the shop and on the stall when required, but she wasn't going to be a greengrocer.

Joe senior was quite strict with the kids and one day when Billy was helping his dad off-load bags of cabbage from the cart, he asked his dad if he could have a bike. The next thing Billy knew was trying to lift himself up off the ground after being knocked down by a flying bag of cabbages his dad had thrown at him. That was Joe's way of telling Billy 'No bike'. Billy didn't ask again.

In 1929 Liz decided to buy a shop in Poplar, and so 126 St Leonards Road was acquired. It didn't have a lot of living accommodation to it and so rooms above another shop opposite Rosenblatt's the bakers were also acquired. Liz and Joe, and the kids Joey, Jinny, and Billy, all moved to Poplar. Joe senior and young Joey would go back to Canning Town to help run the shop and stall with Liz's brother John (Jacky) Watson, and Duck Spicer, Liz's uncle. There was plenty of help. Over in Poplar Liz's younger brothers, George and Henry also know as Harry, would help serve in the shop. The whole family would pull together when required.

As well as moving house in January 1929 Liz realised she was pregnant again. In August 1930 she gave birth to twins, Iris and John. Joe Snr asked Jean what she thought of the new babies. She told him, "She didn't like them and to send them back".

Johnny and Iris were as different as chalk and cheese. Iris was brought up like a little princess in the early years, whilst Johnny, maybe showing some resentment, as he got older, was the naughtiest boy you could ever have.

Joe liked a bit of a drink, and could quite often be found either in 'The Grant' in the Silvertown Way, or 'the White House', proper name Hallsville Tavern, in Hallsville Road. He also belonged to The Buffs or the Buffaloes which was the poor man's Masons. One night he was so long at one of these meetings that he had missed going home for his dinner, so Liz got the twins Iris and Johnny and put them in their prams and wheeled them round to the White House where she informed Joe that his kids were outside and he could look after them where upon Liz flounced off leaving Joe with a red face staring after her.

Liz's sister Maud lived in 49 Brunel Street with her husband, John Murray, and their two children, Annie and John. Annie was a hard worker.

It was her job to walk between Canning Town and Poplar making deliveries for the shops. Each journey took forty-five minutes to an hour and Annie did it without any complaint. She would also fill in time working in either the shop in Poplar or on the Stall in Rathbone Street every day. Annie was a 'happy go lucky' kind of girl, nothing seemed to get her down, Billy got on very well with Annie, and she was his favourite cousin.

In 1933 there was a terrible accident. William Walter Jolley fell between the shafts of his cart and the horse that he was driving. He suffered terrible head injuries. He recovered from the physical injuries but showed signs that all was not quite right with him mentally and he started to show odd behaviour. He was eventually admitted into Claybury Mental hospital in Essex where he died in 1935. Joe was devastated at losing his dad, Mary his sister made all the funeral arrangements with Cribbs, the local undertakers, and he was buried in East London cemetery in Hermit Road.

In 1936 Johnny and Iris were 6 years of age. Johnny wanted some money, but neither his mother nor father would give him any. So he came up with the idea of getting some fruit together, setting them out in an enticing attractive manner in a box, which is called a ' show' and then raffle it off. His mum gave him the go ahead to do this and it turned out to be a nice little earner. Later his dad came along and said that he had to give half the money to Iris but Johnny refused, saying she had nothing to do with the basket of fruit. "She didn't sell any of the tickets, so she shouldn't have any of the money". Without another word his dad gave him a clump round the ear, which knocked Johnny to the floor.

15

Johnny knew he was really hurt when his ear felt sore and was bleeding. Right away he took himself off to Poplar Hospital, which was near the top of the road. The nurses asked him what had happened and he said that he had fallen over. They asked him where he lived and he told them, "Jolley's greengrocers shop in St Leonard's Road". After an examination he was found to have a perforated eardrum. He spent the next five days in the hospital. During that time his mum and her sister-in-law Liley both dressed up in their fur coats went to visit Johnny, standing over him saying, "' How could he, (Joe) do that to the poor little mite?" When Johnny came home nothing was ever said about the incident. However, he was allowed to keep all the money he made on the raffle.

Chapter 3

Soon the talk of war was on everyone's' lips. There were bits of paper being waved about by Prime Minister Neville Chamberlain saying there would be no war and then ultimatums given to Germany of which they took no notice. Finally war with Germany was declared in September 1939. It caused a bit of panic to start with. As soon as war was declared all the sirens went off and everyone panicked thinking the Germans were on their way. But almost a year went by before any bombs were dropped. This period of time became known as the phoney war. When the bombs did start to be dropped, it was decided to evacuate the children. But it was only young Johnny who was to be sent away, young Iris was to remain with her mum. At this time they were about 9 years old. Johnny's mum knew a lady who was a devout Catholic and resided in a home run by nuns somewhere near Portsmouth. She took Johnny to this place and when they arrived Johnny was put in a dormitory with lots of other little boys. He found out from these other boys that they were all orphans. This set Johnny off crying because he now thought he was there because his mum and dad didn't want him. Billy went to visit him a couple of times and Johnny begged Billy to take him back to London. So after a while it was decided to bring Johnny back and Billy was the one to fetch him.

Bombs started to be dropped on London in about 1940. Then all hell broke loose and for the next fifty-seven nights German bombers targeted London. Other British cities also got a caning from the bombers. Canning Town and Poplar both

17

had large dock areas and so they took the brunt of the bombing. One terrible tragedy was on September 10, 1940. The then empty South Hallsville School in Canning Town was used to house 'bombed-out' families waiting to be evacuated. Buses were arranged to transport them out but failed to arrive and the delay meant the school was full when the bomb hit. The official estimate of people killed was seventy-three. Locally it was believed that as many as four hundred died. It was in any case one of the worse civilian disasters of the war. The bombing was terrible and Liz wanted to get her youngest kids, Iris and Johnny, away from it all.

Liz's brother, Alec Watson, was a wholesale fruiterer. He had dealings in Kent buying fresh fruit and taking it back to London to sell. He also wanted to get his wife and his son, Alec junior, away from the bombing. Because of his dealings, Alec knew a lot of places and people in the Yalding and Wateringbury area and somehow he found a place in Wateringbury for his wife, Liley, and their son, Alec junior, Liley's sister, Emmy, with their sister-in-law, Nell, and her baby, Doreen. They also took the twins, Iris and Johnny, with them to stay in a cottage with a Mr Sale of Old Road, (Later to be changed to Pizien Well Road). Mr Sale was the brother of Mrs Nell Bodkin who lived right next door. Mrs Bodkin had a daughter called Margaret, who was roughly the same age as Iris and Johnny who were about 11 years old. Mrs Bodkin also had an older son called Alf but he was away in the army. Margaret and Iris became friends and Alec and Johnny found two local boys, who were brothers, to become friends with. Little did anyone know then that in later years Wateringbury in Kent would come back into the lives of the Jolley family.

Liz's son, Joe, had a friend who lived in Pitsea in Essex with his nan. This boy used to go up to London and pop in to see Joe's mum and dad and told them that it was quiet with little bombing down there, and that there were some new bungalows had just been built.

It was about 1941 now. Liz thought it would be a good idea to go and see the bungalows. This she did, and at the same time decided to rent one. It would be ideal for the family to get away from the bombing. Travelling back and forth to London would be no problem. They knew that the train destination was somewhere near Stepney which wasn't far from Poplar. Liz's sister, Maud, heard about the bungalows too and thought getting away from London was a good idea and decided to go for one of the bungalows herself. By now she had a third child, June. So the two bungalows in St Michael's Avenue became a haven and a bit of relief from the bombing. It was a long journey to and from London by steam train, but needs must. So now the whole family had somewhere to go to feel safe.

The move to Pitsea now meant young Annie would have to travel to London every day, back and forth between Brunel Street and St Leonard's Road and then arrive home in Pitsea very late at night, but like I said she was a 'grafter' (Hard worker) and didn't complain.

Joe Junior enlisted in the Royal Navy and was sent to Scapa Flow. During World War II, the Home Fleet was based at Scapa Flow, from where it helped to protect the Arctic Convoys to Murmansk.

HMS Royal Oak was sighted by a U-boat in Scapa Bay and was hit with a torpedo, blowing a massive hole in the hull causing the boat to capsize. Of the crew of 1,400 men, 833 lost their lives. (HMS Royal Oak is now a protected war grave, and each year on the anniversary of the sinking, there are memorial services.)

Following this event, Scapa Flow became heavily defended with anti-aircraft batteries, minefields and further block ships. Later the defences on the eastern side of Scapa Flow were improved by the setting of concrete blocks between the islands to make causeways. Italian POWs were used to build the barriers. They thought doing this was against the Geneva Convention, but were persuaded that the main reason for the barriers was to provide an easy means of access by road for the people living in the some of the parishes.

Joe served as a steward throughout his service and hated it; he wanted to be in the action. The one good thing about it though was that he was able to get plenty of cigarettes and other items that he would bring home when on leave.

Sometime in early 1942 a letter arrived for Billy in Pitsea. It was obvious that it was his call up papers. Johnny and Iris, now about twelve years old, realised what this letter was and what it meant. They took it and hid it. Between them they discussed what to do with this letter. Should they just hide it or throw it on the fire? They loved Billy so much; they didn't want him to go to war. Finally they realised that they must give Billy his letter. In May 1942 Billy was enlisted into the Royal Army Ordnance Corp (RAOC). He was sent to various places in different parts of the country for training.

He wrote many letters home and would often send a letter to Jinny, usually this letter would start with, "If you could see your way clear", which meant he was going to ask for money. Jinny would often send a ten-shilling note to help her brother out. When he came home on leave everyone was so happy to see him. And no one ever asked him to pay back the money he owed.

Billy had a good friend. He was the son of an Italian family called Nastri who lived in Poplar and whose name was Nonsey. Nonsey was a good-looking boy and they got on well together. A little story about Nonsey is that just before the war he decided to go to Italy to visit family and was promptly conscripted into the army. There was a bit of skulduggery to get Nonsey out of Italy and back to England. Lucky for him or he would have been fighting his best friend Billy on the other side.

Liz would often send parcels of fruit to Billy at whichever camp he was at. In those days fruit was like gold dust. Some were in very short supply, like oranges for instance. While stationed in Darlington a parcel arrived for Billy. It was sitting in the office waiting to be given to him. The aroma of oranges could be smelt through the wrapping. A young Geordie ATS girl caught this aroma and said she would deliver the parcel to

'Jolley Bill'. She found 'Jolley Bill' and gave him his parcel and cheekily said, "It smells like you have oranges in there, can I have one". Billy gave her an orange. He decided he liked this cheeky Geordie girl who was called Bette Taylor and asked her out on a date to the pictures (cinema).

Bette hadn't been out with a boy before and wasn't sure if Billy would turn up at the pre-arranged day and time, so she asked a friend to go with her. Needless to say Billy was quite surprised to find he was taking two girls to the cinema. But being an easy-going chap he didn't make a fuss. Billy did discover one thing on that first date, and that was Bette was not keen on the cinema. She fell asleep during the film. In spite of that, Billy and Bette hit it off right away and started a courtship.

Billy's letters home to his family started to mention a girl he had met, and it wasn't long before he asked if he could bring her home to meet the family on his next leave.

Bette had never been to London before and like Dick Whittington, thought the streets were paved with gold. How wrong she was. She saw the results of the bombing and its devastation to East Enders' homes which was due to them being in close proximity to the East and West India and Millwall Docks.

She also experienced what it was like being in air raids. Liz and Joe and the rest of the family welcomed Bette, but they all had a problem understanding her Geordie accent. Bette in turn was having her own problem with the Cockney accent, but eventually they all got through it.

Iris used to love to watch Bette put her makeup on, and put her long dark hair into the fashionable roll hairstyle. Iris said Bette looked like a film star with her rouged cheeks and red lips. It became a regular thing for Bette and Billy to spend their leaves together, mostly in London and Pitsea, and just occasionally in Bette's hometown Gosforth, Newcastle.

Bette's dad was a regimental sergeant major (RSM) in the Northumberland Fusiliers. He had served in the first war and in

1924 joined the Territorial Army so was one of the first to be called up for WWII. So Bette didn't see much of her dad during the first part of the war, but at home was her favourite uncle, Uncle Ab (Auboney Taylor). Uncle Ab always had a roaring fire going and baked fresh bread most days and made hearty warming meals, which were especially welcome when it was cold. 32 Santon Street was a small cottage house in a row of terraced houses with outside toilets which were back to back with another row of terraced houses separated by a cobbled back lane where the girls would play their games with their dolls and prams and skipping ropes. The boys of course would be playing their usual game of football. Billy and Bette would only make rare visits to Newcastle, because the journey was just too long, and getting to London was just easier.

The romance between Billy and Bette was flourishing. Billy always loved telling the following story about his proposal to Bette. They had taken a boat out on the Serpentine in London, and Bette had a go at the rowing and as it turned out was pretty good at it. This impressed Billy (so he says) and decided that Bette would make a good wife. She was strong and could work on the family greengrocers stall. Yes! She was the girl for him, and so he proposed and was accepted.

For some reason known to them, they didn't go rushing back to tell the folks about their decision. The first the family all heard about it was in a letter Billy wrote home after getting back to Darlington telling them of the engagement, and at the same time asking if his dad Joe would go out and buy an engagement ring for Bette. No mention of Billy paying for it. Joe did as he was asked and bought a three stone diamond twist ring, put it in with a letter then sent it back to Billy, by just ordinary post. It's unbelievable when you think that there was a war going on. People were moving about all over the place, and here was an expensive diamond ring stuck in an ordinary envelope with a letter. No one even thought about registering the letter. Billy gave Bette the ring, and Bette was shocked at how many diamonds there were and how sparkly it was, she was afraid to wear it.

The need to spend as much time with each other got Billy into trouble. He was late getting back to camp one night and was listed as going AWOL (absent without leave). He was in fact on his way back to camp when the Red Caps picked him up and threw him in jail. He was able to explain what had happened and he was let out of jail, but the incident stayed on his service record.

Billy was mustered along with thousands of other soldiers for what was to become known as the D-Day landings. But Billy was stood down from this action. It was found that Billy's eyesight was not A1; Billy's eyesight condition was the result of an accident that had happened some time ago. He was in close proximity to a working crane when the cranes grab swung out striking him in the head. He survived the accident but was left with deafness and a slight weakness in his eyesight, which never seemed to trouble him. Nevertheless these slight impediments were enough to stop Billy joining the D-Day landings. Billy felt terrible that his mates were going and he was being left behind. The first person that Billy got in touch with, was Bette, she was so relieved. It was a scary time for everybody.

Billy and Bette spent another leave together at Pitsea along with Nonsey Billy's Italian mate. They had quite a celebration at The Gun public house and all three were as drunk as skunks when the night ended. Billy ended up carrying Bette on his back, but with all the shenanigans all three ended up falling in a ditch.

Billy had learned quite a bit about Bette during their courtship. He found that she liked to dance; she had attended dancing classes from the age of about 12. When she was 16 she got a job in a chorus line and had appeared at the Glasgow Empire. But on a visit home Bette's mother found lice in her head and wouldn't let her go back again That was the end of Bette's life in show business. But Bette never lost her flair for entertaining, and I will come back to that later.

Billy and Bette's wedding date was set for 24th January 1945. It was to take place in Newcastle at All Saints Church,

Gosforth. Bette borrowed her beautiful satin wedding dress from the ATS, but she bought her own veil.

Billy's dad, Joe, having previously paid for the engagement ring now found that he was footing the bill for the whole wedding as well. Starting with Saville Row suits for Billy and his brother Joe and young Johnny. The bridesmaid dresses, wedding cake, the hall for the reception and the honeymoon in Torquay. Billy's sister, Iris, was one of the bridesmaids and as she and Lilla, Bette's young sister, were of a similar age they used Iris's measurement for Lilla's bridesmaids dress.

The whole family travelled from Kings Cross the day before for the wedding. It was freezing cold on the train, and even colder when they reached Newcastle. Liz was glad she had her lovely mink coat to wear. Some of the wedding party stayed with Mrs Dunch, a close friend of the Taylor family she had known Bette most of her life. In fact she had been a bit of a mother figure to the Taylor children, she lived just a few doors from Uncle Ab where the rest of the Jolley's stayed, including Bette herself. There was a bit of a shock when Liz saw Lilla. The bridesmaid dress that she had got for her was miles too big. Lilla was just a little titch for her age.

Mrs Dunch had to set to with scissors and needle and cotton and make emergency alterations, which turned out perfect thanks to Mrs Dunch's sewing skills.

The next day was still very cold. It had snowed overnight. Billy rose nice and early and was having a wash; he noticed his hair, which was normally straight, had developed a bit of a kink. He thought it looked quite good and made him more good looking than he was and he carefully combed his hair so as not to disturb the wave. It can be clearly seen in his wedding picture.

A few doors away at Mrs Dunch's, Bette was putting on her wedding dress and veil. Her dad handed Bette a bouquet of deep red tulips. January 1945 and wartime was not a good time to have a choice of flowers. The bouquet looked lovely and the red tulips against the white satin dress looked stunning. Mr Jack Taylor was very proud of his daughter as he escorted her to All Saints church and walked her down the aisle. After the church service the wedding party went off to the reception where they had a wonderful meal. Bette and Billy saw the beautiful two-tier wedding cake that Liz had brought up from London. As they cut the cake, Bette's brother Ernie who was getting married the very next day to his fiancée, Ethel, asked if he could have the small tier of the wedding cake for his own reception. Bette and Bill agreed that Ernie and Ethel could have the cake. Everybody had spent so many years helping each other out when necessary even though the war years had been a struggle for everybody.

After the reception the family said goodbye to Billy and Bette, They made their way back to Santon Street for Bette to change into her going away outfit. They then picked up their cases and made their way to Newcastle Station and caught the train to London's King Cross Station. It was a long journey in those days and could take as long as six or seven hours. When they arrived at Kings Cross Station. Bette's feet had swollen so much she couldn't put on her shoes. They had to get from Kings Cross over to Paddington Station where they needed to be to catch a train to Torquay. Billy had to leave Betty at Kings Cross with the cases while he went to find a shop that sold house slippers. He found such a shop in Baker Street and quickly dashed back to Kings Cross and Bette for her to put the slippers on, which thankfully fitted her okay. They were now able to get on their way. They finally made it to Torquay where they had a wonderful honeymoon. But all good things come to an end and both Billy and Bette had to return to their units, as they were both still serving in the forces.

Chapter 4

VE (Victory in Europe) Day came in May 1945 and about three months later, sometime in August 1945, Betty found that she was pregnant, and this was her ticket out of the ATS. Bette first went to London and stayed in Brunel Street, but the family thought it better that she took it easy in the country and so was sent to Pitsea.

While the family thought Pitsea was best place for a bit of peace and quiet for Bette during her pregnancy, Bette hated it. It was too quiet. She was miserable and lonely and would count the days till she could see Billy again. But in the meantime she would have to be content with sending and receiving letters.

While at the bungalow, Johnny asked Betty to make a stew with dumplings. Bette had never made dumplings before, so she asked Aunt Maud who lived two doors up, how to make them. Maud told her what the ingredients were but what she failed to tell Bette was how big to make the dumplings. Bette had made them the size of cricket balls so when they were in the stew they began to swell, pushing the liquid of the stew out of the pot. They finished up with one big dumpling the size of a football. Johnny thought this was hilarious.

Towards the end of the pregnancy it was decided to fetch Bette back to London so that she would be nearer the hospital. Betty was over the moon to be back in the lively atmosphere, but it was still hard for her getting to know her in-laws more, and still having the trouble with the Geordie and Cockney accents. When Billy came home on leave he would fall into the routine of helping out in the family greengrocery business taking the horse and cart to market, and Bette would join him sitting high up on the cart next to Billy. Liz and Joe would shake their heads, afraid if anything bad were to happen to Bette while she was so heavily pregnant. They even said she'd probably have the baby on the cart if she were not careful.

Billy realised that he had made a really good match with Bette; it seems that before Bette joined the ATS she had been working for quite a while in a greengrocer's shop in Gosforth. So Bette was well able to help out in the family business. She knew her onions, so to speak.

It was very cramped in the Poplar shop and the family had to make do and mend with sleeping arrangements. So it was that Betty slept with Jinny on a mattress on the floor in the kitchen, while Billy and Joey slept on another mattress in an upstairs room.

One night Jinny felt a warm liquid spreading next to her and woke Bette because she thought Bette had wee'd herself; in fact Bette's waters had broken. Labour started soon after, and all Bette wanted was a cigarette, but no one had any, so they took to rifling through Billy's dad's pockets looking for dog ends, which they found. While Bette was puffing away, Billy and Joey ran down to Abbots Road where there was a public phone box and called for an ambulance.

As they got back to St Leonard's Road they found the ambulance already there. Bette was taken to St Andrew's Hospital. Billy stayed at the hospital as long as he could, but as dawn was coming up he knew he had to get back to the shop to harness the horse and get it into the shafts so he could get over to Stratford Market to buy fresh produce. So he had to go.

He decided that after he had been to market he would take a roundabout route and go to the hospital to see how Bette was doing. This he did. It was about 8.30 a.m. May 1 1946. He was told he had a baby girl who weighed in at 10lbs. He was also told that Bette had lost a lot of blood and needed a transfusion.

Billy couldn't go in to see Bette or his daughter because he had the horse and cart outside which was heavily loaded with the produce from Stratford Market and the family at the shop were waiting for it. He told the nurses he would be back as soon as he could. He went back to Poplar and announced the news that he had a daughter, He told them about Bette needing a blood transfusion and Jinny said she would go back to the hospital with Billy. They tested Jinny to see if her blood was okay, but it turned out that she was anaemic, Billy's blood was okay and so they siphoned some out of him and pumped it into Bette.

In those days you didn't have all the family going in to see the mother and baby, it was just husbands. But Jinny decided to walk along to where the babies were to see if she could see the new addition, which incidentally was me.

Apparently I was an absolute image of my grandfather, Joe, with a round face and jet-black hair. She had no trouble at all in picking out which one I was. I was to be called Patricia Ann, for no other reason than they were the fashionable names of the day, which is true, as I have met so many Patricia Ann's born in 1946.

This is also where the name Jolley changed to Jolly. The story is this. Although my grandmother's marriage certificate, and her children's birth certificates all have the Jolley spelling, she always dropped the 'e' whenever she had to write the name herself. My dad was so used to seeing the name spelled without the 'e' that he thought that this was the correct spelling. When it came to having me registered, the surname was spelled without the 'e'. Years later I showed my dad his own birth certificate and told him he'd registered my sister and I with the wrong name. He just said, "It doesn't matter, does it?" Too late now even if it did!

When Mum came out of the hospital with me, we stayed in Poplar for a few weeks. There was a lady called Mrs Titterton who was very dainty and very posh and she used to get lots of donated things from quite wealthy people. She just happened to have a lovely pram at that time. Mum was quite proud to be pushing me around in such a nice thing. During that time Mum helped out doing a bit of serving in the shop, and one day while she was doing that, my Nan Liz told Jinny to take me to the Holy Child school to have me christened. The church had been bombed and the school was doubling up as school and church.

Nan said, "'If Bette wants to have her 'done' again in the C of E church that was okay as long as she's 'done' in the Catholic church. So Jinny became my godmother. Another lady called Mrs Payne accompanied us; she had made me a pair of green booties. No lovely white christening robes, just ordinary baby clothes and 'green booties' for me.

I was baptised into the Roman Catholic Church. Dad was of course Catholic, Mum was High Church of England, and so the two religions weren't too far different. It came as a bit of a surprise to Mum to learn that her baby daughter had been christened without her being present. A few weeks later we were sent back to Pitsea. There was no cot for me to sleep in. Iris had a large dolls cot so I was laid in that.

Dad was finally demobbed on the twenty-ninth of May 1946, He went straight back into working with the family between the Poplar shop and the Brunel Street shop and the stall in Rathbone Street Market

Mum was so lonely. Every evening she would put me in a pram and walk to the station, which was about a mile away. There she would sit and wait for the train from London carrying my dad back home to Pitsea. This was her routine for about six weeks, she was so unhappy.

Mum was so low that she decided that she would take a trip to Newcastle to see her dad and show me off to her family. It was only supposed to be a week long visit, but then that turned into two weeks, then three weeks. It was becoming clear that Mum didn't want to go back to Pitsea. My dad wrote letters to her to come back home with the baby. (My dad said years later that he didn't think he would ever see my mum or me again). My granddad, Jack Taylor, was telling her that she must go back to my dad with the baby. Finally after six weeks of coaxing and cajoling we boarded the train back to London.

Mum insisted that we all live in London, she wasn't going to be stuck in the country anymore. Ten months had gone since the end of the war. London was safe again!

We took over living at the 27 Brunel Street shop. We had the downstairs and my great grandmother's brother, George Spicer, known for some reason as Duck, lived upstairs and shared the living accommodation with John Watson. Everybody called him Jacky. He was my grandmother's brother and both would help Dad do a bit of serving from time to time.

My Granddad Joe gave my dad a horse and cart. The horse was called Nobby; he was a big brown Welsh Cob. He was a young horse and had spent his life up till that time grazing in a field in Yalding in Kent. The horse must have got a real shock to find he was now surrounded by buildings and noise and living in a stable and pulling a big old cart every day; no more green fields for him to graze in.

Being a greengrocer was real hard work. Every morning dad would get up about 4 a.m. After getting washed and dressed, he would have to go to the yard next door and pull the stall outside. Next, he would have to drag the cart outside, then put the harness on Nobby and manoeuvre him between the shafts of the cart. After that, Dad would get Nobby's nosebag and off to Stratford fruit and veg market they'd go. Once at the market Dad would put the nosebag on Nobby to keep him occupied while dad would wander along, checking out which was the best produce to buy. Potatoes, cabbage, peas, rhubarb, tomatoes, cucumber, lettuce, and whatever fruit was in season. Or what came in from abroad.

As I mentioned before, Dad's uncle, Alec, was a wholesale fruiterer and greengrocer and he was responsible for allocations of bananas to other greengrocers because rationing was still in place. Dad only held one ticket allocation for one box of bananas, whereas his own dad, Joe, held two tickets. So my granddad would often give my dad extra bananas, because at that time bananas were scarce and if you had them on your stall, the chances are they would attract the housewives causing them to buy some other produce off the stall. It was a good way to draw more customers.

Potatoes came in thick hessian sacks by the hundredweight. Very heavy. All the greengrocers and porters could carry these weights on their backs without any trouble; they were really fit and strong.

Cabbages came in thinner hessian sacks. Apples came in boxes. Tomatoes came in 'boats', not boats, as we know them. These were in thin white wooden shallow boxes with gaps in between the slats that held three or four layers of tomatoes. All the tomatoes were individually wrapped in small squares of paper with the producers monogram on it.

All the greengrocers had to pay extra on the stuff they bought. For example a hessian sack might have half a crown deposit, or in today's money 12.1/2p. The apple boxes may have been anything from 3 shillings, or 15p, to 5 shillings, that's 25p today.

For a box of apples you paid the going rate for the apples plus 5 shillings, then the salesman would hand the greengrocer a brass metal token, called a ticket. Around the edge of the ticket would be the wholesale's name so there was no mistaking which 'stand' (the place where the produce came from) the deposits had to go back to. In the middle was shown the deposit amount on it, and a slip of paper would be given. One day every week the greengrocer would make time to 'take the empties back' to the market to collect all the deposits back. This way the farmers got all their boxes and sacks back to re-fill for more produce to go to the markets.

Dad would get his metal ticket and slip of paper, along with the box or hessian sack; everything had to match before the greengrocer got his deposit money back. Quite often the paper ticket would be lost, and you lost out on getting your money back. So if you couldn't return the box to recover your deposit, you would chop it up and use it for firewood (expensive firewood?).

There were two other big markets in London. One was Spitalfields, which was situated round the back of Aldgate just outside the city of London and the other was in the city itself, which was Covent Garden. These markets were further away from Canning Town, and my dad would only go there if he heard that there was a particular produce that he couldn't get in Stratford Market or if it the produce was cheaper.

Once the cart was loaded, it would be back to Brunel Street and unload the cart, put the horse back in the stable, along with the cart and make sure the horse had plenty of feed and water. Dad would load some of the stuff on the stall that he was going to sell that day ready to start 'making a show'. This means presenting the produce in the best way for the customers to come and buy. But not all of it, and so he would have to go back to the yard at some point and get a barrow with more stuff loaded onto it. Then Dad would have to pull the stall up to his pitch in Rathbone Street. Mum was already to go by that time and would put me in the pram and go along with him. This would be about 8 a.m. All three of us would be at the stall until 6 p.m. Monday to Saturday, with a half-day off in the week and all day Sunday. This was the routine each week rain hail or shine.

Our stall was outside Jack William's cafe. So Mum and Dad didn't have far to go for a cup of tea; especially welcome in the winter months to keep you warm. You could also get a bacon roll, or go in and sit and have a plate of food, usually of the fried up kind.

Mum used to take me to Mrs Olley's Pie and Mash shop which at that time was at the bottom end of Rathbone Street (the bottom end being near the Hallsville Tavern or White House, the top end being up toward Barking Road). It was there I would have a basin of mash and liquor (liquor is a green gravy with parsley in it). As I got older I would have a pie as well. This food would usually keep us all going until we got home and mum would cook a proper dinner. Mum said I got the liking for Pie and Mash because it was all she ate when she was pregnant with me. I'll tell you some more about Pie and Mash later.

Mum would leave me in the pram with my dad looking after me as well as serving on the stall, while she went to one of the butchers in the market for some meat or to get some fish from Thake's the fishmongers.

Now add into this the fact that Dad would have to keep the cart in working order, and the horse would have to be shod by the farrier at Poplar, plus having to go and buy hay and oats for the horse, as well as brushing the creature and keeping its harness in good condition. It all made for pretty hard work. And every day was the same.

At that time there was a young black boxer by the name of Cliff Anderson who came from British Guiana. In his career he had a total of fifty fights. He had thirty wins with fourteen KOs, lost fifteen and drew five. He was a really nice man and he and his then girlfriend, got on well with my dad and they would offer to look after me. Especially in the winter months it was good for my mum to have a break from me so she could concentrate more on the stall. She was still experiencing the problem with her Geordie accent and the Cockney accent. She would tell a customer "threy-heypence" (pronounced with a Geordie accent) for one penny and a halfpenny. The customer would think she was saying three pence, three pennies. The Cockney way of pronouncing a penny and halfpenny is as, 'free-a'pence' and the three pennies is pronounced as 'froopence'. There were other names for the money at that time. A 'tanner', for six penny's, also called sixpence. A 'farving' for a farthing (quarter of a penny). A 'hog' for a shilling. Two shilling, two hog, etc. Add to this as well the rhyming slang that was spoken, it was a nightmare for Mum to come to grips with. Mum decided to make a conscious effort to lose her lovely Geordie accent, and pick up more Cockney. In time she was speaking like a native.

I have memories of being in Brunel Street which I told Dad about; he reckoned that I could have only been about eighteen months at the time. My first memory was sitting on an old iron bed with coloured plastic ABC bricks that also had pictures of farm animals on them. I told him I don't remember Mum being there and he said that she used to take a night off to go to the Queen's Theatre in Poplar. The other memory I have is sitting on a big old brown leather sofa watching my mum at the kitchen sink and watching mice run back and forth under the sofa and cupboards. I guess with the storage of oats and hay for the horse, we must have been running alive with vermin in those days.

Diagonally across from our shop in Brunel Street was a firm called W&C Tipples. They were steel stockholders. They supplied black steel, which looked rusty, and bright steel, which was very shiny and coated in oil. As well as being suppliers of their iron goods they also had a retail-shop around corner in Hallsville Road. There they sold nuts and bolts, washers, nails, screws, ball cocks and other ironmongery. Little did I know that one day I would work in the offices of Tipples. With Dad supplying their canteen with vegetables.

In 1948 Mum got pregnant again; she wasn't doing as well as she did when she carried me. Towards the end of her pregnancy she was taken into Howard's Road Hospital in Plaistow. Dad was still in Brunel Street and couldn't look after me, so I was taken to Poplar to live with my nan and granddad and the rest of the family. Dad decided that he wouldn't come and see me because he didn't want me to keep getting upset when he would have to leave again.

I felt the loss and showed my uncertainness in a few different ways. First by saying I want to do a 'wee wee' but saying it too late and ending up weeing my knickers and leaving puddles everywhere. Then almost every night when we all had to go to bed, I would wake up and cry, waking everybody else up in the house. All I would ask for is 'drinky water'. It seemed as long as everyone was awake I was okay. But I must have settled down at some point in time

There was a butchers shop next door to my nan and granddad's shop in St Leonard's Road; it was known as

Hedges. A man worked there who I knew as Eric. He didn't talk like everyone else; he was a nice man, and very nice to me. But, because he talked different, I would say to him, "You talk funny". I was never chastised about saying this to him. It was years later when I found out that Eric was in fact Erich. He was German and was captured in WW2 and brought to England as a prisoner of war (POW). Whilst here he met a young English girl called Joyce and they fell in love. After the war Erich went back to Germany, but soon came back to England to marry Joyce. I realise now all these years later that my bringing to attention his accent, which I now know was German, must have embarrassed Erich. The war would have only been over for about three or four years, but still fresh in people minds. As I begin writing this in 2010. I am still in touch with Erich and Joyce who are now in their 80s .We speak at least once a month. He still reminds me from time to time those words I used to say to him as a child. 'You talk funny', and we laugh.

My new baby sister was born 31 January 1949 and was named Elizabeth Mary, for no other reason than they were fashionable names at the time, although my Nan Liz liked to think she was named after her. I don't remember much about Liz as a baby. She was no bother to me and I never felt like I had lost any of the attention that I had enjoyed previously from my mum, dad and aunts and uncles. So Mum and Dad must have done a good job there. Years later I would tell people that my sister was named after two ships. I would tell them after a pause, the Titanic and the Lusitania. (famous sunken ships). This usually made them laugh, then I would say, "I mean Queen Elizabeth and Queen Mary". We also learned in later years that my sister was never baptised. This really bothered my sister, and I could understand it. I eventually arranged for her to be baptised in November 2010 which was a surprise for her. It was a very emotional little service. I acted as the parent and a friend was godparent. It made Liz very happy.

While we lived in Brunel Street another man and lady would look after me, they were both black, but I can't remember their names; I wish I could because I would love to have met them again, especially as I got older. I remember the man was very handsome and smart and on Sundays he would dress in a grey trilby hat and a grey mackintosh. He always chewed Wrigley's spearmint gum, the small oblong kind with the sweet hard candy shell coating that you had to bite through to get to the spearmint itself. He would ask Dad if I could have one and Dad usually said yes. The point I would like to make here is that at that time I didn't get the feeling that there was any animosity to black people. They were referred to as 'coloured' people then, but not in any derogatory sense. Anyway, Mum and Dad must have been a very easy-going kind of couple with 'coloured' people because as I said before they let Cliff Anderson the boxer and his girlfriend (He was black she was white.) look after me, and then this black couple who lived just a few doors away from our shop.

Opposite our shop was a family called Street. The old dad was known as Streety and he had two sons George and Bobby, I think he had another son called Len who died from consumption. Streety had a dog, I think it was a Jack Russell and she was called Peggy. I loved that little dog. Streety always had a kind word to say to me, and so did George. Bobby never really spoke to me at all. Maybe he wasn't so good with kids to know how to talk to them. Years later Bobby took over a local pub called The Prince Alfred near Rathbone Street and Ruscoe Road and it gradually become known as Streety's.

I remember, as I got older playing down Rathbone Street Market while Mum and Dad worked on the stall. Most of the other stallholders knew who I was. Some of them would also take care of me. One particular woman made such a fuss of me. Her name was Sarah Thake, and she worked a potato stall with her brother, Bert. They mostly sold potatoes that resulted in a lot of 'tater' (potato) dirt piling up around their stall. She taught me how to make mud pies by mixing a little water with the dirt. Sarah swore like a trooper and every other word was an Eff or a B. She could 'Eff and Blind' like any man and it wasn't long before those swear words became part of my vocabulary too. By now no one could stop me swearing, but I had to learn who I was not to swear in front of. And I learned that pretty quickly.

'The Brothers' had a stocking stall two up from our stall. They were two very smart men who always dressed in dark trilby hats and black Crombie overcoats. They looked like two gangsters, an unlikely looking pair to be selling ladies' stockings. Bert's and Sarah's stall was three up from ours. Next to our stall was Winnie's. She sold a lot of household goods. Further along were Charlie and Emmy Allen. They were also greengrocers.

I have already mentioned Thake's, the fish stall. This stall fascinated me because they had live eels squirming in boxes on the stall. I would watch Kate Thake chop the heads off and slit them open, then gut them. That really was an art in doing that. The eels wriggled about so much. Behind their stall was a shoe shop called Zak's. Mum used to buy my shoes and boots in there.

Further along was a stall that sold a Sarsaparilla cordial in thick tumblers. In the summer it was served cold and in the winter it was served hot. I loved the taste of this drink. I have had Sarsaparilla since but it just doesn't taste the same. On the next stall a lady used to grate fresh horseradish. I remember the lady's hands used to be red raw from all the grating that she did; she was a hard worker. Opposite this stall was Tiggy Rance. He sold fruit and veg, and behind him there was a cleaners. In the front part of the cleaners a man worked on one of those big steam presses, I remember how sweaty he used to get in the summer months.

A bit further along near the Flying Scud pub was Joe Bromley; he was a cousin to my dad. Then there were the Jeffords. Of course they all knew my dad and would jokingly holler out unkind remarks about my dad to me, they knew I would get angry about it. I gave them saucy answers back in defence, peppered of course with the swear words I'd learnt

37

from Sarah Thake that caused them to laugh at me. I guess I would have then been only 3 or 4 years old.

Chapter 5

I was about 4 years old when I remember sitting on the back of our cart with bits of furniture and other household stuff. We were moving. Dad had acquired one of the ten brand new shops with a maisonette flat above it in Tarling Road, about a seven or eight minutes walk from Brunel Street. Before the war Tarling Road was called Alice Street. Since the end of the war there had been a lot of rebuilding going on which included the erection of a large estate of houses. The estate was named in honour of a famous socialist called Keir Hardie. He was the first Independent Labour Member of Parliament. He was also one of the founders of the Labour Party. The area of Stepney, Poplar and Canning Town were populated by many of the working class and had a history of supporting political organisations that fought for their cause. Keir Hardie was a committed pacifist. He put up as a Labour candidate in the East End of London at West Ham South in 1892. He won the seat and the rest is history. In recognition for his work in fighting the cause of people like the East Enders the new estate was named after him. They were good solid council houses that still survive today.

The ten shops and the maisonettes above them were the last buildings to be erected. There was Francis's, the grocer and dairy, next was Laker's sweet shop, then the laundry shop followed by Benny Rand's the butcher, then Jolly's, our shop, Hartman's the baker, John's the cobbler, the Co-op grocer, Desmond's the chemist and then an off licence. A lot of these shops changed business over the years.

Laker's sweetshop and newsagent originally came from St Luke's Square. Their new shop had two shelves along one wall, each shelf holding jars with all different kinds of sweets such as Sugared Almonds, Brandy Balls and Peanut Brittle. You could buy two ounces or a quarter. Your sweets after being weighed would be put into little white bags.

On the counter were the cheaper sweets and those more appealing to the kids, like black jacks, and jujus, gob stoppers, strings of liquorice, flying saucers, pink prawns. The sweets cost anything from a farthing to a penny, so you could get a black jack a juju and a string of liquorice for a penny, or four jujus for a penny. This was back in the 50s. And you thought it was Woolworths that started pick and mix.

Old Mr Laker called all the children 'George'; "whaddya want George". It didn't matter if the child was a boy or girl, he always called them George. During the summertime, Mr Laker used to make lollies from cordials mixed with water. They were red or green; which he sold for a penny. They were ideal to suck on a hot summer's day.

Walter Laker took over from his father and moved into the flat above the shop with his family. The one thing I remember about Walter Laker was how precise he was at wrapping anything. If you bought a large brick of ice cream, he would wrap it in newspaper, to help keep it from melting. It was as well done as if he were wrapping an expensive Christmas present.

A lady called Margaret ran the laundry shop. People would bring their washing in bags and some days later it would be returned, washed and ironed and neatly parcelled up with paper and string.

Margaret was a good knitter, and she was responsible for teaching many of my friends and myself the basic stocking stitch. She had the patience of a saint. We would run into her shop if we dropped a stitch and she would painstakingly work at our grubby attempts to pick the stitch up again. Although I can knit, I am not good at it. Something always goes wrong. I attempted to knit my friend Diane's new born baby boy a cardigan, I knitted most of the parts okay and then made a mistake on one of the sleeves, I had knitted a size up. I never got around to unpicking it and starting again. The boy is now in his forties; I don't think it will fit him now.

On two other occasions I knitted cardigans for myself. With the first one, when I tried it on, the sleeves were that tight around my wrist, I swear it stopped the blood flow up my arm. The second cardigan was totally the other way; you could have got two people in it. I gave it to my granddad from Newcastle. He loved it. He said it kept him warm and he didn't mind that the buttons did up on the opposite side. My success has been in knitting little dolls; these come out perfect each time. So I have no idea where I was going wrong before.

The butcher's shop was Benny Rand, they used to cook pigs' trotters and peas pudding and faggots. I particularly loved the pigs' trotters. I liked all the people who worked in this shop. One was a lady called Nell and she lived next door to us above the shops.

All the butchers used to joke with me. I learned a joke somewhere that had really made me laugh; I was such a saucy little kid. I said to the butchers, "Do you want to hear something funny?" and I started to tell the following joke.

'There was a very large lady and she had a little dog called Titswobble. One-day the lady's dog went missing and she went to the police station to see if they had found it. She asked the policeman, (And this is where I started to laugh and could not stop.). I ran into our shop next door to compose myself, and when I felt that I was, I went back into the butchers to finish telling the joke. But each time I would start laughing again. I don't know how many times ran into our shop to compose myself. My face and my belly by this time were aching with the laughter, but I had to finish the joke. Through howls of laughter I just did my best to get to the end, which was where the lady asked the policeman, "Have you seen my Titswobble?" And the policeman replied, "No! But I like to". By now the tears were streaming down my face, my jaws were aching, I was struggling for breath. Benny Rand and his workers were laughing through tears as well, not at the joke I had told, they were laughing at me.

One winter we had some very heavy snow and I made a snowball, then I started to roll the snowball in the snow and it got larger and larger. It got so large that it took me and two friends to push it. We pushed it in front of the door of our shop and left it there. The customers who were inside couldn't get out and no one could get in. My dad grabbed a shovel and had to go out the back way of the shop and get round to the front to dig the snowball away to let the customers in and out again. I got a clout for that.

Hartman's was the bakers on the other side of our shop. No stories about them, but I can tell you that they made the best cream horns I have ever tasted. And the cream buns were to die for.

John the cobbler was next door. He was a crippled man with one leg shorter than the other and he had to wear a very big built up boot. He was a really nice man, and maybe because of his bad leg, in my child's mind I thought he needed help. All the shoes that were waiting to be worked on were just thrown together in one large pile. I would go in and tell John I'll get the shoes together and then I would try to find the shoes that matched; John never said anything he just let me get on with it. But he did used to thank me when I had got most of them sorted. The next day they'd be all messed up again.

The Co-op shop didn't do so well in trading and didn't survive very long. The shop was taken over by another man called Bacon Bill. He used to trade down Rathbone Street. Bill was a happy character, always smiling. He was a real housewife's favourite; they all enjoyed his banter with them. Bacon Bill had two wheat coloured Bull Mastiffs; they were so large, probably from all the scraps of meat Bacon Bill would feed them. They were such a gentle pair of dogs.

Desmond's the chemist. Not much of a story to tell about them really; they also had a flat above their shop. What I liked about their shop was the two enormous bulbous glass bottles with stoppers in their front window. One had a red liquid and the other had a blue liquid. For some reason they fascinated me.

Mr and Mrs Desmond had a baby girl and Mrs Desmond would let us take her out in the pram around the shops for a walk. In fact a lot of mums with new babies would let older children wheel their new babies about, as long as we didn't take the babies out of their prams. We could be out for two to four hours; we would even bottle feed the baby. Who'd let a 10 or 11-year-old out in the street with a brand new baby today?

The off licence was the last shop at the other end of the row. Dad always liked to drink Guinness and Mum liked a Watney's Cream Label. She would mix it with lemonade, and sip it while she cooked the Sunday dinner. It was my job to take back all the accumulated bottles and get the deposits back to go towards the next lot of beer. All the bottles had deposits on them in those days. The most popular drink for kids was Tizer or Cream Soda; if you found a bottle and took it back to the 'Offy' (off licence) it was money in your pocket, because a deposit would be paid for the return of the bottle.

Chapter 6

Now that we had a nice flat to live in we soon started to get visits from our granddad from Newcastle. Liz and me liked his visits because he made lovely rice puddings for us. He was a good cook and did most of the cooking while he was with us to give mum a break.

He would get me and Liz up in the mornings while Mum opened the shop. He used to bathe us in the kitchen sink; he was so gentle with us. He used to pat our skin dry with the towel. Mum used to scrub us dry when she bathed us, so this was a welcome relief. The only problem we had with our granddad was that we didn't always understand him, with his Geordie accent. He had to repeat himself many times before we understood what he was talking about.

Mum's brothers and sisters all came to London for visits as well. I loved Auntie Ethel. She was very funny. Always talking in a funny voice and pulling funny faces. Auntie Lilla, was always cracking a joke. Uncle Ernie was game for a laugh. Uncle Freddy was a little more serious, but he was a very handsome man I always thought. Then there was Uncle Eddy. He was lovely, he was funny, he was useful as a handyman, and he could play instruments. He was a very hard worker. We got to know Uncle Eddy more than anyone else because he also lived with us from time to time when work brought him to our part of the world. He worked on the building of the second link of the Blackwall tunnel in Poplar and also on the Dartford Tunnel. He used to have to go into a pressure chamber;

sometimes he wasn't decompressed properly and would be in dreadful pain from the air in his blood, which deep sea divers call 'the bends'. He would have to take himself all the way back to be decompressed properly.

The disappointment for us with Mum's family was that they all, her brothers and sisters, died between the ages of 55 and 70.

I mentioned a paragraph or two back that I got a clout. Well, that wasn't unusual. I got a few clouts and clips in my time from my dad. I did, but my sister Liz never ever got a clout.

I think I did try to push a few boundaries. I was over at 'The Arches' once (These were arches below the Silvertown Way Flyover), not a very nice place to be for a little kid. I was on my own banging a German's helmet against the wall, a policeman came along, he must have been 6 foot 12 inches tall. He told me I was disturbing the peace, (obviously meaning I would be better off not being in this area alone). He asked me where I lived, I told him about our shop and he got hold of my hand and took me back. He had a word with my dad, and as I stood looking up at both of them, it was then bang! I got a clip round the ear. I didn't go over to The Arches on my own after that.

Some of my mates and I used to cause annoyance to Mr Smith the local caretaker; we were all a bit saucy to him. But I guess that me being the girl from the greengrocers I stuck out like a sore thumb and he told my dad about it. It was a few hours later that I saw my dad and then bang another clip round the ear. No explanation no question, just a clump and then the words, "Don't do it again!" But somehow I always did because the clouts didn't stop coming. I don't think I was particularly bad, I think my dad was being just a bit too strict. But I have never held it against him.

Nobody had much to fill his or her homes with. When we first moved to the new flat above the shop, we only had a couple of chairs, and a couple of apple boxes to sit on. Army blankets covered the concrete floors, two old iron bedsteads and more blankets. Gradually over a time Mum and Dad earned better money and were able to buy the things they needed. They purchased lino (linoleum), and a carpet that was laid down on top of that. Then they got a nice big comfortable three-piece suite. Kitchenette table and four chairs coloured blue. New beds, it all took time but they got there.

Although the flats and the shops were brand new they were really cold in winter. We had a coal cupboard in the passage, whereas the neighbours across the street had to go up the side alley to the coal shed. But even though we could always re-fill the coalscuttle from our indoor cupboard we were still almost as cold as they were. We used to huddle around the fire, which meant we were warm on our fronts but cold on our backs. Mum and Dad used to look at one another to see who would go and fill the coalscuttle, because once you set foot outside the front room door a blast of cold air hit you.

The windows were set in metal frames and they were freezing in winter. We had a coal fire in the front room, and there was a damper at the back of the chimney to let warmth into the kitchen, which was a waste of time. Coming down into the kitchen on a cold winter's morning, Mum would light the gas rings and shut the kitchen door and open the airing cupboard door to get warmth from that too.

My sister Liz reminded me of the following story.

It was always a bit nippy going up to bed and you didn't hang about if you could help it. You quickly got undressed and jumped into bed and tried to get warm as fast as possible. On one occasion Mum and Dad kept saying it was time for bed, but my sister and I kept saying, "Oh! Just another five minutes". That usually turned into half an hour. But Mum and Dad kept on at us that it was time for bed, so reluctantly we went upstairs. But this time it was a little unusual. Both Mum and Dad came up with us. Usually it was just Mum. Quickly we got out of our clothes and into our pyjamas and jumped into bed. But as fast as we jumped into bed we jumped out again. Something was different? It was really hot in the bed. It turned out that Mum and Dad had bought electric blankets for our twin beds. After the initial shock we both got back into our beds again. It was heaven. Mum and Dad couldn't stop laughing at our surprised faces as they watched us snuggle down under the lovely warm cover of the blankets.

Dad made it his goal to warm the flat up, over the years Dad must have used enough draught excluder around windows and doorframes to circle the world twice. He gradually got old coats and blankets and old rugs and carpets up into the loft to form insulation. He got a gas fire installed. The coal cupboard was cleaned up and painted and it became a place for hats and coats and shoes, and as time went by the flat became a warm cosy place.

At the time when we first moved into the flat there wasn't any television and I can remember playing with the knobs on big old radio. It made noises like a skinned cat as you tuned into a station and out of it again. I used to like it making that noise and it would drive my Mum crazy. I was a case of making your own entertainment. We had a big dining table in the front room and Dad would stretch a table tennis net across it and he and Mum would play table tennis.

Mum decided to go to classes to learn dressmaking. Her first project was a dress for me. I remember standing on the dining table while Mum did the hem to the right length. It was green and white gingham, I can still see it now. She never did become a dressmaker. This was her one and only attempt.

What she did though to get us new clothes was to join the Provident Mutual. You asked for a set amount of money and then went to specific shops that took Provident cheques, and then you paid the Provident man back on a weekly basis. This worked well; we used to get our clothes from a shop called Teddy's in Upton Park opposite the West Ham football ground. They were really nice quality clothes. We usually got new clothes three or four times a year. Christmas, Easter, Whitsun, and also when we went back to school after the six weeks' holiday.

47

Mum and Dad worked hard in the shop. Dad still had to go to market on the horse and cart. By now he had the horse stabled around one of his old customer's yards. Her name was Hannah; a nice old lady and I'm sure the rent helped her out. He took on a lot more home deliveries. This meant an extra few hours going round to various customers with the orders they had previously given to Dad. I would sometimes go with him. He would put me in an apple box and cover me with a hessian potato sack to keep me warm on the back of the cart on cold days.

Nobby had been a good horse, but something happened to him that changed all that, back in Brunel Street. Nobby always slept standing up. He was in his stable one night and Dad's young brother, Johnny, sneaked in and startled the horse. Nobby swung his head up in fright and with great force hit a lump of iron that was sticking out. After this incident Nobby became a little nervous and sometimes when out and about he would bolt for no reason. London in those days used to have what they called pea soup fogs, you couldn't see your hand in front of you. Dad was out on a delivery and while he was taking the veg box off the cart Nobby bolted. He was like a bullet out of a gun. Dad dropped the veg and took off after the horse. But the problem was he couldn't see a thing; he would have to stop and listen for the clip clops of hooves. The fog created a strange echo. The sound didn't always come from where you thought it was. Dad knew the horse would be frightened. He had to find it quickly before it did itself any harm or harm to someone else. Luckily he found him a couple of streets away.

Another time Nobby decided to bolt was on the way back from market. He took off down the Silvertown Way. Dad was standing up on the cart pulling the reins back and "Whoa!" while pressing the footbrake down with all his might. Nobby was flying along; Dad pulled the cartwheels into the side of the kerb to create a further drag. He was like John Wayne with this runaway horse. Nobby finally came to a standstill a couple of miles away at the Connaught Tavern. It was really scary for dad. It brought back the memory of his own grandfather's accident years before. Also, it was luck I wasn't sitting in my box on the back of the cart.

One of the worse things that can happen to your horse is if it gets colic. The pain that they suffer is excruciating. There was no calling out a vet to see to the animal, you had to do the best you could with the knowledge you had picked up. There are different kinds of colic; Dad's only thought was to get as much castor oil into Nobby as he could. To do this he hollowed out potatoes, poured the castor oil into them, then shoved them as far down the horse's throat as he could. It was a real worrying time, but he got the horse through it okay.

Chapter 7

Mum was still going to the Queen's Theatre on a regular basis and quite often took me with her. We would walk up Silvertown Way and cross over to a sweetshop called Tibbs; Mum used to like sugared almonds. She would also buy a bar of chocolate. Then we would cross back over the road to go to the bus stop opposite Canning Town Station and wait for our bus to take us to Poplar.

Arriving at the theatre Mum would go up to the box where you paid your money to get in. But... she never paid any money. She passed the bar of chocolate over and the man gave her two cheap tickets for the stalls. Once inside though, Mum knew the usherette and she would direct us with her torch to better quality seats. I don't remember much about the shows there, the only things that seemed to stick in my mind was that during the course of the show the curtains would part and there would be a tableau vivant. This was the heyday of the tableau vivant with semi-nude poses, also called 'poses plastiques'; they provided a form of erotic entertainment. (By the way I didn't know it was called tableau vivant or poses plastique, I looked it up on the internet.). All I knew was there would be a semi-naked lady in a pose who may have been surrounded by leaves. This pose would have been called something like 'Autumn'. Another pose may have flowers and so could be called 'Summer'. It was all tastefully done, though I suppose a lot of people would have had something to say about that.

The other thing I remember was at some point during the show they would get a few members of the audience up on stage to carry out an act in which they may win a Spot Prize. The way the person was chosen to get up on to the stage was that while some music was played, the compere held a mirror up against the spot light, and directed the lighted beam onto the face of the chosen audience member. I remember one time they had to show how to milk a cow. The funnier they played it out the more enjoyment they gave. My mum was a born entertainer. She made everybody laugh. They must have known my mum because she was up on stage a lot, and she brought home a lot of prizes. At the end of the night they always let balloons down from the ceiling and my mum would race up the aisle to get two balloons, one for me and one for Liz. I'm told I saw a lot of the stars of the day, but it didn't mean much to me, as I was so young.

Chapter 8

I was around about 5 years old by now, time for me to start school. Although I was baptised in the Catholic Church Mum and Dad decided to send me to the nearest local school, which was St Luke's primary school which was part of St Luke's church that stood nearby.

I used to like morning assembly, singing all the hymns. The hall had prints of famous paintings, two of which have always stuck in my mind. The first was *Sunflowers* by Vincent Van Gogh and the second was *Laughing Cavalier* by Frans Hals. I liked *Laughing Cavalier* the best though.

Mr Isom was the headmaster then and he was a very kind gentleman. In fact, all the teachers were kind. There was only one that had a reputation and that was Mr Biddle. He taught the 'A' stream classes. I wasn't clever enough to be in one of his classes so our paths never crossed.

Sometimes I got the honour of ringing the bell to call the children back for the afternoon classes. It was great pulling the rope and hearing the bell as it swung back and forth.

We had a school nurse and her name was Mrs Bacon, she was nice and looked after us if we fell over or weren't feeling well. She also aided the nit nurse when she came to the school. I never ever got nits thank God.

I often stayed to school dinners, I loved the way they put the mash potato on the plate with a scoop. Mum would ask me what I had been given for dinner, and I would tell her what had been served on the plate and how it always ended with how many plops of potato we had, which was almost like a punctuation mark. "And we had two plops of potato", full stop.

I made friends with a few girls at the time and one in particular was a girl called Valerie Melia; her family lived opposite our shop. Another girl was called Irene Ruscoe; she was a relation to the Street family I mentioned earlier who lived opposite us in Brunel Street. Irene had an older sister called Rita and their mum was called Ray.

Ray and my mum were friendly and they used to take us three girls to dancing classes at Trinity church hall on the corner of Barking Road and Hermit Road. The name of the dance school was Peggy O'Farrell's; she was a very good teacher. In later years some of Ken Dodd's Diddymen were drawn from Peggy O'Farrell's school of dancing.

There was to be a show held by the school and my big piece was to sing, 'How Much Is That Doggie In The Window?' But the first thing us little ones had to do was a Hawaiian dance behind an older girl.

All my family came to see me make my debut at Canning Town Public Hall. There were about six of them all sitting in the front row. The show started and the Hawaiian set came on. I was nowhere to be seen. Mum came backstage to find out what had happened to me, and there I was asleep among the costumes.

Mum carried me out to where they were sitting and I watched the show sitting curled up on my Dad's lap. (So much for my big debut in show business.)

Another of my little friends was a girl called Maureen Allen. She was a nice girl. Her dad died whilst we were still at primary school. I didn't know what death was or how it made you feel. I remember talking to Maureen about it, and she began to cry. I felt so bad that I had made my friend cry; I carried the guilt around with me for ages. I never said anything about my guilt to Maureen, until I got the opportunity years later. In 2009 I got a message via Friends Reunited. It was from Maureen. I had often thought about her over the years. In short we met and we were just mates again. I decided now was the time to apologise for making her cry all those years ago. When I reminded her of the course of events, she laughed and said she didn't remember. So I carried the guilt all those years for nothing. Maureen did say, "although I don't remember, I forgive you".

Something quite unexpected happened in the early hours on the 1 February 1953. Mum and Dad woke my sister and I and told us to come and look out of the window. I couldn't quite believe what I saw, there was water everywhere, and a boat was being rowed up the street. I think it was firemen looking to see if anyone needed rescuing.

The living quarters of our home wasn't affected because it sat above our shop, so it was the shop that took the brunt of the flood. The next day the water was still lapping the houses and the neighbours were calling out to one another from their bedroom windows. We had gas in our maisonette so my Dad was able to tell the neighbours in the houses opposite to bring a teapot with tea leaves in it and we would boil kettles for them to have a hot drink. Many of the neighbours took advantage of Dad's offer with the result of them paddling across to us. It was a strange sight that evening to see rowing boats coming down Tarling Road and up Bowman Avenue with firemen in them handing out packets of sandwiches.

The yard to our shop was an open one and Dad kept all of his apples boxes, banana boxes, and other empty wooden boxes that produce came in, so it wasn't surprising to find that most of these boxes had floated away. As I explained before, each apple box had a deposit on it. You might as well say that quite a bit of money had floated away. When the waters eventually went down (I can't remember how long that was.) he had to search around the local area, under the Silvertown Flyover and up Silvertown Way looking for his apple boxes. Luckily he found most of them. Most of our fruit and veg had to be condemned as it was unfit for consumption. It hit Dad very hard financially. He couldn't open the shop, he lost a lot of his stock, and it took quite a while to get the shop shipshape again to open.

In hindsight I realise that although this was an interesting adventure in my life it hit other people a lot harder with the loss of life. An elderly man who was a night watchman in Ritchie's the Sack Factory behind our shop lost his life, as did many living on the East Coast. At that time in 1953 it was a much more serious situation.

Chapter 9

One day in April or May 1953 something was delivered that was to change our lives. It was brown in colour, stood about three feet high and had a square face and below it was some round knobs. Further below was a kind of thick knitted type of material that covered a speaker. It was a Baird standard television set, from Radio Rentals. The only thing I can remember watching in the early days was the Coronation of Princess Elizabeth in June 1953. Which reminds me of the coronation street party we had in Tarling Road.

There was one long table, stretched along the road. We had to take our own knife and fork and a teaspoon. So as not to lose the cutlery our parents were told to put a plaster on the end of each piece and write your family name on the plaster. My mum took great care marking the entire cutlery items but we lost them just the same. Whoever organised the event in our street, bought a big box of oranges from my dad for every child to have one each along with the presentation of a commemorative mug. Naturally of course, my sister and I both got an orange, but when we got home Dad took them from us to put up in the shop for re-sale again.

Getting back to the television set, I think the thing I remember most was how the picture would roll every now and then and Dad would sit on the floor and stick his hand behind the set and gently twiddle the knob to get the picture to slow down and stop. Mum would be sitting in her chair telling Dad that he's gone too far and it's rolling the other way. Between

Dad's twiddling and Mum's coaxing the picture eventually came to a stop. We often had to have the Radio Rental man in to replace a valve or something; he came so often to fix the 'Telly' I thought he was an uncle. As years went on we all became adept at being able to stop the rolling pictures, yes, even me

We had several new television sets over the course of time. One of them stood on the floor with a massive magnifying glass over the top to make the picture look bigger. After that we got a table top one. With each new television the screens got bigger resulting in bigger pictures.

The memory of the war was still pretty fresh in most people's minds. Most of the kids knew that their dads were soldiers or sailors. We also knew the name Winston Churchill. I remember sitting on my dad's lap watching television with him and I asked him if he was a soldier in the war. He said "yes". He told me of the time when he was fighting at the front and a telegram arrived for him from Winston Churchill. When he opened the telegram, it said, 'Bill Jolley, you must come home at once, you have killed too many Germans, you must leave some for the other soldiers'. I thought my Dad was a hero, and told all my friends at school. Two of my Dad's customers, who were mothers of my school friends, came into the shop. They told him that they had heard the story of his 'heroic deeds' during the war. Dad had to admit he never left the country. They all had a good laugh about that.

I don't remember too many things about my sister Liz when she was younger, but what does stick in my mind was that from about the time she could walk up until she was about 8 or 9 I rarely saw her without a fat lip, grazed knees or a scrape on her face. Dad used to call her rubber legs, because she fell over so often. The other thing I remember about her was she had a bottle up until she was about 5 or 6. In those days the bottles were glass. Liz loved a bottle of tea with a bit of sugar in it. She would walk about holding the teat between her teeth and the bottle dangling. She loved that bottle.

Although the war had been over some time now the elder people like my Mum, Dad, Aunts and Uncles never forgot the hardship of rationing in those dark days.

During the war food supplies were cut off because of the sinking of ships by U-boats. The government issued everyone who had an identity card with a ration book. The ration books contained coupons that had to be handed to, or signed by the shopkeeper every time rationed goods were bought. This meant that people could only buy the amount they were allowed. Rationing still continued after the war into the fifties. I remember going into Francis's, the grocer shop where a lady called Becky worked behind the counter. She was probably in her late forties or fifties. She was very short and round and she had a big bust; she was just tall enough that her bust used to sit on the counter top in front of her. It always looked so awkward as she cut up the little bit of cheese or butter. Becky would be so precise with her indelible pencil as she put a cross in the ration book indicating that we had received our small amount of butter or cheese or whatever it was you were buying. Another lady worked there too called Mickey who was like a painted lady. She had jet-black curly hair and she used to wear mascara and had ruby red lips; she looked like a film star to me.

Because of the scarcity of foodstuff, my Dad's Uncle Alec would drive down to Kent and buy direct from the farmers and then take it back to London for our shops and stalls. Rationing ended in about 1954.

Going on errands for my Mum has reminded of somewhere else she used to send me. I mentioned earlier that among the ten shops in Tarling Road there was a Co-op grocer. If you belonged to the Co-op you were given a number; our number was 299869, or as it was said 'two double nine eight six nine'. You would make your purchase and then the shopkeeper would ask if you had a Co-op number and you would rattle it off. I have forgotten a lot of things in my time, but I have never forgotten that number.

As Liz started at St Luke's in the infants, I had moved up and had become a junior. I didn't have much to do with my sister at school. But I have to tell you this little story. Liz was placed in Miss Elliot's class, a very elderly teacher; her hair was pure white. One day I was called to Miss Elliot's class, they told me my sister had been crying and needed to be taken home. I could see all this water on the floor, and thought to myself that Liz must have been crying a lot to create that pool on the floor. I took her hand and we walked out of school, Liz was sniffling a bit, and the tears were still falling. When we got to the shop, I told Mum about all the water on the floor where Liz had cried so much. With that mum stuck her hand up Liz's dress, and said, "She's wet her knickers". I was relieved to hear this; I thought it was way too much water to produce just for crying.

Chapter 10

Around this time I started to go to Saturday Morning Pictures up the Imperial Cinema on Barking Road opposite Canning Town Station. Dad had a Saturday Boy Ronnie Pigeon working for him. He used to take a couple of mates and myself to 'The Pictures'. It was sixpence to get in then. It was so exciting. All the noise of the other kids, it was almost deafening. Bits of paper being thrown this way and that and the usher who was a man trying to keep order by calming us down always gave it up as a lost job. The lights would go down and the kids would scream, 'Hooooooooooraaaaaaay!'. I used to like 'Our Gang', who were also known as the Little Rascals, with Alfalfa and Buckwheat and Porky; I can't remember the other names. They were a pack of young boys and girls getting up to all sorts of mischief. But they were so funny. I wonder if they would make me laugh as much today.

The morning always ended with a serial with each episode leaving us on a knife-edge wondering what was going to happen next. The film was usually about cowboys fighting on the range, with goodies versus the baddies. The goodies were always dressed in white and the baddies were always in black. I think the only time this wasn't true was when Hopalong Cassidy (Hoppy) appeared on the scene. He was always dressed in black even though he was a goody. When there was a chase and the baddies were shown, everyone booed, and when the goodies showed up everyone cheered and stamped their feet. Just the thought of it brings a smile back to my face. After the 'pictures' we would go down Rathbone Street and have some pie and mash before going home. I have to tell you this little story before moving on. In Mrs Olley's pie and mash shop, like all pie and mash shops, all the tables were marble and you sat on long benches on either side of the table. Also, in Mrs Olley's shop there was a lip that went round two sides of the walls that you could also sit at. This is where I would always sit. The reason for this was I hated sitting opposite old men and women with no teeth in their mouths and watch them trying to suck the eel meat off the bones. Believe me it was not a pretty sight and it used to put me right off my food.

The first grown up film I ever saw was *Seven Brides for the Seven Brothers*; it was about 1954. My dad gave me the money to take my mate, Val Melia. It was a matinee performance in the afternoon. Val and I sat in the stalls. The film seemed to go on forever, and although we were enjoying it we were worried that it might be getting dark outside and we didn't fancy walking home in the dark. We started to make our way up the aisle, when out of the shadows crawling towards us was Val's older brother, George. He asked where we were going and we told him we were worried it was getting dark. "Go back to your seats, it still only the afternoon and still daylight outside," he said. Once we knew that, we sat back down and carried on enjoying the film. I can't stand the film now!

I also remember our Mum and Dad taking us up the West End. I don't remember which cinema it was but the film was in Cinemascope. It was like a wrap around screen, and it made things seem more real. They were showing what it would be like to be on a toboggan going down a run. I have always suffered from motion sickness, but can you believe watching that film made me travel sick? I told my Dad I didn't feel well and he got me out into a corridor area in the nick of time.

The emergency exits from the Imperial cinema lead you into Silvertown Way. Some of the boys, once inside the pictures, would go down and let their mates in through these doors. Another new piece of technology that film makers were experimenting with was 3D. We had to wear cardboard glasses with paper plastic lenses, one red and one green. We were supposed to see things shoot out at you from the screen. I didn't see it, I thought it was a waste of time. But as I write this over fifty years later, the 3D technology actually does work.

Opposite the Imperial in Silvertown Way was a bombsite with rubble and debris still left there from the war. It was a wonderful place for us to play on. Us local children called any piece of waste ground a 'debris'. It was also a place where people sold second-hand stuff like bicycles and prams and clothing. The biggest customers were black men that we called 'John Johns'. The reason we called them John Johns was because whenever they wanted to know the price for anything they would say "Johnny, how much?" These men were actually Lascar seamen from the ships in the nearby Royal Docks that sailed from places like India. As well as buying second-hand stuff they brought beautiful goods from their own countries. As our shop was just across a road and railway lines from the Royal Victoria Dock, we would get the odd seaman come in to try and sell stuff, usually some sort of textile. I know Dad bought bits and pieces here and there over the years, but I don't know what happened to any of it; maybe he sold it on to someone else.

Photographs

Annie (Spicer) Watson
my
great gandmother

George Watson
my
Great Grandfather

Joseph Edwards Jolley aged 17

Elizabeth Ann Watson
aged 17

Bill
Jolly

Bette
Taylor

Iris   Lilla   All Saint
Church
January 1945

Billy   Bette

Bette   Pat   Billy
          Southend on Sea

AWARDED SILVER CUP 1938

Bill Jolly on stall
Rathbone St
outside William's Cafe

CUP 1938
Mum
Bette Jolly

Dad
Bill Jolly

Mum Dad & Me
Rathbone Street
1947

Jolly's
Greengrocers
23 Tarling Road
Canning Town
E.16

Mum
Bette

Elizabeth   Patricia

Bill Jolly

Ronnie Pigeon
Saturday Boy

Nobby the Horse

Bill Jolly

Liz (Watson) Jolley   Joseph Jolley

Tommy Morrison John Palmer Bill Jolly Tom Nisbett Bert

Pam Morrison Meg Morrison Nancy Palmer Bette Jolly Rose Nisbett Esther

The Lord Nelson Public House
Victoria Dock Road E.16

Ashburton
Secondary Modern
School

Russell Road

Freemasons Road

London Borough of Newham

Ashburton School
1st Year

Maureen Allen · Madeline Fitzgerald · Christine Neal · Val Morris · Henry Hawkins · Martin Brown · Ricky Springford · Arthur Bennett · Irene Ruscoe · Jimmy Heggarty · Frances McKay · Miss Harvey · Pat Jolly

Revd Sydney Goose at the time of his retirement in 1978. Known by all as 'Father', he served as Curate and later Vicar of St Luke's church. He devoted his life to serving the people of the parish and he was held in high regard by them.

Mrs Olley's
Pie n Mash
Shop
Rathbone Street

St Margarets Church
Canning Town

Father
Papworth

Liz
Jolly

Barbara
Neal

Stan Morse Mickey Grainger Pat Jolly Colin Ebsworth Tony James

Pat Morse

Denise Kay Claire Jackie Pat Barbara

Mickey John

Pat Jolly
Rathbone St
Behind
Ron's Record Stall

Ron
(Ron's Records)

Liz
Jolly

Johnny
Thompson

Johnny
Thompson

Liz
Jolly

Rathbone St
Behind
Ron's Record Stall

Chapter 11

The seasons played a big part in the life of a greengrocer, because in those days you could only get the fruit and vegetables that were in season. There was a season for Spring Green, Brussel sprouts, Savoy cabbage, and Primo cabbage these all came in Hessian sacks and were sold by weight.

The cabbages were so fresh from the farm, to the market, to the greengrocer that they still had the snails on them. My sister and I would pick them off and paint numbers on their shells with shoe whitener and then we would put them on long pieces wood from an old orange box and race them. I'll tell you another use for orange boxes later.

Although I was only young I got the job of scrubbing the celery. In those days the celery, as with most all root vegetables, came in still with some root and the earth attached. Dad would fill an old tin bath and give me a scrubbing brush to get the dirt off, and then he would chop the root off. I also dipped the cabbage to get the dirt off. In the winter my hands used to be red and blue with the freezing cold, but as young as I was I didn't think much about it because that's what I had to do.

Fruit that you can't get in supermarkets so readily today are Laxton Apples, Winter Pearmain apples, Worcester Apples, Jonathon apples from America, Spartan Apples, Bramley's, Cox's Orange Pippin apples. You'd be hard pressed to find which supermarket might be selling any of these apples. Jonathon apples, I don't think they have come to this country since just after the war.

All you see are Pink Ladies and Red Delicious and Golden Delicious. They just taste pappy, no flavour at all. Same with pears. You don't see the Comice Pear so much these days in supermarkets. Having a local greengrocer was so much better than being replaced with supermarkets; the produce is nowhere near as good.

Tomatoes! There were different types and qualities. I can't remember how the colour grade for the quality went now. It was something like Pinks were big fat round tomatoes; they looked good, but they weren't as good and flavoursome as a Pink and Blue which were smaller. Then there were tomatoes that were sold for frying, and tomatoes sold for salads. The customer would ask for either salad tomatoes or frying tomatoes, although people could still eat a frying tomato with a salad, it was just a matter of the quality.

Packaging was different then too. Green grapes came in small wooden barrels would you believe? Packaged in grated cork to save bruising them. To display a bunch of grapes Dad would hang them on metal 'S' hooks and hang them from a metal bar. Black grapes would come in a tray of about six bunches all carefully packaged in a very soft tissue paper made into a wad. Bananas were hung up on the metal bar too to keep them away from the other fruit as the gas from bananas spoils other fruit near it.

Nuts and tangerines we only saw at Christmas time. There would be baskets of Walnuts, Almonds, Chestnuts, Hazel nuts, and Brazil nuts. Dad would take some of each of these nuts and make a further basket of mixed nuts.

Dad's Christmas 'show' (display of fruit and veg) used to look spectacular. Packing the fruit was an art. For example, the tangerines would be layered on top of one another sitting cushioned on its own piece of square paper that it came wrapped in.

As Dad worked up the layers he would wrap a tangerine in coloured metallic paper. Working up further he would wrap more tangerines in the metallic paper. Finally there would be a diamond shape or a star shape in the coloured metallic wrapping. It used to look wonderful. The top of the bins would be decorated with holly and laurel and tinsel hung. In the window there would be twinkling Christmas lights. What with the smells of the lovely fruit and veg and the decorations, it was magical. I loved our shop at Christmas time.

Dad sold mistletoe laurel and holly, and of course, Christmas trees. There would be small ones that would sit on a table top that you could buy that for about half a crown, or a bit bigger for five shillings. Bigger still, for ten and six. St Luke's church always bought their tree from us; it would be about fifteen feet tall. I think one as big as that must have cost about thirty shillings.

I remember when I was quite young the Christmases our family enjoyed so much. The tree that we had in our house was usually the one that nobody wanted to buy from the shop so we didn't get our tree till late Christmas Eve. While the shop looked like a magical fairyland our house was bare of decoration. Mum and Dad just didn't have the time to put anything up. So it was left to our childish attempts at decorating the Christmas tree. My sister and I used some of the metallic paper and wrapped tangerines in the different colours then threaded cotton through and hung them on the frail branches of the little tree. The best thing about our tree was the fairy. She was celluloid and had on a beautiful white crepe paper dress with silver cardboard wings, and she held a wand with tinsel on the top. Dad would try to hang the paper chains made by us but in his attempt would break them and we had to make some more. In the end there would be little bits of coloured paper chain draped over the top of a mirror or a picture hanging on a wall.

Every Christmas day after dinner Mum and Dad would put us in the pram when we were very young, and walk us over to Poplar. All of Dad's brothers and sisters, as well as some cousins would gravitate to my nan and granddad's shop in St Leonard's Road. My sister and I looked forward to this as we got lots of presents from everyone. I remember one year we were both given little pink and white slippers shaped like a bootee but on the front in the same material was a bunny rabbit's head. I loved them. After all the present giving, my Uncle Joe would put records on. They were all 78s then. It would usually be Al Jolson because he was Uncle Joe's favourite singer. Everyone would get up and dance and have a good time. Sometime during the evening Iris and Jinny would go down to the kitchen and make a massive tray of turkey and pork sandwiches. There were pickled onions and red cabbage and piccalilli and gherkins. The sandwiches were like doorstops. I never tasted sandwiches so good. Later Liz and I would be put back in the pram for the walk back to Canning Town.

I explained earlier what Dad had to do to get the horse and cart ready before he could set off for market. Now we were living in Tarling Road, dad had a fifteen minute walk to get to where his horse was stabled. He had to go through the rigmarole of getting Nobby harnessed and into the shafts before setting off for the market. Mum opened the shop about 8.45a.m. and Dad would be back from market by about 9.15 a.m. with all the produce. He would get it unloaded and put up all fresh fruit and veg on the bins. (The wooden displays were called bins).

Apart from the fresh stuff that was sold, he also sold tins and jars of produce. You don't see the names now. There were tins of Benedict peas. Jars of Pannet & Neden mint; Pannet & Neden grated horse radish. We also sold 'loose vinegar'. By that I mean that we would measure the vinegar, by half pint or a pint. The vinegar came in a wooden barrel and Dad would knock a wooden tap into it and people would bring in a clean empty bottle for the measure they wanted. This vinegar was called non-brewed vinegar and had a lot of acid in it. I know because the vinegar barrel occupied the same place for years and over that time the drips from the tap wore a dip hole of about 2-3 inches into the cement floor. I enjoyed the job of selling the vinegar to the customers. It was much better than scrubbing celery or dipping cabbage. We also used to sell bundles of firewood; I liked that job as well.

After Christmas and New Year it was the time when the shops took their decorations down. Dad always removed his decorations from the shop. But in later years he didn't bother removing it all. When Christmas time came round again he just freshened it up. But what used to make me laugh was that customers didn't seem to notice that the decorations were still up. Yet every Christmas you'd hear every other customer say, "Cor Bill, yer decorations look lovely". Obviously the freshening up paid off.

I look at the Halloween celebrations that go on today and wonder at how much effort people put into it. Back in the 50s and 60s no one celebrated Halloween. But my sister and me knew all about All Souls' Day. Halloween. Dad used to scrape and remove the inside of a couple of swedes. If anyone has ever cut up a swede they'll know how tough they are just to dice them. But Dad would spend his spare time hollowing out a couple and then cut a face into them, stick a lighted candle inside and stand them in the window of the shop for the kids to see. We didn't see pumpkins; no one would have known what to do with one then. The only pumpkin I ever saw as a kid was a picture of one in a Cinderella story. The local kids loved seeing the 'Swede Heads'. Mum and Dad were Trojans when it came to working in the shop but they always found time for other people not least of all my nan and granddad.

We were usually taken over to see my nan and granddad in Poplar once or twice a week. My nan suffered from osteoarthritis and my granddad suffered from gout. When we arrived at the shop in St Leonard's Road my nan would usually be found in the front room above the shop, while my granddad was always in bed. We always asked if we could go and see granddad. He was a nice granddad to my sister and me. We didn't know that the reason his left foot was always out of the bed was because of the pain in his big toe from the gout. We would get hold of his toe and bend it; He must have been in so much pain yet he never said anything to us to stop it. Sometimes if we were tired we would ask if we could get in bed with him. His answer would be to push the blankets back for us to jump in beside him. On one of these occasions he produced a harmonica and started to play tunes to us. My Dad heard the harmonica being played and asked my nan who was playing it. She said, "It's yer father". My Dad never knew till then that his Dad could play the harmonica. He also found out that he could play the trombone and trumpet. I mentioned earlier how he came by these instruments. (Through loaning money to people.) It just goes to show that even in your own families you still don't know everything.

As we left our granddad always gave us some money to treat ourselves with. On one occasion he gave us the option to either have a £1 note or eight half-crowns (before decimal coinage.) It was 240 pennies to the pound, two ten-shilling notes to the pound, ten two-shilling pieces twenty, one shilling pieces to the pound. If you were born after decimalisation this won't mean very much to you. But this is how it was. Anyway, we had the offer; my sister and I both opted for the pound note each, which he gave us.

He then said, "Close your eyes", which we did, and he said, "Drop the pound note on the floor", which we did. Then he said, "Did you hear it when it reached the ground?"

Both Liz and I shook our heads saying, "No!"

He asked us to give back the pound notes, which we did and he gave me the eight half crowns. He told me to close my eyes again and to drop the coins, which I did; he said, "Did you hear them drop?"

I answered, "Yes."

"Now don't you think you would be better off with the silver money, because if you drop the paper money, you'll never hear it drop and it will all be gone, whereas if you drop any of the coins the chances are you'll hear it and so you won't lose it." Aren't granddad's great?

Dad liked to go horseracing and the two meetings he liked most at that time were Derby Day at Epsom and Gold Cup Day or Ladies Day at Royal Ascot.

In 1955 there had been a rail strike and the Royal Ascot meeting was moved from its usual slot in June back a month to July. The Gold Cup meeting was on a Thursday. The day for us started off okay. Mum and Dad took us in the Silver Ring because there was a crèche there run by nurses. But first we would be taken down to the rails to watch the Royal Party go by in their landaus and we would wave to the queen, then we would be taken to the crèche where my sister, Liz, and I played quite happily. Mum and Dad always came back to check on us between races, it was okay. Sometime in the afternoon it started to rain and it began to come down really heavy. At that same time there was a violent thunderstorm. It was around the time when the Gold Cup had been run. The rain was torrential. With the downpour of the rain there came the deafening sound of thunder. Suddenly there were flashes of lightning that went to earth on a metal fence near to where the bulk of the crowd were sheltering. The shock threw the race-goers to the ground with many of them experiencing temporary blackouts. Scenes in the enclosure were chaotic. The nurses gathered me and my sister and some other children and raced us across to a white building that I remember had a big red cross on it. I have checked back on that event and found that forty-two people were injured, and eighteen were kept in hospital at Windsor. But worse still was that two people died of the injuries they had received in the storm. One was a lady who was pregnant, and the other was a man. I was worried that our Mum and Dad wouldn't know where we were now, but they found us okay. I think it was just a matter of waiting till the rain eased off so we could make our way home.

Chapter 12

I want to tell you about some of the children's games that we played. The East End took a knock in the war, especially in the dock area. It had suffered a lot of bombing. There were still many area's that were derelict with debris and crumbling buildings. These areas and bombed out buildings became our playgrounds. One of these buildings was a pub called The Railway; it was on the corner of Tarling Road and Victoria Dock Road. All the boys and girls were able to climb through a window. There was a wooden beam to throw a piece of old rope over to swing on. I can't ever remember anyone telling us, "Don't go there, because you could get hurt." Another place was in the opposite direction. We called it the nursing home, but whether it ever was or not, I really don't know. It was just another good place to have an adventure in.

Behind our shop was 'debris' (A bombed site relic of the Blitz) that we played on. There was always plenty of wood around and we would make little bonfires. I would get potatoes (taters) from our shop and we would cook them over the fire; they tasted delicious.

We played all the other normal games, like hopscotch, and one we called bally hopscotch. Instead of throwing a piece of slate we rolled a ball. Then there was skipping. In the summer the mums would sit on their walls in front of their houses and we would have a really long rope, long enough to stretch from one side of the road to the other. The mums would turn the rope for us and we would run in and out of the rope singing our songs:

'All in together, girls, never mind the weather, girls, when I count to twenty, the rope must be empty.'

'Jelly on a plate, jelly on a plate, wibble wobble wibble wobble, jelly on a plate.'

'I am a Girl Guide dressed in blue, these are the actions I must do:

Salute to the Captain, bow to the Queen, and turn my back, to the boy in green.'

And my favourite one. 'On a mountain stands a lady, who she is I do not know. All she wants is gold and silver. All she wants is a nice young man so come in (call the name of a boy e.g. Billy) Billy dear, Billy dear, Billy dear, so come in Billy dear while I go out to play.' The boys in our street always joined in the skipping with the girls, who made us proud to think that they didn't mind playing some of the girl's games.

We also played with balls, one of the well-known ones was: 'One, Two, Three, O'Leary.' You would bounce the ball and chant 'One, Two, Three, O'Leary. Four, Five, Six, O'Leary. Seven, Eight, Nine, Ten O'Leary.' But every time you said 'O'Leary' you would bounce the ball and swing your leg over it. You could do all kinds of stunts.

We would play cricket and football with the boys. As well as Tin Can Tommy, Knock Down ginger, Run Outs, and Kiss Chase.

All the games came in seasons each year. Roller Skating became popular. All the kids were getting 'Jacko' skates; they had rubber wheels with ball bearings. I asked Father Christmas to bring me some skates but I forgot to mention in my letter that they should have been 'Jacko' Skates. I thought Father Christmas would have known, but no He didn't! He brought me all metal skates. I was so upset; it was my Mum who sorted out Father Christmas's balls up. She went straight to the toyshop and came back with the right skates. Once those skates were on my feet, they never came off except when I went to bed.

The surface in front our shops was so smooth, which is where I learned how to skate. But I wanted to learn more, I wanted to turn round by gliding my skates at the ends of the smooth patch. I practised that glide so many times, and finally I cracked it. I skated back to our shop and called out to my Mum.

"Mum! Come and watch me skate and turn round."

Mum came and stood at the shop doorway watching me. Off I went. I didn't do very well with the turning and fell over at each attempt. Mum started laughing; she said to call out to her when I could do it.

"But, I can do it, I do it all the time but every time I call you, I fall over." Eventually I did become quite adept at skating and could do all sorts of tricks. Dad decided to take us to Forest Gate, Skating Rink, I thought I'd died and gone to heaven. Mum and Dad put skates on as well and I couldn't believe my eyes to see that they could both skate. You don't think your Mum and Dad can do those sorts of things.

I spoke earlier about oranges boxes and another thing you could do with them. Orange boxes were about thirty inches tall and were divided into two; each orange was individually wrapped in a square piece of paper, that's how the oranges came in. All the boys and girls started making carts, my sister and me were too young to make a cart ourselves so our Dad made one for us; mind you we had to give up our dolls pram to get it.

Dad made the basic cart and then went one better, he got an orange box took one end out so you could sit in it. It also gave the front passenger a back rest and then the compartment behind would take a smaller person, my sister. He put the string onto the front axles and hey presto we had a Rolls Royce cart. Dad pushed us up and down the road and we thought it was fantastic. But the problem with that was, the cart was only a good game when you had someone to push you. My sister was too little to push me, and there wasn't anyone else, it wasn't so good after all. I got more fun out of the dolls' pram that we could no longer use because there were no wheels on it.

Dad often made things for us to play with. He got two tin cans, punched two holes in the end of each can and threaded string, long enough for us to hold. So we would walk on the tin cans holding the string. Dad also made me some stilts, from a couple of bits wood he pinched from a lady's garden fence; he nailed a block of wood to each length of wood and I became a good foot taller.

I could play out in all weather's. Talking about what Dad made out of different things, let me tell you about another one of his ideas. One terrible rainy day I was getting soaked but it didn't stop me from enjoying playing, but Mum and Dad were obviously concerned, and called me to come in a few times, but I wouldn't. Dad came and caught me and took me back to the shop, I told him I wanted to go out and play and he said I still could but I had to wear something to cover me up. What he then did was to get a heavy potato sack he pushed one corner in the other, and then used it to cover my head and shoulders and back, The sack was so long it clipped the back of my heels as I walked. I bet I looked a right picture, but I didn't care I was having fun and nothing would stop me. The coalmen used to wear a coal sack this way too in bad weather, to save all the water dripping off the coal falling on to them.

A bunch of friends and me used to sit on the corner of Tarling Road and Victoria Dock Road and collect car numbers. Why? I have not got the faintest idea why. We never did anything with them, yet we would sit there for hours watching the cars and fill pages and pages with letters and numbers.

This spot was particularly good when it was coming up to Guy Fawkes night. The boys would make a fantastic guy and on the days leading up to bonfire night we caught many of the dockers for a, 'Penny for the guy', as they were going home. We did all right. We were rolling in money. The money was put into a pool, shared with some other groups of kids with whom we had one big bonfire on the debris. The bigger boys would collect the wood and build the massive bonfire. I remember one time the boys told me to go into the local undertakers and ask if they had any empty boxes, for which I was chased out of the shop. The boys were all laughing at me but I didn't know why. It was years later that I realised what the joke was.

A couple of adults bought our fireworks and sparklers and let them off for us. I loved the Rockets and the Jumping Cracker Jacks, and even the silver and golden fountains. But what I couldn't stand was the Catherine Wheel. Year after year someone would nail a Catherine Wheel onto a standing piece of wood, and year after year the bloody thing hardly ever spun round, if it did ever spin it would drop to the ground and make off never to be seen again. I'd have rather had another silver fountain and forget the Catherine Wheel altogether. As the bonfire died down leaving a rosy glow of red ashes we would sit there while Dad got out a couple of dozen potatoes distributing them to all present for them to roast their own. We had a cracking night.

There used to be a man who came round the streets with a horse and cart. The back of the cart had been adapted to hold a large round drum that had a seat which went all the way around inside for four or five children to sit on. He would spin the drum just with his hands. We would pay a penny for a ride in this contraption, but it was great. Sometimes he would take jam jars as payment.

I must tell you about getting my first bike. I was playing in the road at the back of our shop. It was afternoon time. I heard the clip clop of Nobby's hooves coming down the road; it was Dad and Nobby coming back from Stratford Market after taking the empties back. I stood and watched waiting for them to come around the corner. What followed next appeared to happen in slow motion. First I saw Nobby, then I saw my dad sitting on top of the cart, and then my eye caught sight of a three wheel bike on the back of the cart. I waited as he pulled Nobby up and Dad jumped down from the cart. "Who's that bike for?" I said. "What bike?" answered Dad, "That one there," I said. He walked to the side of the cart and lifted the bike off and put it on the ground. It was red and white with a white metal basket on the front. My eyes were popping out of my head at this beautiful piece of metal. After a long pause, he said that it was for Liz, and me, and we had to share it. I thought to myself that it would be fine; Liz wasn't quite big enough then to actually ride it on her own. So I will get the most use out of it. Liz was able to stand on the back axle and hold on to my shoulders while I peddled. It wasn't long before she was able to peddle it herself. The memory of my first sight of that bike on the back of the cart still takes my breath away.

Chapter 13

I'd like to mention a few traditions that people don't do now or that have since fell out of favour for one reason or another.

There were the New Year traditions. It was lucky for the people who lived in the house if the first person that called on them brought a lump of coal. Imagine over fifty years later I find out that this tradition actually has a name and it's called 'First Footing'.

The kids would come out front and bang the dustbin lids and everybody would be calling across the street to one another 'Happy New Year', That's if you could hear them over the noise of all the ships in the docks blowing their hooters. What a sound that was, the docks were filled to bursting point with all the ships moored there. The sounds filled the night. Just thinking about it raises the hairs on the back of my neck.

It used to be traditional for a bride to have a sprig of myrtle in her bouquet, for fertility.

When a new baby was seen out and about with its mother, and you were seeing it for the first time you would put a silver coin in its hand for luck.

When you went to the cinema or the theatre, at the end of the evening the national anthem was always played and everyone stood up and waited till it was finished before leaving the cinema or theatre. I think they should bring this one back.

Another time the national anthem was played was every single night at the end of the night's television broadcast. Then the TV being switched off while we watched the white spot in the middle of the screen disappear.

If you saw an ambulance, there was a little rhyme we said. 'Touch your collar, touch your toes, hope never to go in one of those.

Another little rhyme we sang when it rained was 'Rain. Rain. Go away, come back another day'.

Chapter 14

Thursday afternoons were mum and dad's half day off from the shop. Dad always took us out for the afternoon. I don't know how my sister and I were allowed to get away with having most every Thursday afternoon off from school, but we did.

My sister and I were taken to museums, and parks and places like Hampton Court and Greenwich Observatory. But what we enjoyed most was going up the West End and having a walk along Oxford Street and Bond Street. Sometimes our Dad bought us something; my sister and I didn't ask for anything, Dad just treated us.

On those days up the West End we would always go to the brasserie at Lyons's Corner House near Oxford Street. It was a beautiful restaurant. All the waiters wore black suits, bow ties and white aprons. There was a small band that played all the music from the current shows in the West End.

We weren't very adventurous with trying things on the menu and so we always had minestrone soup, which was delicious. Fish and chips followed this. I can remember the first time we went to the brasserie, there were bread sticks in the middle of the table and my sister picked one up and started to eat it. My Dad told her to stop it in case we had to pay for them, but a waiter overheard and said they were free, and so after that we devoured them all and the waiters always brought more.

Many times whilst at the brasserie a waiter would trip up and all the plates and their food covers would go flying, and the next time we would go we would try to spot the waiter who tripped to see if he would do it again.

After having our meal we would either go to the London Palladium or the Prince of Wales to see a show. In those days a variety show would run for two weeks and so we could see a new show every week almost. Sometimes we would see a film instead. I think somewhere near the Strand there was a theatre that showed all cartoon films like *Tom and Jerry* and *Tweety Pie*.

When it got dark we would walk round to Leicester Square. It was fascinating seeing all the ladies and men dressed up in their evening clothes going from one venue to another. The ladies wore beautiful dresses. Sometime we would see someone famous. We saw Petula Clarke once just walking along the street. Another time we saw Max Bygraves. Dad was always good at spotting the celebrities.

In the middle of the road outside the Leicester Square Empire there were two men who did a sand-dance just like the one that Wilson, Betty and Kepple did. They were very funny and were always having a bit of banter with the taxi drivers.

By the end of the day, my feet and legs were aching, but I was too big by that time to be picked up and carried, but my sister wasn't and Dad would scoop her up in his arms, and I would wish it were me.

Mum always dressed Liz and me to look very nice for our trip up the West End. We usually caught one of the 669 buses from the Silvertown Way to Plaistow Station. On one occasion Dad's brother, Johnny, came over to drop something off and when he heard we were going up the West End he said he would give us a lift on the lorry. Dad said okay and when we got to Johnny's lorry is stunk to high heaven. He had out of the blue decided to become a pig farmer with his brother-in-law, Alf Reeder. The pig farm was near Whalebone Lane, which was on the outskirts of East London. Johnny used the lorry to take the swill to two hundred pigs three times a day, so you can imagine the smell. We just stood on the back of the lorry holding on for dear life trying not to let our clothes touch anything. The smell was so strong it made you want to gag. I tried holding my breath but when I had to breathe I had to take in bigger breaths, which didn't help. It was easier just to breath as shallow as possible.

I have to tell a story here about, George, the pig. Johnny turned up at my nan's shop one day with a tiny piglet, the runt of the litter. My nan never batted an eyelid when Johnny gave her the piglet. She straightaway started to treat it just like a puppy dog, and like any dog it had to have a name. So she called it George. It wasn't very long before George was following her around just like a puppy. He would walk around the shop and the customers would pet him, he looked so cute. But in a short time with all the good food my nan fed him he started to grow. When it came to feed times she would shout, "George, come and have you dinner", and the pig would come running. George finished up a fine figure of a pig, he was enormous. George was a health hazard in a greengrocer's shop and so he was finally given back to Johnny for slaughter. I bet whoever got a bit of George on their dinner plate either as a pork chop, or piece of bacon or a sausage, had a real juicy meal because all the lovely grub he was fed.

Chapter 15

When the darker nights of late summer set in we would go to Southend by train to see the lights. There would be crowds of people who had come down on a 'Beano' by coach. The young men and women would all be wearing 'Kiss me Quick' hats, walking arm in arm along the esplanade. Popping in and out of the places with slot machines or going from one pub to another. Buying souvenirs of their day trip, pink rock, with Southend written all the way through it. Eating fish and chips or ice cream. The ice cream was delicious. It was made by Rossi's and this was the first place I ever tasted chocolate ice cream.

We would go on the Southend Pier and get the train to the end. You could walk it if you wanted to, or pay to go on the train. I guess it depended how much time you had to spare because the Pier was the longest in the world at over a mile long. Southend Pier has always been popular, and pleasure steamers such as *Crested Eagle*, *Royal Daffodil*, *Golden Eagle*, *Medway Queen* would take you from the end of the pier to Clacton, Margate, Walton-on-the Naze, and a few other places.

When my Dad was younger he wanted to go to sea. My nan knew a man who worked on the *Crested Eagle* and he got my dad a job as a steward. He did all sorts of jobs like washing up and serving food, or getting drinks for people. The *Crested Eagle* was travelling between Southend and Clacton and my Dad said he was seasick five times. He only lasted one day. It cured him of wanting to go to sea, and he became known in the family as 'The One-day Sailor'.

Along the esplanade was a cabin where you could make your own record. A man would play a piano and he would do the recording as well. My Mum was a pretty good singer. My sister and I even made a record with her. It was called 'Heart of my Heart', originally recorded by the Four Aces. Mum made quite a few records over the years; we just haven't got the record players these days to play them on.

The records were made of shellac and very brittle. They weren't very big, about the same size as a 45, but had to be played at 78rpm. The ordinary 78s were larger and heavier. Later in the 60s when 45s came out people found that if you put an old 78 record in hot water it would become pliable and people started making flowerpot holders out of them by making them into a kind of frilly shape.

The Kursaal was another attraction. It used to cost sixpence to go through the turnstiles, which were operated by uniformed ushers who looked very smart. You were undercover for the first part of entering the Kursaal. There was a big ballroom and bar. I never ever saw inside it. Then there were a few sideshows; one was 'Tip the Lady out of Bed'. A ball was thrown at a target and if successful a scantily dressed lady was tipped out of the bed to roars of wolf whistles from the young men

The next big thing was the cakewalk. These were two walkways that had a moving motion that threw you forwards as you tried to walk. The operator could speed it up or slow it down. There was an unsuspecting thing that happened as the ladies got off. As they trod on a pressure pad a whoosh of air blew their dresses up.

There was a water chute, People got into a boat that held about twelve people and then it was manoeuvred toward a ratchet system and taken high up and then rolled round the to the chute. The boat was released to come down under its own weight. It came speeding down and into a pool of water; the people got wet but the rush of excitement was clear on their faces. The boat would then be pulled to the side by men with hooks and loaded with people again then dragged to the ratchet to take it up again.

There was the wall of death where motorcyclists rode round a small area at high speed high up on the wall you could almost touch the rider.

Another ride that was good to watch was the 'Wall'. People went inside this circular area and were told to stand with your backs against the wall. The whole thing would then start to revolve and get faster and faster, then the floor would drop away and the centrifugal force would keep the people stuck to the wall. My Dad went on this once and all the change came out of his pockets. After the thing had stopped spinning he had to scramble on the floor to recover it.

Canvey Island was a nice little place to visit; it was small in comparison to Southend. It did have a funfair and not much else apart from a pub for the grown ups. The thing I liked best was the Helter Skelter. At the bottom the Helter Skelter you rode on your mat into a big wooden bowl. We used to call it the Sugar Bowl. It was very slippery trying to get out and there was a rope with knots in it on the side that you had to pull yourself up on.

My sister and I used to go on the beach and collect seaweed for my nan to put in her bath. My mum told us that seaweed was good for arthritis, which my nan had very badly.

Canvey didn't get the same crowds as Southend so it was more comfortable to sit and relax if you wanted to.

Chapter 16

I was about 9 or 10 when my idyllic little life of being happy and carefree, and unafraid was to change.

It was wintertime. The dark nights had set in and all the shops in our parade were closed except the sweet shop Lakers and the off licence. It was about 6.30p.m., our shop shut at 6 p.m. and I was having an extra bit of playtime while I waited for Mum to call out of the window to come and get my dinner.

I was playing with my best friend, Val Melia. She had her skates on and I was pulling her along by her hand and then letting her go, and off she would go at high speed. We came to a standstill outside the off licence. It was there when a man approached us. He started to talk to us and told us that he was supposed to be going to his niece's birthday party but he wouldn't be able to get there and asked if we would take a message. He would give us five shillings. The money didn't faze me, because I more or less took what I needed out of the till in our shop. But Val came from a large family and money was tight for them, so the prospect of five shillings for an errand was acceptable. The man said he had to write the note and invited Val and I to go with him around to the back of our parade of shops, to where the debris were and all the factories. I was scared, this didn't seem right.

Some kids had left a small bonfire burning on the debris and the man said he should put it out and asked us to go with him. I was really scared by now and hanging back. Val was right behind him even though she still had her skates on. The man then led us to the back of a factory wall and told me to stand in one place and for Val to stand in another place and to tell him if anyone come along. By now I was shaking, my heart was pounding, my teeth were chattering, my throat was constricted with fear.

Suddenly the man called out, "Oi! Turn round, do you want some more money?" I turned round and saw that he was playing with something in front of him, and knew that whatever it was it was he was doing was really very wrong.

I found my voice and screamed, "Run Val!" and we both ran as fast as we could off the debris. I remembered that Val still had her skates on. She skated straight home, her house was opposite our shop. I ran up the stairs to get to the flats where I lived. I was screaming and crying and knocking on the front door of our house. My Mum opened it and I tried to tell her what happened, she called my Dad and I tried to tell him. He understood and grabbed my hand and dragged me out of the house to see if we could find this man from the description I gave. We walked around a lot of places but we never found him. We had to walk because we never had a car or anything at that time.

I remember having to go to bed that night, I couldn't get the pictures out of my head and I was still shaking and shivering. My sister was already asleep. My Mum and Dad came and stayed in the bedroom with me because I couldn't stop shaking. I remember them giving me my sister's Teddy bear to hold, it was a musical one and played four and twenty blackbirds.

I was scared for a long time after that, and ended up having a bit of a sixth sense about dirty old men. I encountered a few more of them as the years passed, but not as frightening as this first experience.

Chapter 17

At the end of Tarling Road was a building called the Victoria Dock Mission. A man called Mr Reeves ran it and his wife helped him, but he was the mainstay of the mission. They held a Sunday school and at every attendance your Sunday school card, would be stamped with a star. Sunday school was held in a small room upstairs and we would sing catchy little songs. I am 'H.A.P.P.Y' was one, and, 'Give me oil in my lamp keep it burning', was another. I liked Sunday school. At the end of each lesson we were given a little coloured religious card depicting the lesson we had just received. I still have my Sunday school card and many of the little religious cards. When we got older we could go to another part of the Mission and sing normal hymns with the rest of the congregation. I will talk more about Mr Reeves later.

At the other end of Tarling Road was a very large imposing church, almost cathedral like, called St Luke's, it was magnificent inside. It had a vaulted ceiling, large pillars, beautiful stained glass windows and a wall painted with all the saints in shiny gold leaf. I've check and found it was consecrated in 1875. I never heard that it suffered at all during the bombing in WWII. I believe it has now been turned into a community centre.

As the church was part of the primary school of the same name, we would also go there for services too. The biggest service that we would go to that I really enjoyed was Harvest Festival. My granddad sent prize leeks down from Newcastle, they were enormous. They certainly looked good sitting up there under the altar. I bet there wasn't much taste to them though, so I feel sorry for the person who ended up with any of them.

I have to mention Father Goose, he was a priest at St Luke's Church and was tall and thin with a long neck. I was really young when this event that I am about to relate to you happened. Father Goose would often come into the shop at just about the time Dad was about to close. I often heard my dad curse about this by saying, "That f**ing Father Goose came in again just as I was about to shut up".

One late afternoon just before Dad was about to close up shop, Father Goose came in, and I was heard to shout, "Dad, that f**ing Father Goose is here again". My Dad came running in the shop, pulled me round the back, gave me a good hiding and then apologised to Father Goose. I was bewildered; I couldn't understand why I got a hiding. I only repeated what my Dad always said.

As I grew a little older I came to realise that Father Goose was really a nice man. However, with a name like that, it just begged to have the nursery rhyme Goosey Gander sung. I was walking home from school at lunchtime one day just as Father Goose was getting off his bike. I was holding a bag of coconut chips singing Goosey Gander, very quietly under my breath, (so I thought). The next thing that happened, Father Goose came over to me and held my hand with the bag of sweets and turned it over so that all the sweets fell to the ground, telling me what a naughty girl I was.

The Sally Army (Salvation Army) regularly used to come around the streets. They had an organ on wheels and the lady would sit at it and pump a couple of treadles with her feet which were foot bellows to keep the air flowing through the pipes. It fascinated me. Other ladies dressed so smartly in their uniforms would do all the fancy bits with the tambourines and the streamers hanging from them. I loved it.

I told you earlier that I was baptised into the Catholic Church. The first time I ever went inside a Catholic church was just before I was to be a bridesmaid to my Aunt Iris. It was St Mary's and St Joseph's in Upper North Street, Poplar, You had to go to church for six consecutive weeks before the marriage was to take place. So I went to Mass with Iris. At the Mass we were up, we were down, then we were kneeling, then we were up again. I didn't understand a thing that was going on because it was all in Latin. But for all that I felt something. I felt that if I said a prayer here there was definitely someone listening. From then on I came to adopt the religion that I was actually baptised into. I was 10 years old.

The year was 1956, it was a lovely wedding, and me and my sister Liz felt like little princesses in our pink, with net overlay bridesmaids' dresses, and silver shoes and our little bouquets of fresh flowers. The reception was held in a beautiful hall near Aldgate, it had parquet flooring and there was a big glitter ball in the centre of the ceiling. After the sit down meal and before the grown ups got on the floor to dance to a proper band, the MC (Master of Ceremonies) coaxed the children into playing a few games, one of which was musical chairs. My sister won the musical chairs game, and the MC said that her prize was the glitter ball hanging from the centre of the ceiling. He went on to tell her that they should leave it there for the time being for grown ups to dance under. There were many tears and tantrums at the end of the night, as we got ready to go home when Liz was told that she couldn't have the glitter ball.

Today at some weddings you often see horses and carriages used for taking the bridal couple back and forth to the church. I know I could be accused of being bias towards our workhorse Nobby being able to do the job quite well if he were called upon. But he was by now getting to be a bit ancient.

One day I was playing outside our shop and a large lorry was standing there with its tailgate down on the floor. The next thing I saw was my Dad coming round the corner leading Nobby. He led him right into the lorry, or tried to. Nobby didn't want to get in the lorry so another man helped my Dad to get him in there. They shut the tailgate up and the lorry drove away.

I asked my Dad, "Where is Nobby going?"

He answered, "Oh he just going for a little holiday."

Every other day or so I would ask when is Nobby coming home, or can we go and see Nobby until weeks went by and I forgot about the big brown horse. It was a couple of years later that I thought about Nobby and asked my Dad what happened to him. Then he told me that poor old Nobby went to the Knacker's Yard. In later years I went to live almost where the abattoir was and where poor old Nobby ended up.

Chapter 18

In mid-1956 Dad bought a thirteen- seater Austin Omnibus or Omnicoach or Dormobile as we called it. There was a side door that had a drop down step, and also a back door. He paid something like £600 for it. He paid a bit extra to have it dual coloured. It was grey on the top half and maroon red on the bottom half, apparently no purchase tax had to be paid because it was classed as a public service vehicle. Therefore, the driver had to have a PSV licence. Obviously I didn't know this bit of information, I just checked up on it so I could tell you. I can still remember the number plate LAN 569, funny how some things stick in your mind.

This van became our adventure-mobile. It was a cracker. We never used to take holidays, but dad decided we would go camping in the van on a bank holiday. As children Dad and his brothers and sisters were taken down 'Hopping' in Goudhurst in Kent. The farm was Three Chimney Farm. Dad wrote to Farmer Benson and asked if we could park on his land for the weekend and the farmer gave his permission. Mum had made some curtains for the van. The sleeping arrangements were solved as follows. Dad took the lids from some banana boxes and laid them side by side over the aisle between the seats he then put a four foot mattress on top and Mum made it up with sheets and blankets, Mum, Liz and me all slept on the mattress. Dad had a lilo that he blew up and slid up the aisle from the back of the van, so in effect he slept under the bed, He didn't have much room but we did this way of camping quite a few times so it couldn't have bothered our dad too much.

We had a single camping gas ring that my Mum did unbelievable things with. Like make a pot of tea and cook a full breakfast of bacon eggs and tomatoes for four people and it was all served hot! I still don't know how she did it.

Just through the woods was Bedgebury Park Lake. At that time there was a building across the lake that was a girls' school. We could hear but we couldn't see the girls laughing and splashing about as they enjoyed themselves. It was at this time that Dad decided to try his hand at fishing, it was crude at first; with some fishing line a hook and a pole that we cut down in the woods, and some bread. But it worked and Dad caught a couple of small fish.

We could walk through the fields to the village of Goudhurst, where Mum and Dad would have a glass of beer and Liz and I would have lemonade. Everything we did was so simple, yet we had the best of times. Dad bought a camera and he became quite a keen photographer. He loved to do funny trick shots. He got a couple of bales of hay together and made me sit at one end. The hay hid my legs. Then he got Liz to lay down and just have her legs sticking out from the other end, so the photos showed a little girl who looked like she had extremely long legs.

Soon after Dad had bought the Dormobile he joined the Automobile Association

In those days the AA man was on a motorcycle. He was dressed in a khaki uniform, and as he came towards you, if he saw you had the AA badge on your front grill he would salute. I also think there was something about that, if no salute was made it was a warning that there was a speed trap ahead. Well that wouldn't have bothered my Dad as the Dormobile only had 60 on the clock anyway. My Dad loved it when he saw an AA man coming towards him raising himself by straightening his back and at the same time giving a salute. It made him feel proud. It was one of those nice little AA customs that sadly ended somewhere in the early sixties.

Having the Dormobile gave Dad the opportunity to take me with him to Stratford Market. The market is adjacent to an area, which is now the site of the Olympic stadium for the 2012 Olympic games.

This market was mostly all under cover and the wholesaler's mostly lined one side of the market, raised up on what they called the bank. Imagine if you were standing on railway lines in a station, then the platform would be like the bank. The other side had a few wholesalers and large openings to the goods yard where wagons from trains stood, and in one little spot there was a place where you could get a cup of tea and food. This was Dinny's place. He made the best sausage sandwiches you could ever taste. They were the size of doorsteps. After eating one of these delicious sandwiches you would be hard pressed to eat another one but because of them being so nice, you would force yourself.

The porters pushed barrows up and down the market and helped to load the lorries belonging to the greengrocers. Some wore leather aprons but all wore caps. Although there was much work to be done nevertheless the market people went about their business with huge smiles on their faces. There was much larking about.

Dad would leave me sitting in the motor while he went and did some buying. A porter came by marching with an exaggerated limp, holding a long runner bean up to his lips and whistling a tune that went with in time with his marching. The show was put on purposefully for me. A couple of other porters, pinched the cap of a third porter and had him running back and forth playing 'Piggy in the Middle', again all put on for me. There was a lot of joking and playing around and later on I will tell you of some jokes my Dad and his Uncle and brother got up to.

Chapter 19

About April of 1957 we got a new addition to our family, it was a little dog, a smooth haired Griffon Bruxellois. If you have never see one they look like a very miniature boxer, but with Pekinese eyes. Dad had bought him from a breeder in Todmorden. The little dog travelled down in a black box and Dad had to go and pick him up at the station. Dad would have liked to have got the dog out of the box right away but didn't know how it would be and so he waited till he got home. When he opened the box he found two big brown eyes staring up at him. I came home from school and was told that the dog had arrived. He was so tiny.

After a day or two Mum and Dad took Timmy to the vet to have his jabs, all seemed well, but then the little dog became ill. Mum nursed him with the medication she got from the vet. It was touch and go but Timmy did get better except for his right foot; it kept twitching. Back to the vet they went and were told that Timmy had probably caught distemper but in a mild form and it had left him with this twitch, called St Vitus dance (An involuntary muscular movement). The vet's advice was that Timmy should be put down. Dad asked if the dog was in pain and the vet said no, but that the twitching will get on your nerves. Well the vet was wrong it didn't get on our nerves, we loved that little dog and we kept it. He was over 16 years old when we finally had to have him put to sleep. It tore our hearts out losing him. I will have to tell a story later about Timmy's departure from this world.

In 1957 Dad's young brother, Johnny, had been to Cornwall on holiday and came back singing its praises and saying, "You must go Bill, take the kids, they'll love it".

Johnny said he would look after the shop; it would be too much to close the shop for a week. He had a word of warning though. He had caught sunstroke in the past and emphasised that if the kids go in the water making sure they cover up when they come out. Dad said we could go and we were taking Timmy our little dog. We were heading for Newquay. I told you I suffered travel sickness. Well it was a six-hour journey and I was sick six times. Anyway, we duly arrived at Newquay and parked the van on a lovely bit of green on the cliffs. Mum cooked our breakfasts on this single little gas burner, and we would have the rest of our meals out, either in a café or we'd get Fish and Chips from the chip shop, Most of our days were spent on the beach, We were all in and out of the water, and Dad, heeding Johnny's words, made sure we covered up when we came out of the sea.

Our little dog Timmy loved to run around free on the beach, usually he was always on a lead. But he became a target for seagulls, they would come down and dive bomb him, so we had to keep him close to us after that.

Some few hundred yards from where our van was parked, was a large building that turned out to be quite a posh hotel, and one day when we came back from the beach a man was waiting for us and he told us that we had to move as the guests didn't like the fact that when they looked out of their window they saw a van with swimming costumes drying in the wind and people cooking over a gas stove. So without argument we moved on, and found ourselves in St Ives. It was such a pretty place; we parked the van in a car park just around the corner from the harbour. Two ex-fishermen ran it. When they heard our plight they said we could camp in their car park for the rest of the week.

Even though we had done as Johnny told us and covered up as much as possible, all of us still got burnt. Most evenings we spent like monkeys sitting behind one another peeling the

111

flakey skin of each other's backs. At one point Dad had run out of money so he had to ring Johnny to wire him some money through to the bank. I didn't know you could do things like that. No more cooking for Mum! We found a lovely café called the Jolly Sailor, where we would have breakfast. It tasted delicious as we sat there overlooking the harbour.

Dad decided to get a rowboat and take us out in the harbour. He rowed quite a distance. The water was so clear you could see the sand right at the bottom, but the old queasiness started to creep up on me again. I held out as long as I could before telling Dad that I felt sick. He started to row back to shore; I was so pleased that he was rowing so quickly to put me out of my misery. A little later I overheard him telling my mum that he too was feeling queasy and wanted to get back to shore and was glad when Pat said she felt sick.

One evening a flare went up and the lifeboat had to be launched; it came back some hours later, with a dead person. They loaded the covered body into a waiting ambulance. All the lifeboat men looked very sombre. I didn't really know anything about the RNLI. My Dad explained that they were just ordinary people, probably fishermen, that answered the call for anyone in distress at sea, and they don't get any money for doing it. After what my Dad told me and because of the events of that night, I decided then that the RNLI would become one of my favoured charities.

One little amusing story I'd like to tell. (It gave us a giggle). Mum and Dad sometimes had a glass of beer in a pub called the 'Union Inn'. One evening my sister said, "Dad are you going to the 'Onion' pub?" She was only eight years of age. My sister had been wearing very thick glasses since the age of about 18 months old; she also suffered from a nervous deafness. School was a bit of a struggle for her, but she still laughs when this story is repeated.

Our holiday in Cornwall ended, and we bought the two car park attendants a little plastic silver cup each, and Dad wrote on a card, 'To the best car park attendant'. They were pleased with this little gesture. The journey home was a bit better for me, I was only sick five times coming back. 1957 was an eventful year and went by so quickly, but the festive season was on its way.

Christmas that year, old Santa made another mistake; I was old enough now to progress to a two wheeled bicycle. But I hadn't learnt from the past that Father Christmas needs specifics when you ask him for presents. So when I got the 'Blue Lightning' instead of the 'Pink Witch'. I was really upset, but for some reason my Mum couldn't work her magic and get it changed, so this time I was stuck with the 'Blue Lightning'.

I was pretty pleased when I found out that there was no Father Christmas, and that it was your parents all along buying the presents, because I could now cut out the middle man and get the right information across to my Mum and Dad. There weren't any mistakes after that.

Leading up to that Christmas, The building opposite St Luke's Church, which was called The Boyd Institute, as far as I remember it was a boys' club. Someone there decided to show a film for the local children. It was called *A Christmas Carol*. My Dad sent me along there; I had to ask for Mr Andrews, who was the churchwarden for St Luke's Church. I knew him well from coming in to the shop as a customer. I found Mr Andrews and he found me a seat on a bench right in the front row, although I was surrounded by lots of other children who seemed to know each other. I didn't know anyone else there but the film began and straight away I became drawn into it. It was like there was no one else in the room except me, I was completely mesmerised. As the film went on, especially when it got to the three ghosts of past, present, and future, I felt a bit afraid, and then started to weep silently with a lump in my throat as big as a house brick as I watched Scrooge being visited by The Ghost of Christmas Present who showed just how ill Tim really was, and said that Tim will die unless he receives treatment. When visited by The Ghost of Christmas Future all he sees of Tim is his crutch. Tim had died. Of course the film had a happy ending because this

113

made Scrooge change his ways and become a better person. The famous line said by Tiny Tim, 'God Bless Us, Every One.' comes at the end of the story.

Chapter 20

Dad sometimes took me down Petticoat Lane, a Sunday Market in Aldgate. East Enders referred to Petticoat Lane, as 'The Lane'. The large area surrounding 'The Lane' was in Stepney where the Jewish people lived and worked in the textile trade in the making of clothes, or garments as they used to call it. It was known in the area as 'The Rag Trade' You could buy almost anything up The Lane, There were exotic animals like snakes and monkeys, tortoises, or you could buy budgies and parrots and dogs, and pigeons. There were bits of debris (waste ground) where anyone could set up and sell their goods.

But I liked going down The Lane for the Jewish food. There were potato latkes. These are shallow-fried pancakes of grated potato and egg, usually flavoured with grated onion. They would be hot off the griddle and wrapped in greaseproof paper. Then there was salt beef beigels with mustard, lovely. The salt beef was all freshly cooked so it was nice and juicy. This was the first takeaway food I ever knew of apart from fish and chips. Our visit to The Lane usually was to get schmaltz herrings, or you might know them as roll mops, The Lane was the only place we knew where to get them. Then we would go and get the shellfish, prawns, cockles, whelks and winkles.

You haven't lived if you have never had a winkle sandwich. After picking the winkles out with a pin, soak them in vinegar, butter two slices of bread and spread the winkles on one slice and cover with the other and enjoy.

The Jewish community having occupied the area for so long obviously had some influence on the Gentiles living in the surrounding areas and beyond, possibly without them even realising it. I have been going over how many Yiddish words that I have used and still use from time to time. Like schmutter, meaning clothing. "Nice bit of schmutter you're wearing". Schtum, means keep quiet. Nosh means snack or food. Shmutz means dirt, "You have a bit of Shmutz on your face", we pronounced it Smut. Everyone knows Kosher meaning genuine. Schmooze means small talk or a chat. Schpiel is a sales pitch, Schnozzle a big nose. Schemozzle a row or a fight, Schlep means a tedious walk. Tukhas actually mean Buttocks, but the cockneys picked it up and made it mean testicles. Schmaltz means sentimental. And another one that everyone would have known is Mazol Tov, which means good luck. There are a few more that we used in everyday talk but that is enough to be going on with.

At the top of Gaulston Street, Aldgate, off Whitechapel Road there was a couple of stalls that sold jellied eels. The most famous was Tubby Isaac, I believe there is still a stall that sells jellied eels called Tubby Isaac's. But It was the original Tubby Isaacs himself that was there serving when I was a kid. I think the other stall was Tubby's brother and they supposedly had a row and didn't talk, I don't know if that is a true story or not. Around the corner was the famous Bloom's Kosher Restaurant, they sold hot salt beef sandwiches on rye bread with hot mustard.

There were two other markets attached to and close by Petticoat Lane. One was Club Row where you could get really cheap second hand stuff, and the other market is Columbia Road where you can buy lovely plants and flowers.

This particular area has always taken in refugees from other parts of the world. One of the first groups were Huguenot refugees. They flocked to Petticoat Lane and Spitalfields areas. They established a major weaving industry in and around Spitalfields. The fleeing of Huguenot refugees from Tours, France, virtually wiped out the silk mills they had built.

The next to come were the Jewish community, they were a colourful race of people with the way they talked, their food, their clothing factories, they were what Petticoat Lane was all about when I was a child growing up, and even up on to the early sixties.

In the Sixties the Bangladeshis arrived and the Jewish community all but moved out. They took over the garment trade to some extent. The only people that remained throughout these changes were a little further away in Limehouse, and that was the Chinese community.

Chapter 21

The Woolwich Free Ferry was just a short distance away from the 669 trolley bus route (this later changed to 69). We would go quite often in the summer just go for a ride back and forth across the River Thames. We would walk down a jetty, and wait till the ferry came in. The crewmen would jump off and tie the mooring ropes around the capstan so that the people could get on. The ferry had paddles, you couldn't see them but they churned the water up as they started it made the water frothy, and you got the smell of the river. I loved this smell. There were lots of seats around the ferry, and in the middle were all the wooden floats stacked up in case of disaster. I used to like to go inside and watch the big piston engines turning, and watch the men looking after them. The smell of the hot oil was a heady aroma. It was just like being on a big ship, you heard the bells clang its message from the bridge to the engine room indicating what was required.

Sometimes Mum and Dad would take us to the pictures on the 'other side' of Woolwich. The problem was that if the film was running late you could miss the last ferry back so there would be a mad dash from the cinema to the ferry jetty. I think the last one was about 10 p.m., if you missed that ferry you had to walk through the foot tunnel beneath the river. Although there were lifts to take you up and down to the foot tunnel, the lift operator also finished about the same time as the ferry, so you had to walk down a spiral staircase, then up another at the other end. I didn't like to think that as we walked through that tunnel there was a whole river on top of us, and I couldn't wait till we were back safe above ground again. The ferry was an afternoon out for many families in the summer time, our own little mini cruise.

Chapter 22

Dad's Dormobile was the ideal transport for our large family trips to the Epsom Derby. It used to be held on the first Wednesday in June. My grandmother, Joey, Iris and Alf, Jinny and Frank, Johnny and Jesse, a couple of their kids who were really young, me and my sister, and of course Mum and Dad.

Iris and Jinny, and my Nan would prepare loads of food the night before; enough to feed the five thousand. There was fish, chicken, pork and egg pies, sliced ham and sliced pork, boiled eggs, and cheese, then there was all the salad stuff, tomatoes, cucumber, lettuce, celery, cooked beetroot and boiled potatoes. There were apples, oranges and bananas. There was sliced bread and bread rolls, cake and sweets. A feast. The men sorted out the drink, there was whisky and rum and ginger ale and lemonade and beer, and we always had champagne. All this stuff was wedged under the seats. Then we had the blankets and pillows to sit on. It's amazing how my Dad got it all in.

We would arrive at the course and head for the Epsom Downs. As we crossed over the racetrack onto the Downs we could see the bright coloured ostrich feathers, and the exotic clothes of Prince Monolulu the racing tipster. He was the most famous black man around the racing scene and was at all the most important horse race meetings. He would shout, "I gotta Horse, I gotta Horse", and for sixpence he would hand you an envelope with his prediction. His clothes were all billowy and his ostrich feathers so tall on his head, to me as a child he looked enormous. Prince Monolulu died in the mid Sixties; I think he was in his eighties by then. You don't see characters like him anymore, I suppose John McCririck is as close as you can get.

My first Derby was in 1953 and my last Derby was in 1978. In that time the only Derbys we missed were 1955, 1973 and 1976. We stopped going after 1978 because the meeting really started to get too commercialised. Helicopters flying in, more and more coaches and buses and we were getting edged out further and further from the area we usually parked in.

We had a lot of fun, laughing and joking, seeing who won and who lost. My nan always seemed to do well. So I thought I would back the horses she did. I asked her what horse she was betting on and copied her, but every time I did that, she lost, and so did I, or rather my Dad did because I kept borrowing shillings off him to place bets with.

We always walked over to see the Derby Race start, and by the time we got back to the van, it was over; it was quite a walk. With all races we only ever saw from our vantage point the tops of the jockey's caps as they came into view rounding Tattenham Corner. So it was just as well that Dad used to take a portable TV, which ran off the engine battery to see the races properly. Can you believe it?

There were two fairs at the Derby; one in the Dip almost opposite the grandstands and the other was over at Tattenham Corner. After the racing was over all the family would go down to Dip to see the 'dirty ladies'. Now these ladies were dirty in more ways than one. They were in fact striptease ladies and they would do a little bit of a free show in front of the tent on a stage. The 'Barker' (A Barker is a person who tries to attract customers, to see a show inside a tent or onto a funfair ride. He would describe the attractions of the show or ride and emphasizing all the attributes. He would try anything to get customers to pay up. He would conduct a short free show, introducing performers and describing acts to be given at the feature performances) would bang his drum and shout to attract the people to come and see the show.

These (dirty) ladies would have been working since early morning, and by the time the day's racing had finished, their skin and feet were filthy from all the cinder dust that had been kicked up during the day. They weren't pretty, and their hair was bleach blonde straw. They all looked rather faded, not a pretty sight at all. We just wanted to go and see how dirty they had got from the day, and how fed up they looked, and to hear the barker's schpiel. Still for all that, lots of men did pay their money and go inside.

There was a tent with a big billboard outside that read SEE FRANKENSTEIN IS HE DEAD OR IS HE ALIVE. The men in our group had been standing in front of this tent when the rest of us caught up with them. They persuaded the women and girls in our group to go inside to see Frankenstein. There was me, Mum, Liz, and Iris a couple of others, and our Aunt Jesse, who at that time was heavily pregnant, we paid our shilling and walked in. There in the dark was a big chair made to look like an electric chair with coloured light bulbs, and sitting in the chair was the figure of a large man that looked like the figure we have seen depicted in Frankenstein films. We all stood in front of this set and were saying how we had been 'done' again, paying a shilling only to see a model in a chair with a couple of coloured light bulbs. When all of a sudden this figure jumped out of the chair and ran towards us screaming at the top of his voice. Well, you never see a bunch of females move so quickly, and it was a wonder Jesse didn't give birth to her baby there and then in fright. We were all fighting for the exit to get away from this 'thing'. When we got outside the men were in fits of laughter. We then stood for some time while we watched others go in and then come running out screaming, and that was the men as well.

We would go on the shooting galleries, which was my favourite thing to do, and I usually came away with a prize. The men would try the coconut shies, and usually miss.

Another big sideshow was the boxing tent. Here the barker would ask for challengers to come up and try to win a prize

122

against his fighter. That used to get a lot of spectators in. All the men in our group used to go inside to see a fight.

Boxing was a popular sport, and used to be on the TV a lot in those days.

Three British boxers I remember from that time were Don Cockell, Freddy Mills, and Randolph Turpin. The American boxers I remember from that time were Rocky Marciano, Floyd Patterson, and Sugar Ray Robinson. Boxers used to fight on a more regular basis than they do today, and so they stayed around for a longer time. I suppose one of the last boxers to stay around for a long time was Henry Cooper. These boxers really did fight for a living. Nowadays they have a fight here and a fight there all for massive purses so it doesn't matter whether they win or lose, get a title or not.

At the end of the day at Epsom we would pack up all the blankets and cushions and what was left of the food and drink and start heading home. With so many people having had such a good day we would sing songs all the way back home.

Chapter 23

During the 50s Mum and Dad became friendly with a group of his customers who used to go out every Saturday night to the pub. The one they went to most was The Lord Nelson in the Victoria Dock Road, below the Silvertown Way flyover. In those days it was very strict and you could not take children into any pub. Just opening the door and put one foot inside was a definite No! No! It was a boundary you just weren't allowed to cross. Two of the couple's had children so we all played together outside the pub. The pub was on an island and so we would have races around it. Another thing we liked to do was get the coloured bottle tops from the beer bottles. They used to have a little round disc made from cork inside. We would remove the cork disc, put the bottle top on our jumper then push the cork back in from behind our clothing, it looked like you had a load of medals on your jumper. The problem was the crimped edges of the bottle cap also used to tear your clothing, so our mum's weren't too pleased that we did this.

The grown ups kept us topped up with lemonade and packets of crisps or salted peanuts. The crisps then only came in one flavour, Plain. And as far as I know, only one maker, Smith's!

This was all good fun in the summer but in the winter, for my sister and I it was awful. The children that we normally played with had older brothers or sisters, or grandparents nearby to look after them while their mums and dads were at the pub. My sister and I didn't have anyone to look after us and so we would have to go along to the pub with our Mum and Dad. The owner of the pub used to let us sit in the passage on the stairs. It was nice to be sitting on the pubs stairs keeping dry, but there was no heating so we used to be really cold. There was nothing for us to do except sit on the stairs and talk to each other. It was so boring. We didn't ever used to drink lemonade during the winter, because we learned that the lemonade was freezing cold and so it made us even colder. So we just ate the crisps. We were so bored and so tired, the only thing to do was to try and get a little sleep. We would snuggle up really close with each other, just for a bit of warmth. We were unhappy children at those times. Our Mum, ever the entertainer, used to dance to the music and everyone used to egg her on. She was a really good tap dancer. But my sister and I didn't like it and we used to shout through the door to our Dad to tell her to stop dancing.

Nearly every Saturday night through all the seasons, there would be a party round somebody's house. There were four main couples. Mr and Mrs Nisbett, Palmer, Morrison, and my parents. Mostly the Nisbetts had the partys in their house. The men would have a whip round and buy some crates of beer. They would buy some whisky and gin and some ginger ale and orange juice to mix with the spirits. Then we would walk back home and everyone would be singing. We would run into other people coming from a different pub and they would be singing at the tops of their voices too. Sometimes they would join up and they would come to the party. 'The more the merrier', as the old saying goes. We would get to the house and the carpet would be rolled up. Nisbett's had an older daughter Sheila; she was a friend with the elder daughters and sons of the Palmer's and the Morrison's, so they would turn up at the party as well. They were good parties. Everyone used to join in. There would be the pop records of the day, plus the old knees up records. The parties would go on till about two or three in the morning. Mum and Dad would have to get up on a Sunday morning to open the shop for half a day's business. I don't know how they did it.

Sometimes they would leave the pub and go up to Aldgate to Tubby Isaacs for jellied eels, or maybe Blooms for a salt beef sandwich. Then another place we started to venture to was Limehouse. Here, some of the Chinese people would open up their front room and put in a few tables and chairs and you could go in and have a Chinese meal. There were no menus. It was very basic. Chow Mein with or without bean shoots, Chow Mein with shredded chicken and curry sauce and a cup of tea. That was it, but boy did it taste good. These were just ordinary families who did this to earn a few extra shillings. At that time in the early 50s I can still remember seeing a Chinese man with a long plait and wearing the silky type of pyjamas and pillbox hat that you once associated with a typical Chinese man. It was from these humble beginnings the Chinese restaurants that we know today grew. Limehouse was the original Chinatown, before the one we now know in the West End.

Chapter 24

Around about the time of the 50s one of Mum and Dad's customers started to talk to them about Spiritualism. Dad was always willing to learn a little about different things. The customer, a lady called Kit Smith was a medium and she would hold séances in her house. Mum and Dad were invited to one of these. The Smith's house was just across the road from our shop. My sister and I would be in bed and asleep. There obviously hadn't been any problems before with my sister and me waking up, so Mum and Dad felt okay to leave us to go across the road to the séance. They started off with the ouija board. As I explained earlier, the letters of the alphabet are laid in a circle along with the words 'yes' and 'no'.

Apparently the glass started to move towards different letters and it started to spell out the words 'Bill Jolly GO HOME'. This scared the hell out of Mum and Dad. The glass started to go wild and kept spelling out the same thing. Mum and Dad decided to remove themselves from the séance circle and just watch the others. But still the glass kept spinning around the letters, repeatedly spelling out 'Bill Jolly GO HOME'. Dad was really frightened and he and Mum decided to leave. They came back home and as they walked in the front door my sister and I greeted them from where we were standing at the top of the steep flight of stairs. My sister was about 2 years old and I was about 5. Dad was amazed. What if they hadn't come home as they were told to do by the Ouija board, and there could have been a terrible accident.

This incident whetted my Dad's interest about spiritualism, and he started to go to the local Spiritualist Church in Cumberland Road, Custom House. At that time Dad used to suffer terrible migraines. He was having one of his migraines during a spiritualist meeting. No messages were given to him by the medium, that night. A man had been sitting next to my dad that evening and he turned and asked Dad how he was feeling.

Dad said, "Funny you should ask, I have been having a terrible migraine attack."

And the man said, "I know, I could feel it, but you won't get them any more."

It was true, Dad didn't get the attacks ever again.

You can imagine that with these couple of incidences Dad was being drawn towards spiritualism and he wanted to find out more. So he started to do the ouija board himself. He also began to go to more séances; at one of them he received a message that he should get the wheel fixed. Dad didn't know what to make of this. He had the cart, and barrow, and there were bikes and skates, there were lots of things with wheels on so he didn't know what to make of it.

One night he was closing the shops and had pulled the shutters down and was about the shut the door when he forgot something and went back inside. I was waiting outside for him, but he was taking a long while, so I decided to get my sister's scooter out for a while. I put one foot on the scooter and tried to push off with my other foot, but the front wheel stuck and I went over the top of it and hit my face hard on the concrete floor. Of course I started to cry and Dad came running, picked me up and was shocked to see that I had smashed both my front teeth. It was sometime later that he put two and two together and realised that this was the wheel that should have been fixed. It had needed oiling for a long time, but he never got round to doing it.

Chapter 25

I remember doing some sort of tests while I was at St Luke's school, the 11plus. I didn't realise what it was for. I did not know that this was to sort out where you would carry on the next part of your school life, be it a grammar school or the secondary modern school. I also didn't know that it gave an indication of what stream you should be in. As it turned out, I went to the secondary modern school called Ashburton in Russell Road Custom House. (It was previously known as Russell Road School before the war). We heard all sorts of rumours about what it was like for first year kids starting at the bigger school. The worse one was that the older kids would put your head down the toilet and flush it. Or you just got beat up for no reason. I was really scared about starting at this school. But when I got there it was nothing like it at all. Who starts these scary rumours?

The school was a big old Victorian building over three floors that housed about eight classrooms to each floor. Although the classes were mixed, the boys had their own staircase and the girls had theirs at each end of the building. Outside in the playground area there were two prefab type building that held four more classes. One of the prefabs buildings housed the woodworking and metal working classrooms. There was also a gymnasium.

I was placed in 'F' stream. The stream went from 'A', being the highest to 'G', being the lowest. But me? In 'F' stream? What was I doing there? This was wrong; I knew that I was no dunce.

The first year was a bit of a blur at Ashburton, settling in, making new friends, learning all the different classes, periods and teachers. I realised that St Luke's only taught us the basics of reading and writing, and not much else. Everything else I knew was what I had learned from my Dad taking us to museums, and buying me books.

The first couple of terms were a bit changeable with teachers and classes. But nevertheless I found myself moving up into stream 'E' and my teacher there was called Miss Gold. This was getting better. I still had a couple of friends from my primary school classes, but I was beginning to make new friends, Christine Neal, Valerie Morris, Madeline Fitzgerald, Pauline McMahon. These were a nice bunch of girls.

By the time I got into my second year, I found teachers that opened up a whole new world to me. Mr Barraclough was the most wonderful teacher of History. I couldn't get enough of his lessons. I began to eat up the knowledge that was being given to me, except for maths. I hated this subject, I never had a teacher that could make the subject interesting enough.

This all sounds like I had hit the jackpot and everything were going to end happily ever after. Far from it! As well as soaking up all that I was being taught I still found time to string along with a naughty faction in my class getting into trouble at least twice a week. I found myself sent to the middle floor to stand beneath the window of the headmaster, Mr Chenappa. At some point he would look out from his window to see if there was anyone there, and if there was he would come down and ask us why we were there. Regardless of the explanation we would receive the cane twice, once on each hand.

There were several teachers that gave the cane, Mr Barraclough, Mr Townsend, Mr Mays and Miss Ball the headmistress. I received the cane from Mr Barraclough and still suffer to this day from a pain in a bone in my thumb. I don't blame Mr Barraclough; the stick just caught me wrong.

I narrowly missed getting the cane from Mr Townsend, he was the science teacher and had a reputation for being the one to give the stick the hardest. I found myself sent out of a music class because I was talking instead of singing. The reason for that was, I was trying to get my friend, Val Melia, to put back some nail varnish that had been confiscated by the music teacher from a pupil from a previous class before we got into trouble. But I was the one that did get into trouble. I expected to be sent to stand beneath Mr Chenappa's window, but instead the teacher said I was to go to Mr Townsend and ask for four. (Two strokes of the cane on each hand.) My mouth dropped, my eyes were wide open with absolute shock. What should I do? Could I feign illness and be sent home? Should I just walk out of the school? All I knew was that I did not want to go to Mr Townsend. After much pleading with the music teacher I finally went to Mr Townsend's class, and knocked on the door.

'Enter' I heard Mr Townsend say. He was in the middle of teaching a bunch of third year boys, one of whom I had a crush on. The boy had a bit of a bad boy reputation, but I really liked him. I was blushing to the roots of my hair by now as well as being scared of the teacher who was about to cane me four times. Mr Townsend stood on a dais about eight inches high off the ground, so I really had to look up to him.

"What do you want," he asked.

"I have come to ask you for four, sir." He turned toward the blackboard to get his cane, and came back and stood in front of me.

"Hold your hand out," he said. I raised my hand, but it wasn't high enough for him and so he put the cane beneath my hand and raised it higher. I looked at Mr Townsend and gave a weak smile and shrugged my shoulders at the same time. I don't know how this must have looked to him, but something must have stirred him because he said, "Get out of here and don't let me see you again." I sighed the biggest sigh ever and closed my eyes.

I looked at Mr Townsend again and said, "Thank you sir, you won't see me again sir." Someone was looking down on me that day, that's for sure.

I still managed to get into trouble most weeks and one time just for a change I was sent to the middle floor, not to stand under the headmasters window, but to clean the silver. The silver being all the cups and shields that Ashburton had won from netball and football and swimming and other stuff, there was a hell of a lot of silver. I started this little job, and was half way through when the bell rang to change the lessons and along came the boy who I had a crush on, he took the lid from one of the cups I had cleaned and started to run away with it, I took chase pleading with him to please let me have it back. He ran up the boy's stairs to the top floor and I was right behind him, he was dancing in front of me and teasing me with the lid. Finally he gave me the lid. He then asked me if I would go out with him, I said, "OK". He told me he would meet me after school near where I lived. I danced all the way back to the middle floor and cleaned that silver as fast as I could.

I didn't tell my Mum and Dad that I was meeting a boy for the first time in my life, in case they wouldn't let me go. Later, I met the boy and we went to a fair that was being held in Beckton Park. It was raining and we got soaked, but I didn't care. We went on all kinds of rides and he made me laugh. Then I felt it was time for me to get back home before I got in trouble with my parents. The boy said he would take me home and we walked up the stairs to my house and he said he would wait at the end of the veranda until I went in the house. I knocked on the door, but there was no answer, I knocked again and still no answer. I walked back along the veranda and told the boy that my parents must have gone out. He said he would stay and wait with me. We walked down to the shops below and stood in the doorway of the laundry shop and it was there that this boy with the bad reputation kissed me for the very first time. He was so gentle.

Finally my parents came home. I introduced the boy to my Mum and Dad and told them he had looked after me. My parents knew his parents anyway, and they also knew the boy's reputation as well, but they thanked him and that night I went to bed and dreamed of this lovely boy. I soon found out that we were never going to be boyfriend/girlfriend. But we would be good friends for years to come.

I was now moving up from'3D' stream into '3C', my hard work at paying attention to my lessons was paying off. From the second year onward we were taught domestic science. The cookery teacher was Miss Finch. It was a good lesson to be in, we could have a joke around, but it was good groundwork for later in life.

During cookery lessons Miss Finch would nominate a couple of girls to start making the tea for the teachers on 'break time'. I did one of these duties one time with another girl. When the teachers came in we would pour tea for them and they would take their tea and sit down to chat with each other.

I overheard one of these chats and I became so angry at what was being said. I heard a teacher (thankfully not one of mine) say to another teacher. "There's no point teaching this lot much, they are only going to finish up in Tate and Lyle's sugar factory". I wanted to tell someone what had been said but who would listen to me?

Tate and Lyle's was a sugar refinery in Silvertown. There was also Lyle's that made the syrup. They were the biggest employer of people in the area, and gave thousands of people all a good living. The workers were extremely well cared for. I knew a lot of girls and a few boys that went to work at 'Tate's'. I never heard a bad word said against working there. The boys and girls worked hard and they had to do shift work. 6 a.m. to 2 p.m. 2 p.m. to 10 p.m. 10 p.m. to 6 a.m. Tate and Lyles always reminded me of a massive heart beating, and the people that worked there was the blood that flowed in and out each day and night. What an awful thing for a teacher to say.

The first few times I did cookery, I didn't think Miss Finch gave us the right weights for the ingredients for fairy cakes, so I added more of everything. I knew I was wrong to do this when I found that all my mates had twelve fairy cakes and I had thirty-two. I didn't learn my lesson when it came to making bread; I overdid the yeast and flour. The bread dough found a life of its own as it tried to escape the oven because there was so much of it. And why didn't I listen when Miss Finch said to strain the gravy off the vegetables before putting a layer of mash potato on top for the vegetable hotpot. The potato had dissolved in the gravy before I got home. Nevertheless, my Mum dished it up on a plate and my sister thought it was lovely.

I used to love the way my Dad would praise my cookery efforts that I brought home. Apple dumplings that were like cricket balls? He would go, "Mmmmmm lovely". Rock cakes, that were as hard as cement? "Mmmmmm lovely".

Going back to my first year. I told you that I had smashed my front teeth. I ended up at Eastman's dental hospital in Grays Inn Road. I was going to be fitted with crowns. While they were being made I had to wear temporary crowns and because they were going to have to come out at some point they weren't cemented in very hard.

This being the case got me into trouble with the PE teacher, Miss Handley. We had come to the end of the PE lesson and were lined up to make our way out of the gym. I sneezed and one of my crowns flew out and slid across the floor. Without thinking I stepped out of line to go and get my tooth back. The teacher asked me where I was going. I told her I was going to get my tooth back. She told me to get back in line and to stop messing around. I told her I wasn't messing around and picked my tooth up and showed her how I could just pop it in and out. She thought I was acting like a clown on purpose. By now half of the girls in my class were laughing their heads off, the teacher was really angry and I was sent to stand underneath the headmaster's window, again.

By my fourth year I had moved from '4C' up into '4B'. When you reached the fourth year, you were given duties to do; each class in the fourth year took turns at these duties. Each pupil did one day each. The first duty was to hand out all the registers to the teacher and then collect them after the registers had been marked. The next part of the duty was to sit outside the headmaster's room and act as a runner or messenger; you took a book along with you to read while you waited for instructions. This obviously made a change for me, sitting outside the headmaster's room rather than standing under his window.

Another part of the duty was to answer the telephone when the headmaster was out of his office. The telephone was a plan 1A system. It was one of those large old fashioned Bakelite telephones and on the base was a white lever that could be moved into a certain position to call the headmaster's secretary, it also acted like an intercom system. I already told you that the headmaster's office was above the middle floor of the boy's stairwell. But the secretary's office was above the top floor of the girl's stairwell.

Our class was told how to work the phone to contact the secretary. I didn't pay too much attention to the instructions, as in my experience the head master was nearly always there. I should know, I stood under his window often enough.

The day came for me to be on duty. I distributed all the registers first thing and after assembly I went to collect them all back in. Then it was back to the headmaster's office to be the messenger. I had my book; I got myself nice and comfortable on the bench outside Mr Chenappa's office. This was going to be 'a doddle', nice easy day, no lessons to do. I ran a couple of messages. Then Mr Chenappa came out and said he was going out for the rest of the day. What! Go out. Go out! He can't go out, he never goes out. Where was he going for goodness sake? He told me to take messages if the phone rang. I just said, "Yes sir".

Off went Mr Chenappa, and there I sat there with my book No more than ten minutes went by before my worst nightmare

135

happened. The phone started to ring, I sat bolt upright wondering what to do. I decided to ignore it, it'll stop soon and I won't have to enter the office with the dreaded mechanical contraption with its loud ringing bell.

But then a teacher came dancing down the stairs and said "Aren't you going to answer that?"

"Yes sir, I am sir, just on my way now sir", I said. I walked into the office over to the big telephone and picked up the receiver. I said, "Good morning, Ashburton School, Mr Chenappa's office may I help you?" A man's voice asked for Mr Chenappa, and I told him that Mr Chanappa was out for the rest of the day. Job done I thought. But, Oh No, it wasn't. The man said he wanted to speak to the secretary. My heart was sinking by the minute. I said, "Yes sir, just a moment I will try to connect you."

I moved the white lever at the base of the phone and pressed the plungers, and then I said, "Hello."

The man then said, "Hello."

I said, "Sorry sir I am not talking to you I am trying to talk to the secretary, just a moment."

I moved the white lever again, and then said "Hello' and the man said, "Hello". Again I told the man I wasn't speaking to him. This went on twice more and in the end I just put the receiver down, hoping the man would get cut off and go away. I walked outside the headmaster's office and sat down with my book. I just opened the page and the phone started to ring again.

I ran into the office and picked up the phone and said "Good morning Ashburton School, Mr Chenappa's office, may I help you?" It was the same man calling again.

He said, "I think I was cut off."

I said, "Yes I think you were. Sorry about that. I will try the secretary for you again, just a moment." Rather than go through all what I had done previously I thought I would go direct to the secretary herself.

I put the receiver down next to the phone, ran out of the office up the boy's stairwell to the top floor, ran from one end of the floor to the other where the girl's stairwell was and ran up another three flights of stairs to the secretary's office, I knocked on the door and she told me to enter. I quickly told her about the man on the phone and the difficulty I was having putting him through. She decided to tell me how I should be doing it. But I do not understand what she's telling me; I am not telling her that though, I said okay. I ran out of her office all the way down the girl's stairwell to the middle floor, ran from one end of the floor to the other end, back to the boy's stairwell, I ran up two flights to the headmaster's office, ran across the room picked up the receiver and tried again moving the damn white lever again. I said "hello" and the man said "hello." I said I am sorry I am still trying to connect you. This just wasn't working; the secretary was just going to have to come to Mr Chanappa's office herself. I ran out of the office up the stairs to the top floor ran from one end of the floor to the other, across to the girl's stairwell, up three flights to the secretary's office, I knocked on the door, no answer, knocked again, still no answer. I opened the door. She wasn't there! She wasn't there! Where the bloody hell had she gone? I had no time to run around looking for her. I ran all the way down to the middle floor, ran from one end of the floor to the other, across the floor to the boy's stairwell, up two flights into the headmaster's office.

I picked up the receiver and said, "I am sorry sir, I have just been told that the secretary has gone out with Mr Chenappa, can I take a message?"

"No!" he said. "Don't worry I will call back tomorrow." Phew!

It was now lunchtime, I dashed out of school across the playground and within in ten minutes I was home. I told my mum all about what had happened with the phone, she couldn't stop laughing.

I said, "Mum, I can't go back in case the bloody phone rings again."

She said, "All right, stay home, I will write a note for you to take in tomorrow." Thanks Mum.

I was 15 years old in 1961, I left school having reached stream 4B. Four years of applying myself to learning as much as I could to work my way from 1F up to 4B. I often wonder if I hadn't spent so much time under Mr Chenappa's window, could I have made it 4A, I'll never know. But I proved I wasn't a dunce. I was pleased with myself.

Chapter 26

I belonged to a youth club at the Victoria Dock Mission at the end of Tarling Road; Mr and Mrs Reeves ran it. I mentioned Mr Reeves earlier; he was the man that ran the Sunday school I went to when I was younger. Mr and Mrs Reeves were an elderly couple or seemed so to me. They were a very dedicated couple, but I did not appreciate that at that time. Mr Reeves organised lots of games for us to play. He acquired a record player and some records for us to play. . Some of the girls got a netball team together. Every now and then Mr Reeves would get a coach and take us out for the day to Southend. We weren't very nice to Mr Reeves, he was a gentle man and we used to run rings round him and play him up.

Sometime we used to attend the afternoon service on a Sunday, and Mr Reeves would take the service wearing just a normal suit. But he suffered a runny nose; he would constantly have a dewdrop hanging from his nose until he got his handkerchief out to wipe it away. We used to giggle at this and this would disrupt the service.

Mr and Mrs Reeves used to take four services on a Sunday. Sunday school was followed by morning service, afternoon service, and evening service. In between times they would go to their home, which I learned years later was Hammersly Avenue, this was a good twenty-minute walk away, and Mr Reeves did not drive.

I remember one evening about 7p.m., it was winter, it was dark, and it was snowing, and it was very windy. The snow was a good six inches deep. I looked out of the window to see what was happening with the snow and there, by the lamplight, I saw Mr Reeves trudging through the snow, his collar up on his overcoat. He had a black hat on and the wind was driving the snow into him. I knew that he had already done this walk back and forth three times and now he was going home for the fourth time. All of a sudden a feeling came over me for this man. He was a good man, doing the best job he could spreading the word of his faith to others, as well as taking on a bunch of thankless kids, keeping them off the streets and giving them something interesting to do. I vowed then that I wouldn't hurt this man again. No more being cheeky and taking the micky out of him. I would try to tell my mates the same, that they should be kinder to Mr and Mrs Reeves. Years later I saw many streets named after people, even Mr Chenappa had a close named after him. But I think Mr Reeves more than anyone deserved to have a street named after him. He was a lovely man.

The new friends I made at school Christine Neal, Val Morris and Madeline Fitzgerald invited me to go along to The Mayflower Family Centre, also known as The Docklands Settlement. It was the Tuesday Club. There was a church and some buildings where helpers stayed and joined onto to all of this were many rooms for different activities, there was even a swimming pool.

Youth leader Miss Jean Lodgepatch led the Tuesday Club; she was a tiny dark haired, attractive lady. The Rev David Shepherd (Yes, it was the same David Shepherd who played in the test matches for England.) and his wife, Grace, over saw the whole thing. These were good people; they did so much for the community, especially the kids. It was a beginning that kept a lot of my generation on the straight and narrow, especially the boys.

I already told you earlier that I was baptised into the Roman Catholic Church. But what with Mr Reeves and now the Rev David Shepherd teaching us about religion, I began to take more of an interest in the subject and felt that I did want

140

this to be a part of my life, but Mr Reeves's religion wasn't doing it for me and neither was Rev David Shepherd, but it would suffice for now. Miss Lodgepatch obviously noticed my quest for more information about religion. She presented me with the New English Bible and wrote an inscription inside and marked off Revelation 3. 20. When I looked it up it read:

Here I am! I stand at the door and knock. If anyone hears my voice and opens the door, I will come in and eat with him, and he with me. [21]*To him who overcomes, I will give the right to sit with me on my throne, just as I overcame and sat down with my Father on his throne.*

It was the perfect verse, and meant so much to me.

Two things that stick in my mind from my time at the Dockland Settlement was, our friend Val absolutely loved Tommy Steele a young English rock and roll star of the day who had found fame after being discovered in the Two Is coffee bar, Soho. Val persuaded Miss Lodgepatch to get the van and take us girls over to Bermondsey to see Tommy Steele's house, which she did. When we got there, we didn't do anything except sit on the wall in front of his house for a while then we all piled back in the van and came back to the club.

Val also got me to go to see Tommy Steele in the film *Tommy the Toreador*. Not once, not twice but seven times. By the end I knew the whole dialogue and every song by heart. I hated Tommy Steele.

The other thing we did was to persuade our cookery teacher Miss Finch to come to our club, The Docklands Settlement, or the Mayflower as it was also known. After a lot of badgering she agreed. There is an ending to this little story. In May 2009 there was an invitation that went out for 'old boys and girls' to attend a reunion at the Mayflower. I went along with my friends Barbara and her husband Jimmy Nicholls. I have to tell you here that Barbara was the younger sister to Christine Neal, and Jimmy was in my class at school. For some reason I found I got on better with Barbara and we have stayed friends throughout our lives. Back to the story of Miss Finch and the reunion. They held a lovely service and it was nice to see other friends from my old school days including Christine and Val.

Sadly by this time David Shepherd had passed away. In his career he had captained the England cricket team, been Bishop of Woolwich, and Bishop of Liverpool and finally became Lord Shepherd. However, his lovely wife Grace attended the service.

There were speeches by different people, one by the former Miss Jean Lodgepatch, who sadly didn't recognise me at all, when I re-introduced myself to her. And one by Miss Rosemary Finch who during her speech related the story of how some school children introduced her to the Mayflower. Barbara and I were nudging each other excitedly because we were two of those children. Afterwards, we went and spoke to Miss Finch and she remembered us right away. I finally confessed to her about my adding extra ingredients to the recipe's she taught us. She thought it was very funny. It was a happy ending to a story for me starting many years ago.

Chapter 27

Around 1957 my Dad got himself a transistor radio. This was extraordinary, a radio that didn't have to be plugged in to an electricity socket. He didn't have it long before I claimed it. It had an earpiece so you could listen without anyone else hearing it. This was great. I started to take it to bed and tune in and out of stations and then one night I found Radio Luxembourg. I was listening to my very first disc jockeys. Sam Costa, Jack Jackson, and Pete Murray, these are the names I remember most. More or less at the same time there was a show on the television called *Six Five Special* introduced by Pete Murray and Jo Douglas. It had a catchy signature tune by the same name and was sung by Don Lang. I began taking a real interest in the music being played. A lot of it to begin with was country and western based, and so I was listening to people like Nancy Whisky who sang 'Freight Train' in about 1957, Johnny Duncan sang 'Last Train to San Fernando' around the same year. Paul Anka was singing 'Diana', Guy Mitchell was 'Singing the Blues'. In 1958 the charts were showing artists such as Connie Francis and The Everley Brothers, The Platters, Pat Boone. And young man called Elvis Presley was doing all right for himself with a song called 'Jail House Rock'.

Up until about 1957 records had been made of a material called shellac. The records were quite heavy and were played at a speed of 78 rpm. Popular music started to really take off, a younger generation was starting to buy the records. The records became smaller, they were made out of vinyl, and they were a lot lighter and were called 45s because that was the speed they were played at. Also record players were changing and, instead of being able to play one record at a time as they did with the 78s, these new record players were able to take a stack of eight records and drop each one automatically, so you had a continuous play of your favourite music. I bought my very first record in 1959. It was called 'Dream Lover' and the artist was Bobby Darin, the second record I bought was 'Donna' by Marty Wilde. After that I was buying records every week. I used to buy my records from Sellman's in Barking Road opposite the Trossachs public house. Other records that had caught my attention around this time were 'Blue Moon' by the Marcels, 'Forty Miles of Bad Road' by Duane Eddy. We were in about 1958 or 1959 and at this time the girls of my age started following fashions, as the thing to do. Girls started to wear kitten heels, and lots of petticoats under their dresses. I also got my first bra at this time, and I have to say for me, it was like wearing a horse harness; it was awful and took me a long time to get used to it. Everyone seemed to know a dressmaker. A stall down Rathbone Street that sold lovely fresh patterned cotton was doing a roaring trade selling material to young girls like myself to have lovely flared dresses made. The lady who made dresses locally for us was called Mrs Scarborough and she would knock up a dress in two days. It didn't matter that most of the girls wore the same patterned dresses; they all had slightly different details to them. Peter Pan collars, or a sweet heart neckline, Sashes that tied up at the back or tied at the front. There was enough to make them look different to each other.

I remember the first teenage magazine for girls that came out was called *Romeo*. Two other well-known magazines for girls at the time were *Bunty* and *Judy*. Dad even helped me into teenage years; he took me and my mum and sister to see Elvis Presley's first film, *Love me Tender*. This wasn't Dad's kind of music at all; he liked Frank Sinatra and Bing Crosby. He subsequently took us to see *Loving You* and *King Creole*. So

144

fair play to him for taking my sister and me to see these teenage films. These were the beginning of exciting times.

Chapter 28

A tragedy hit our family in November 1960, I was 14 years old and this was the first time in my life that death had come so close to me.

We learned that my Dad's young cousin, Iris Watson, had suffered a heart attack on the back of her boyfriend's motorcycle. She was only in her early twenties. I never really knew Iris as well as I knew her older sister, Doreen, and her younger brothers, Peter and David, but I do know that she was a pretty girl with blonde hair, whereas all the rest of the family had dark hair.

This part of the Watson family lived in Joshua Street Poplar, just around the corner from my nan and granddad's shop in St Leonard's Road, Poplar. My Dad spoke to me and said that if I wanted to I could accompany him and Mum to go and see Iris in her coffin. I told him I was frightened of seeing a dead body. Dad said that dead bodies don't hurt you; the person just looks like they are asleep. He told me that he would be with me and that if I wanted to leave he would make sure we did with as much haste as possible. He explained a lot more to me and I knew that this was another of his wise teachings that he handed to me over the years. So we went to see Iris.

Dad went in first and left me with Mum, then he came out and said that because Iris had come off of a moving motorcycle she had a few grazes on her face, but she did look like she was asleep. So then I went in with my Mum and Dad to see Iris. She was shrouded in white silk or satin, and with her blonde hair and deathly pallor and light overhead she looked almost translucent, she could have been an angel. Seeing Iris lying there completely changed my thoughts as to what a dead body looked like. Which of course means that Dad was right to let me experience my first involvement with death.

The funeral was to be held on the 21 of November. As we prepared to leave Canning Town to head for Poplar for the funeral, Dad got a phone call, and the next thing I know we were speeding over to Poplar as fast as the little dormobile would take us. My sister and I had no idea what the excitement was all about. As soon as we pulled up outside of the shop, Dad jumped out and ran inside while Liz and me and Mum got out in our own time. As we entered the shop I saw my Uncle Alf and Uncle Frank both dressed in dark suits ready for a funeral, my Uncle Joe was standing around not sure what to do or where to be. There was one or two others standing around as well. When my uncles saw my sister and me their faces seemed to change from serious to pleasantly happy, there was an awkwardness as they spoke to us that made me realise something was really wrong. You could see that everybody was trying to hide something from my sister and me. My Dad came back to us and he told us that our granddad (his dad, Joe Jolley) had died, as he was getting ready to go to Iris's funeral. He had a died of a cerebral haemorrhage, they seemed to think that when he was first told of Iris Watson's death he thought it was his own daughter (who is also called Iris) that had died. Whether shock could cause such a thing I don't know. What a sad day the twenty-first of November was, a burial and a death on the same day.

Within a few days I was going to see my second dead body. This time my dad decided that my sister Liz should see her granddad, she was 11 years old, so she was being introduced to death at a much younger age. But my Dad was wonderful at explaining things and making things easy to understand, Liz had no problem at all seeing our granddad laid out in his coffin.

Whoever embalmed my granddad was an artist; he really did look like he was asleep. So much so I turned to my Dad saying that I could see him breathing. My granddad was laid out in a lead lined coffin. He wore a pair of red and white striped pyjamas, red carpet slippers and a deep red dressing gown. My Dad asked if we wanted to kiss our granddad and we said we did. I was tall enough to lean over and kiss him, and my dad lifted Liz up to place her kiss on his forehead.

I do not remember one thing about Iris Watson's funeral; I can't even remember where she is buried, or even if she was cremated. But I remember every detail of my granddad's funeral. He was buried in St Patrick's Catholic cemetery in Leytonstone, along with his mother-in-law Annie Watson and his brother-in-law John Watson.

After the funeral we came back to my Dad's sister Jean's (Jinny) café, she had laid on a lovely big spread of food for the mourners. A little later, after a lot of people had gone we went back across the road to my nan's shop and the front room above. Aunts and uncles were talking and chatting, and then someone got some drinks out, and the next thing I know everybody is laughing and joking, I couldn't understand how people could be like this when we had just buried my granddad. What happened to the serious faces earlier that day? I didn't understand.

I can't remember exactly when it was, but within in a few years I was to see yet another dead body, this time it was very moving. It was a young girl the same age as myself, Barbara Chambers. Barbara had suffered heart problems. Maybe as a result of a bout of rheumatic fever, I'm not sure. However, around this time surgeons had been pioneering the operation for replacement heart valves and Barbara was one of the early patients. Sadly it was not a success. Barbara was a lovely girl from a very nice Catholic family. Barbara's mum said that I, along with some other of Barbara's friends could go and see her if we wanted to. I was the only one of all my friends that had seen a dead body, so I explained to my mates as my Dad had explained to me that it was nothing to worry about. So

148

three of us went and knocked on Mrs Chamber's door and she let us in and led us into the front room. It wasn't a big room, and apart from the coffin and a few chairs it was empty. All of the walls had been draped from top to bottom in pale mauve silk or satin, black velvet ribbon made to look like crosses hung two feet apart all around the room. Mrs Chambers led us over to Barbara's coffin and there she was, our dear friend. The tears welled up in my eyes, and a lump formed in my throat. This was the first time death had really touched my heartstrings. I didn't have any of these feeling with Iris or my granddad; my feelings with them were bewilderment.

What a devoted mother Mrs Chambers was, every year for the rest of her life a memorial notice was put in the Stratford Express that became the Newham Recorder, twice a year, once on Barbara's birthday and once on the anniversary of her death.

Chapter 29

My Dad was always thinking up things to do. He bought a Grundig tape recorder; it was a big thing that had large reel-to-reel tapes. It was so strange hearing your own voices, and when I heard mine I hated it. Did I really sound like that!

Dad would set up little sketches of one person interviewing another on the silliest of subjects. The fact that we had to try to be serious would send us off into fits of laughter. My Mum was the worse one for doing this. In the theatre they call it corpsing. Corpsing is a theatrical slang term used to describe when an actor starts laughing during a scene and by doing so causes another cast member or more to laugh. It is believed the term 'corpsing' originated whenever a living actor played a corpse on stage; there was sometimes a tendency to try to make that actor laugh.

Anyway Mum was the world's worse, she would just start to laugh and we would all be on the floor, not really knowing what it was we were laughing at. Then we would get ourselves straight to have another go at the staged interview, and Mum would set us all off again. The one who laughed the most at this was my Dad.

Out of the blue one evening he said we are all going to be birds, he looked at my mum and said, "What bird do you want to be?" She said, "Oh! What about a sparrow?" Dad turned to me and said, "What bird do you want to be?" I said a blackbird. I had no idea where this was leading. Then he asked what bird my sister Liz wanted to be and she said a budgie.

Dad said he would be a seagull. He then went and got the tape recorder ready to record, He got the microphone and hung it from the light pendant in the middle of the ceiling, then he turned to us all and asked if we knew the tune to the 'Chocolate Soldier', we didn't and so he la la lahed the tune for us, then we realised we all knew the tune. He told us to stand in a circle around the microphone that was hanging down. Dad said, "Right, I want you all to whistle that tune when I count to three, ready, one two three." We all started to whistle the tune, It all started okay, then Mum started to laugh, Dad tried to keep me and my sister going, but then I started to laugh, then my Dad and sister. We kept trying to whistle the tune, the more we tried the more we laughed, our faces ached. I can't tell you how many times we stopped and then started again, only to start laughing again, I also can't remember if we ever got right the way through the tune, probably not.

Chapter 30

There seemed to be electricity in the air at the start of this decade 1960 it was as though we had been looking at everything through gauze and suddenly this was lifted and there was vibrant colour. Everything was sharper.

I think the first thing I associated with the swinging 60s is the 'The Twist', sung and danced by Chubby Checker. People everywhere were doing this dance. I bought the record and played it till it was almost worn out. The carpet in front of our radiogram became threadbare with all the twisting that I and my sister and even my Mum did to this record.

May 1 1961. I was 15 and by the summer of that year I had left school.

Mum and Dad gave me a party for leaving school and I invited all my friends. My Aunt Jinny and Uncle Frank, and my Aunt Iris acted as chaperones. Uncle Frank made a punch for us to drink; I didn't think this was very 'cool'. But the punch went down a storm and my friends were asking for more.

Dad expected me to go to work for him in the shop but I wasn't interested. He made me a couple of offers; the first was to buy me my own little greengrocer's shop, which I declined. Once Dad knew I was serious about not going into the greengrocery business, he went on to make a couple more offers. The next one was to go to art school, which he would pay for. Art school may have appealed to me and I did have a relative who was an art teacher who said I would benefit from going but I still declined. The third offer was he wanted to send me to a finishing school in London, and again I declined. Years later I regretted not taking either of the last two opportunities. I guess I was going through that stage of making my own mind up rather than your parents making it up for you.

One thing I did know was that I was not going to work in Tate and Lyle's. I'd prove that the teacher I overheard several years before in the teacher's staff room was wrong. I wanted to work in an office, doing what? I had no idea. I did go to night school to learn typing and shorthand. The typing I didn't do so bad at, but the shorthand was like hieroglyphics to me. I gave up.

In those days work was plentiful and you could just go and knock on doors and ask if they had any job vacancies. I was called in for several interviews, but they didn't take me on. I knocked on doors almost to the end of September. Eventually at one door I knocked on they took me on. Not because of any skills that I may or may not have had. I was taken on purely because my name was Jolly. (They remembered the name from years before.) The company was W&C Tipple Ltd in Brunel Street. It was the firm that I had lived opposite to in the early years of my life, the firm whose canteen Dad used to deliver produce to.

A Miss Halls interviewed me. She was the secretary of the company and the sister-in-law to Mr Tipple. Miss Halls spoke of my family and said she remembered my dad. Finally she offered me a job, and I was to start the following Monday at 8.30 a.m. I asked her if she would write a letter for me to take home to my dad telling him I had a job with the firm, which she did. I went skipping home and plonked the letter in my dad's hands. I think he was impressed.

Monday came around and I had butterflies in my stomach, I had no idea what to expect. All I knew about Tipples was that they sold steel and they also had a shop where you could buy screws and nails and stuff like that.

I was introduced to a lady called Miss Thompson. She was a secretary to Miss Halls who saw to the general overall running of the office. She had shoulder length jet-black hair that was bobbed with curls, and a curly fringe. She had features that showed her to have at least one Chinese parent. She was about 5 foot 3 inches tall with a slim figure. This lady was to become another teacher to me, and I was going to be her best pupil. The first thing she said to me, was to call her Miss Thom

The first thing I was introduced to was the clocking in machine. We clocked in at 8.30 a.m. and we clocked out at 5 p.m. It was not tolerated being late and if you were late your wages would be reduced accordingly. If you were late more than three times in a month without a good enough explanation, you were sacked.

My wages were £3.15 shillings per week, (£3.75) it doesn't sound a lot but in those days that kind of money went a long way. It was expected that once you started work that you would give up part of your wages to your parents for 'your keep'. My Mum didn't make any stipulations what amount of money she expected off me. I just decided myself to hand over £1.10 shillings per week, (£1.50) and she was okay with that.

The first task I was given was as a filing clerk, which was a lowly job, but it did give me time to see how the office worked, and who was who in the hierarchy, and also what it was exactly that Tipples was all about. I was a fast learner, and it wasn't long before I was given another job to do, which was as an invoice clerk. This meant that I worked direct to Miss Thomson. There were three of us sat around a very large table, Miss Thomson, the Order Typist and myself. The room we were in was adjoining the one Miss Halls occupied.

We worked hard but we had plenty of chatty conversations. I learned that Miss Thomson was in fact married to a Mr Richard E. Baker, known as Reb, (because of his initials). He was a travelling salesman with routes around London touting for orders for the firm of Tipples. Reb had a brother George Baker who was the head buyer for the firm. I guess in all there were about twenty-five people that worked in the different departments of the offices.

Then there was the shop, and this was staffed by two people, plus a supervisor. The despatch office was overseen by a manager and his assistant and below them was four workers. There were six lorries and their drivers that delivered steel and nuts and bolts etc, and then there was the Bright steel department manned by two workers. The product Bright steel was shiny and oily. Two people also manned the Black steel department. Black steel was rusty. Then there was another building called the iron works where things were made by welding it together. I never really had anything much to do with this department; it seemed a law unto itself, although I did know the manager and his assistant.

There's a special memory I have about the manager of this department. His name was Mr Luft; he had very bad feet that required specially made shoes. He was probably in his late 50s when I came to know him, but seemed much older. He wasn't a talkative or friendly man, he just got on and did his job. But something about him made me feel sorry for him. I used to have to deliver papers to him every day, I would just say good morning and leave the work for him. Usually he just gave a grunt. Over the course of time after bidding him good morning, I would add, "How are you today?" And again I would receive just a grunt. But, perseverance in the end paid off and one day after a very long time, I received back a proper good morning with a smile. I had pierced Mr Luft's armour. From little acorns as they say. Over more time I got to know Mr Luft a little more, and we would have pleasant little chats about different things. I didn't learn anything about his private life except that he was a bachelor. I was pleased that I opened up a door between Mr Luft, and me, which led us towards being friendlier.

I enjoyed talking to people, and still do. One of the lorry drivers told me of his experiences being a prisoner of war in Germany during WWII His POW camp wasn't far from one of the death camps where many Jews died. He said they would

155

often get an acrid smell come over the camp when the wind was in the right direction from the crematorium ovens which they used to dispose of Jews.

My friendliness toward people in Tipples got me in a difficult situation once. Most of the men who worked in the Black and Bright Steel departments were black men and some were illiterate, this I know because when some of the men had to sign something they put a cross in the signature space. The colour of someone's skin had never bothered me having been looked after by several black people when I was very young. But in my naivety, I didn't know that many black people weren't so welcomed by some white people. A man in the Black steel department handed me a package and walked off.

I went up to the office I shared with Miss Thomson and told her about the package I had been given, we opened it together and there was a beautiful pearl necklace. She quizzed me on who the person was and why he should give me such a gift. She told me that it was inappropriate to accept this gift and that I was to give it back immediately, as accepting it could mislead the person who gave it to me. So I did go to the man and explained that I couldn't accept the gift, and I was sorry if he mistook my friendliness for anything more. The man above him that he worked alongside, who was also black, also explained that it was wrong for him to give me such a gift. That was my first encounter of a 'them' and 'us' culture with black people. Not my feelings, but other peoples.

As time went on a young man came to work in the shop, his name was Lenny. I became friends with him and soon we became boyfriend-girlfriend. We got on well. Lenny was very charming and got on with everybody well, especially the girls. After about ten months of going together, Lenny turned up at work one day with a big love bites on his neck. We had a blazing row and that was the end of our romance. Which was a big disappointment to Lenny's mum and dad who I got on extremely well with. I think Lenny's Mum always thought that Lenny and I would end up getting married. I couldn't stay mad at Lenny so we still remained friends. More will be written about Lenny later.

I carried on working hard at Tipples and was made Order Typist. I never really trained properly at typing, but I picked up speed through repetition and a good memory. In the beginning I could only manage about twenty orders a day, but once I got proficient I was typing up to 100 orders a day.

From typing orders I was put into the Buying office under Mr George Baker who as I said was the head buyer. He was a nice man to work for, very kind and easy going. I was one of three people to work under Mr Baker. I started off doing clerical work and filing, but soon I was promoted and became assistant buyer to George Baker.

I worked at Tipples for five years. In that time my salary hadn't gone up by much. I was now earning £9.10 shillings per week. I decided to go and ask for a raise. Which was the done thing in those days, if you didn't belong to a union. You were more or less paid for what they thought you were worth, there were no pay scales to go by. So I went in and asked Miss Halls for a ten bob (shillings) rise and she said NO! I came out of the office and got talking to a senior member of staff who was also related by marriage to Miss Halls. I told him that I had been turned down for a ten bob rise and was making my disappointment quite obvious with some well-chosen remarks spoken in a raised voice.

I then went back to my office, but was shortly called back to Miss Halls' office. She told me that she had overheard my conversation and was very disappointed with me for discussing the issue with another member of staff. I got quite belligerent with her attitude and ended up having a few words, lost my temper and handed in my notice walking out of the job. Two weeks later I had a new job earning £11.00 per week working as a typist for Rye Arc, a ship repair company. Now I was really in the money, I gave Mum a raise in my 'keep money'. I was now giving her £5.10 shillings a week. She always got half of whatever it was I earned. She never asked for it, I just gave it.

About 1961 a new family moved in on our communal veranda. They were Mr and Mrs Hickey. They had a son and daughter, Diane and David. Gradually I got to know Diane and we became friends. Her family had moved to Canning Town from Stratford so most of her friends were still there. Diane's family were Catholics and she still had another year to do at St Angela's school for girls while David still had a couple more years at St Bonaventure's school for boys.

Diane and I got on well and as time went on she introduced me to many of her friends from Stratford. One of her friends Marie had a brother Philip and he had a lot of mates and so it was quite a large group of boys and girls. Generally all the girls went and did their thing while all the boys went and did theirs. Quite often there would be a party at someone's house and there we all joined in, enjoying whatever was going.

Diane and me and a couple of girls from Stratford would often go to Stratford Town Hall which was run by Kenny Johnson, he was the brother to Eddie Johnson who ran the Two Pudding Pub in Stratford. Kenny's Dad used to take the money in the little box office of the Stratford Town Hall on a Saturday night. There would be a live group or two provided to dance to. As there wasn't any alcohol served we would wait for the intermission, and that would be an opportunity to nip round the corner to get a quick drink in the Queen's Head in the tramway and a meat pie from of Vi's stall. 'Vi's Pies' as we called them.

I used to love getting dressed up to go out on a Saturday night, putting my makeup on. I never wore a lot of makeup, as it felt too much like I had a mask on. But I would really do my eye's up. I would put my eye shadow on and then the eyeliner and then the mascara. Mascara used to come in a little plastic case with a black block and a little brush. You had to spit on the block and rub the brush in it, then when there was enough mascara on the brush you would apply it your eyelashes, you would do this until you built up thick layers on your eyelashes.

Doing my hair was another long job. It was all backcombed up to puff it out. It was called a bouffant. You had to make sure that you didn't have the backcomb showing through, this was okay from the front as you could see what you were doing, but you needed another mirror to get the back of your hair right. And then you lacquered it. We didn't have aerosols in those days. We used to go to Feldman's in Barking Road, who would sell a little plastic bottle with a spray on it, and fill it with a light brown liquid. You would keep squeezing the bottle for the spray of lacquer to come out. Once you had squirted the stuff all over, your hair was as stiff as a board. Believe me, force ten gales would not move one hair out of place with this stuff. You didn't bother to comb your hair out for a few days. It took a long time to get enough lacquer on it, and back combing in it to have a bouffant that any grenadier guardsman would have been proud to wear instead of a bearskin.

Most of my clothes I bought during the sixties were in Jackson's next to Woolworths in Barking Road. My shoes I bought in Midgeon's, also in Barking Road.

In Rathbone market there were a couple of sister's who sold lovely tops and jumpers.

Once you had your outfit on, no self-respecting girl would go out if her shoes and handbag didn't match in colour. It was, 'de rigueur.'

The biggest killers for me in those days were the high heel winkle picker shoes. They crippled my toes. The heels were never more than about three inches high, but the fact that your heel was higher than your toes meant that your toes slid forward and tried to squeeze into the narrowest point, agony for me. Plus I couldn't dance in high heels either. And I loved to dance.

It was vital whenever I was choosing the handbag that matched my shoes that I had to make sure a pair of flat comfortable shoes would fit inside. Size was everything then, the bag I mean. Who cared that my shoes and bag didn't match when I came home; everyone was too merry to take any notice by then.

Rathbone Street was originally one of the old markets that had stalls either side with shops behind them. It ran from Barking Road down to Hallsville Road. Markets like this were both colourful and noisy. It was a good market. In 1963 Newham Council decided to modernise it and move it up to Barking Road, There were about sixty shops and over one hundred and fifty stalls. The local populace didn't popularly receive it and thought the move to be ill judged.

One of the stalls in the old market was Ron's Record stall. This had been a popular stall for teenagers to hang around and listen to all the latest music. But fortunately for Ron when he moved with his stall to its new location up on the Barking Road it became just as popular. I was one of those teenagers that hung around listening to the latest music. Ron was a great bloke, but the one who really ran the stall was his assistant Johnny Thompson. He was of our age group. I never got tired of flicking through the LPs looking for the one I wanted to buy. We used to exchange knowledge of different artists that we had heard about. One such artist was a young American Jewish girl called Timi Yuro; she had a most powerful voice. She never really made it over here; I think it is because she didn't come to the East End where she had the biggest following.

Nothing would keep us away from Ron's Record stall on a Saturday. We were there in all weathers. There was an ABC cafeteria above the shops opposite Ron's stall and we would go up there for cups of tea to keep warm in the winter. It was a good meeting place as everyone would pass Ron's stall at some point and stop for a chat, find out who was going where and make arrangements of where we were all going to meet up that night.

Getting back to Stratford again, it was a lively place, with its own street market 'Angel Lane', and just around the corner was the Theatre Royal, also known as Joan Littlewood's workshop. She put on many shows there before they went into the West End, such as *Sparrows Can't Sing* that was made into a film starring Barbara Windsor. I think a *Taste of Honey* started there and also *Oh, What a Lovely War*, and *Fing's Ain't What They Used T'be,* by Lionel Bart. I know Princess Margaret and Anthony Armstrong Jones and Jess Conrad used to go along and see these productions. I went with my parents to see *Sparrows Can't Sing*, which was much better than the film in my opinion.

I think it was Kenny Johnson who ran the Lotus dance hall in Woodgrange Road Forest Gate. We thought we were really sophisticated there as we could order drinks and have supper too; chicken in the basket with French fries how posh is that, not chips anymore? Other places we used to go dancing were The Room at the Top, and the Ilford Palais. They were great nights out. I wonder how many girls remember that we used to put a spare fiver in our bra or in our shoe just in case we lost our handbag and needed emergency money to get home, or was that just me?

Around this time we started to go to pubs, when I first started drinking it was port and lemonade, (port and lemon). It didn't take long to progress to scotch and coke, then rum and coke, then vodka and coke or lemonade. I was quiet pleased when we got to martini and lemonade, I never really liked any of the other drinks, but I drank them, Why? I dunno.

Some of the pubs we used to go to were The Lord Rookwood, the Adam and Eve in Abbey Lane, Stratford, The Two Puddings, and The Aberdeen, also the Dueragon. It was the Dueragon Arms that was run by the well-known female impersonator Gay Travers, for many years. Gay built up a large following in pubs in the East End in the sixties. He also appeared at the Theatre Royal, Stratford East in variety shows. As well as working as a singer and comedian, he compered many shows and was known for his theme tune, 'I Won't Send Roses'. He always played to large audiences and many East End publicans were grateful to him for the business he attracted. I got to know Gay when he did the compering at Daniel Farson's pub, The Waterman's Arms. Gay was great company to be in, he knew just about everyone there was to know and he drew you in, his quick wit had me almost peeing myself.

Locally in Canning Town we would go to the Essex Arms in Silvertown Way or the Ground Rent in Rogers Road. There were lots of other pubs where we went to for a quick drink. To name just a few, The Chandelier, The Windsor Castle and The Ordnance Arms.

Talking of pubs has just brought a thought to mind. There were so many pubs at that time; practically every street corner had one, you didn't need a fancy SAT NAV then. If someone stopped you for directions you could direct the person for miles just by the locations of the pubs.

Back to Diane and the boys and girls. I don't know how but at some point all of us girls would meet up with the boys for a party at someone's house. We had a few parties at Marie's. Then Diane also had a party at her house. Everyone was having parties! So, I asked Mum and Dad if we could have a party at our house and they agreed. The other boys in the group were Danny and George and Bob. Now Bob was gorgeous and real charmer, just like Lenny from a few years before. But Bob was a better kisser. Somehow at the end of each party the boys and girls would pair off for snogging sessions and I got Bob; I got the jackpot. We were never boyfriend/girlfriend, he was just fun to be with. Somewhere along the line Bob and John (Candle) ended up working as Saturday boys for my dad, I don't know how that happened. I often wonder where they all are now?

Sunday was spent in bed getting over the night before. Dad would bring me up a cup of tea and a newspaper and there I would stay till my mum called me down for Sunday Dinner, then I'd go back to bed again.

Fashion and music was everything in the 60s. There was a choice you could make. You could either carry on listening to Elvis Presley's and the Tommy Steel's music from the 50s? Or you could embrace what was now happening on the streets. For me the choice was easy, either Rockers with their drab black leather jackets, with grease slicked backed hair, or clean-cut smart boys who rode Lambretta and Vespa scooters? Sorry if I offend some people but 'Rockers' just weren't my scene, I was a 'Mod'.

Being a Mod in the 60s was a complete lifestyle choice - clothes, music, clubs and scooters. Mods did normal jobs, but once work was over, we drowned ourselves in the lifestyle of being a Mod. Mod bands such as The Who, the Small Faces and the Kinks also adopted the Mod style, Rolling Stones, Manfred Mann. London was mostly at the forefront of music. One of the real Mod bands of the day that had a big following were the Dave Clark Five, we used to go down to Locarno in Basildon Essex to see them; they were gorgeous.

There was also a strong influence from black American music artists R & B (Rhythm and Blues), and there were black artists that released songs under the Tamla Motown label. For any self-respecting Mod teenager in the mid-1960s, tuning into the Friday night pop show, *Ready Steady Go*. To watch Patrick Kerr demonstrate the latest 'in' dance craze was an essential weekend ritual. *Ready Steady Go* (or RSG), was first broadcast in 1963 from Wembley. The programme's hosts were Keith Fordyce and Cathy McGowan. Keith was the mature host, I guess he had the TV experience, Cathy was the Mod 'it' girl. She also wrote for 'The Mod's' monthly magazine. RSG brought all the music and dance we liked to our very own front rooms.

I used to go to a tailor in Dalston and have suede jackets made to my own design. Cherry Red, Bottle Green, Midnight Blue. four-inch vent, or a six-inch vent, and leather collar on this jacket or a ticket pocket on that jacket, leather flaps on these pockets, no flaps. If you could dye your hush puppies to match your jacket even better. We were so smart; we walked around with our heads held high and our shoulders back.

The boys were really smart and usually went to bespoke tailors to have their clothes tailor-made. The Mod haircut was the 'College Boy'; derived from the 'American Ivy League' look, of the late fifties. They bought the Lambretta and Vespa

GS scooters and started wearing 'Parka' jackets over their smart suits. Just about every girl wanted a bloke who had a scooter. The places to go to on a summer's weekend were Southend or Brighton or Margate, There were some clashes with Rockers in Clacton and Hastings that hit the headlines, but mostly Mods wanted to stay away from that sort of behaviour.

I had a couple of groups of friends on the go, one was with Barbara, she was a couple of years younger than me, her sister Christine was in my class at school, I got to know Barbara over time when I used to call for Christine to go to school. Another was with Theresa. I had known her a long time because her Mum and Dad used to be customers in our shop but we became friendly when I was about 11, and then there was Diane and I've already told you how we became friends.

Diane took me to a Catholic youth club that had been started in a new building at the back of St Margaret's Church, it was owned by the church. Downstairs there was a bar you had to be twenty-one or over to get into. Upstairs there was a hall and coffee bar and a games room; there was a juke box in the corner of the hall with all the latest records on it. Diane introduced me to her friends, Denny Pullinger, Jackie Stevens and Kay Deliue. I said I would like to bring another friend of mine into the group, Barbara Neal. Up until this time Diane had been my dance partner, but somehow, in a short space of time Barbara became my dance partner and we were good, but good wasn't good enough, we wanted to be the best. We practised dancing with each other and when we were apart we practised with the doors in our own front rooms. We watched other people and learnt some of their moves, made up some of our own, we got to the point that people would stop and watch us, and copy us. We had become the trendsetters.

We started having Sunday dances in St Margaret's club and we would have a live band come along to play. Everybody used to look forward to these dances. Until one day the group let us down, we had all the teenagers present but no music. I forgot to mention that I was on the youth committee at this

164

point. I suggested to the warden that if someone could drive me home I would get all my popular records and my record player, and with the clubs record player we could have non stop music from the charts. This was quickly arranged. It didn't take long to set up, as soon as the first record player was plugged in and a record slapped on, it gave enough time to get the other record player set up and another record waiting to be played. This was 1963. Inadvertently I had created a disco, but I didn't know it. If I had had the brains to slot these two turntables into one unit I would have created the first piece of disco equipment. (I missed the chance of that invention.) The only DJs up till that time were on Radio Luxembourg, More popular DJs weren't to come along for another eighteen months in 1964 when Radio Caroline, the pirate radio station started broadcasting.

This one off Sunday dance without the group was a success and I learned that being a DJ was hard work, keeping everybody happy and keeping them on the floor dancing. More about DJs later.

Father Papworth used to come up to the youth club and we would have group chats about anything and everything, he was interested in all of us and we were interested in him. Because we all knew what he could and couldn't do we used to wind him up a bit, but he would get his own back on us. He had a great sense of humour. Father Papworth was a good looking young priest (what a waste). One time when we were chatting, I saucily said to him, "You know Father, if you didn't have that dog collar on I could really fancy you," and with that he whipped it off. I was in shock and dumb struck. He certainly called my bluff. When I became twenty-one, Father Papworth bought me my first legal drink in the bar below the youth club.

I guess we were pretty lucky in Canning Town. St Margaret's youth club was more or less open every night of the week except Saturday. There were a couple of other clubs that some of the teenagers went to, like St Andrew's at the Greengate, or St Cedd's on the A13.

Our group got bigger as the boys joined in with us. There was Johnny Reynolds, Johnny Hill, Tony Delamura, Tony Wiskin, Johnny Hooper, Brian Westwood, Bobby Hoares, and a quite a few more.

I don't think the 60s would be entirely complete without mentioning The Beatles. My Uncle Alf had a greengrocer's shop in north London and he heard that the Beatles were coming to the Astoria Cinema at Finsbury Park. Uncle Alf had a few connections and was able to get some tickets to see the show. He gave me three tickets so I took my sister and my mate, and he told me that there would be a couple of boys sitting next to us as well, one of which used to help him out in the shop. It turned out that the boy who worked for him was Pat Rice, who eventually played for and captained Arsenal, and subsequently became assistant to Arsene Wenger.

This would have been about 1964. I enjoyed the show right up until the Beatles came along and after that I never heard a word for all the screaming that was going on, didn't see much of them either with all the jumping up and down. Still at least I can say I was there!

As for Pat Rice, he remained a family friend up until about the late 70s. Thanks to Pat Rice's generosity with supplying tickets, I did get to see the FA cup Final in 1971 when Charlie George scored the winning goal in extra time against Liverpool. We had fabulous seats sitting right in front of the Royal Box. Pat was a nice lad. He kind of went his own way when he started courting his wife; and I think her name was Betty.

Chapter 31

Our country retreat was a caravan in the county of Kent in a village called Wateringbury.

Sometime around 1961 our little family were travelling in the van coming back from a weekend camping break at Three Chimney Farm in Goudhurst, (still in Kent). Dad decided to change route and make his way through the village of Yalding taking us towards the river Medway. As we crossed the river via Bow Bridge at Wateringbury, Dad spotted a couple of caravans up on a bank along by the river. Dad decided to investigate further. So he looked for and found the owner of the site, a Mr Burt Buffrey. The owner said that he was going to let about ten plots for caravans. Dad right away asked him to reserve three plots for him. Within in the next couple of months Dad had bought a caravan and soon had it placed on site. My Aunt Jinny and Uncle Frank and my Nan and Iris had their caravans along side of ours, which was great. Three in a row! The site was all very basic, just a cinder path, a stand pipe for water and a ladies and gents toilet. And we loved it, much more comfortable than sleeping in the van. And we could go down every weekend in the summer months.

Soon after getting the caravan Dad bought a boat, it was a two-berth cabin cruiser. At this time there weren't any boats on this stretch of the River Medway. Dad had to moor the boat on the opposite bank. At first this meant that he had to walk up and over Bow Bridge then down a flight of iron steps, then walk along the bank to the boat. Then he had to start the boat up and bring it to the side where the caravans were for us all to jump on and go for a ride. Later he bought a dinghy so that he could row across to the boat. As time went on a few more people got boats and they now were able to moor them in front of the caravans. At that time it was sixpence per foot, per week. Our boat was sixteen foot long. You do the maths. I think the rent for the caravans worked out about £250 per year.

Mr Buffrey and his French wife lived in the upstairs part of a brick building. Down below they kept all the stuff for his large boat that he often took across to France. At one time he turned part of this into a little café. You could get a cup of tea or an ice cream. It was handy as there were a lot of fishermen that came down and lots of day visitors that would come down and have a picnic.

Having the caravan in Wateringbury acted as a base for us to get out and about. It was in easy reach for going to Folkestone, Herne Bay and Whitstable and many other places including Folkestone Race Course. But mostly we stayed around the caravan and on the boat. We enjoyed going to the nearby pub called the 'The Railway' for a lunchtime drink on a Sunday. But it was on a Saturday night that we liked going to the 'Telegraph' pub because it had bar billiards and a couple of slot machines. We more or less had the place to ourselves.

Opposite our caravan across the river was a field. It was so pleasant watching the animals grazing which were usually sheep and sometime cows. We would take many pleasant walks around the village and up in the fields and orchards. We always made our way to the Mill Pond area having a browse through the Mill Potteries admiring the work of a potter who had set up his workshop there in the old mill. I bought several of his pots which I still have to this day.

Our holidays were now spent in Wateringbury. During the school holidays me and Mum and Liz would stay for the week, but Dad would drive back and forth every day to run the shop in London. We couldn't wait for market day to go into Maidstone. In those days it took nearly the whole day to go around the market. It was wonderful. It was here I developed my taste for rummaging through the junk on the little so-called antique stalls. I also enjoyed bidding on the auctions that were held there. I could buy great stuff, useful stuff, for next to nothing.

The Medway often flooded in the winter, but my nan's caravan and ours were higher up on the bank so we were never flooded. But Jinny and Franks caravan did and they often had to renew their contents over the years.

A couple of little stories come to mind of our times in Wateringbury.

The family had been staying at the caravan, but my sister and I planned to go back to London on the Saturday for her to meet her boyfriend and for me to go to a party. We packed the one suitcase between us and set off on our journey to London From Wateringbury station. It was raining, it was that fine rain that soaks you to the skin. The train we were catching would only take us to Paddock Wood where we would have to change to wait for another train to take us to London. To catch this train meant crossing over a bridge to another platform, and that's where the trouble started. Because of the rain the steps were very slippery and I fell very hard on my knees. A young girl behind me laughed. That made me angry and I knew if I opened my mouth I would blow up like a volcano to anyone around me. Liz knew this and after checking that I was okay she didn't talk to me again. We boarded the train taking us to Charing Cross. There was no conversation the whole way until we were almost at our destination and I spoke to Liz and said sorry about being miserable. She said it was all right she understood.

As we pulled into the platform I got off the train first, and Liz handed the suitcase to me. I set it down on the platform. When Liz got off she grabbed the handle of the suitcase and started to walk on. But there was a problem. All she had in the grip of her hand was just the handle; the suitcase was still sitting on the platform. I started to laugh and then Liz started to laugh. Somehow between us we managed to carry the suitcase out of the station. A young gypsy woman came up to us

169

carrying a basket and said. "Buy some lucky white heather." To which I replied, "You're a bit f**king late with that luv." This caused Liz and me to laugh even more.

Some years later the caravans and site was taken over by Ivan and his family. They brought about many changes, which were quite good. The first was to upgrade the toilets and put in showers. Then he laid a tarmac path over the cinder track that was more suitable to cope with the rain. In time he also put up electric lighting. While this was going on he also had a house built and turning part of it into a restaurant, which was named The Riverside Restaurant. Things moved on again and slowly a marina started to take shape on the opposite side to the restaurant. We used the caravan that my Dad had bought right up until 2008 when the family finally decided to give it up.

Chapter 32

I told you about my first experience with a dirty old man. There was another when I was a teenager. It was a summer's evening and I was on my way up to St Margaret's. I had to pass a lorry driver's motel at the bottom of the Silvertown Way. This was a stop off for lorries from all over the place. As I passed a lorry I heard someone call out and I turned to where the voice came from. There stood a short, balding little man in his forties, with his penis hanging out. Well I turned and ran like hell back home, to tell my Dad. Straight away he called the police, and from my description the man was picked up. I can't remember the time scale now, but at some point we had to go to Stratford Magistrates court. To my surprise, we had to wait in the same area as the man who had exposed himself to me. I was really scared. Someone in the court said that the man was pleading not guilty and so I would have to go in and give evidence. But right at the last minute, the man changed his plea to guilty and was fined £5 for indecent exposure. I heard too that he was a father himself and had a couple of young children of his own.

Over a long period of time I encountered loads of flashers. After all my experiences I was so frightened walking home alone in the dark. The Silvertown Way was always deserted; you had to pass either a lot of factories or St Luke's church before you got to the housing estate where I lived. The factories had so many places a person could hide, and the church was all in darkness looming up. I would ring my Mum and she would come to meet me. The time usually coincided with Timmy the dog's last walk. So she would have him with her. It never occurred to me that she might be frightened from any kind of danger from these dirty old men. But she was always there, like a safe harbour always waiting for me.

Thinking about Timmy our little dog again, I have to tell the story of when we had to have him put down. As I said before he was over 16 years old when we had him put to sleep. The day was a Thursday and it was summertime, we were so upset, all of us cried. Mum wanted to bury Timmy, but our yard at the back of the shop was all concreted over, so the only place we could bury Timmy was down behind the caravan in Wateringbury. However, we wouldn't be going down to Wateringbury till Saturday evening after Dad had shut up shop.

In Dad's shop he had a big freezer. We called it the Birdseye freezer because most of the stuff were items made by Birdseye, fish fingers and steak and kidney pies and chicken pies as well as frozen peas and runner beans.

We had to keep Timmy fresh for his burial or else he would have stunk the place out as he started to decompose.

Dad placed Timmy in a curled up position in a box lying on a blanket so he looked like he was asleep. Dad wrote on a brown paper bag, 'Our Timmy died aged 16 years and 8 months', and placed it just above Timmy, then he scooped out a potato and used it as a candle holder. Every day, Timmy laid at the back of the shop with his little death notice and a lit candle. We would look at him and stroke his little body. It was a sad time. Then every evening after the shop shut and unbeknown to all of dads' customers Timmy was placed in the Birdseye freezer. God only knows what the customers would have said if they knew there was a dead dog in with the fish fingers they were likely to buy. Saturday finally came round and we were able to bury our dear little dog.

Chapter 33

I was nineteen years of age when the Sixties was in full swing; it was like being on a roller coaster ride.

In January 1965, Winston Churchill died. It may seem strange reading that a teenager having such a 'swinging time in the sixties' would care about something like this, but I did. I suppose being born in 1946 you heard so much about the war and the major players who took part such as Field Marshall Montgomery, General Eisenhower, and the great man himself, Churchill.

I came home from work one evening and Dad asked Mum and me if we would like to go and see Churchill lying in state at Westminster Hall, we said okay. We thought we would just park up the van, go into Westminster Hall and then home again. We would probably be there for only a couple of hours at most. (Or so we thought.) We parked up the van, and then found a queue quite close to Westminster Hall. However, we didn't know that the queue snaked on right past Westminster Hall and went round and round for what seemed to be forever. Once we got into the queue that was it. You just had to see it through to the end. Little did we know then that the end was six hours away? We had just started to file past the coffin and just as we got in line with the catafalque we witnessed something amazing. The queue was stopped and we were to witness the changing of the honour guard. The soldiers guarding the coffin did a changeover, without a word being spoken, only soft taps were heard, the soldiers made the change and the new guard took up its position, I'll never forget that moment, it was amazing how they did it.

Meanwhile back at home, my 16-year-old sister Liz was frantic with worry. Because we thought we would be just a couple of hours, we didn't bother to leave a note to tell her where we were. Once we got in the queue we had no way of contacting her, we didn't know where any phone boxes were.

Liz was ringing family members, and then she rang the police telling them that we were missing. The police were telling her that everything would be all right and she was worrying for nothing. We didn't get home till about 2. 30 a.m. the next morning. It must have been awful for her not knowing all that time where we were.

Chapter 34

1967 It was my 21st birthday and I was starting my second job with Rye Arc in Peto Street Canning Town E16. Rye Arc was a ship repair company that worked on the Shaw Saville Line, the Furness Withy line and Royal Mail Line ships in the Royal docks.

I was secretary to four ship managers. Each time a ship docked, one of the ship managers would go on board and write up a list of repairs that needed to be done or new work that was required. He would then hand me his written list and then I would type it up and hand it out to the relevant workshops, which were the Sail Makers, the Carpenters, and Engineers, etc. It was very interesting work.

There was a switchboard operator who worked there her name was Joan, I knew her from school days. Part of my duties was to man the switchboard while Joan went to lunch. The switchboard was a PBX ten plus fifty dolls eye. It meant it could support ten incoming/outgoing lines and have up to fifty telephone extension. You'd think after my experience with Mr Chenappa's phone at school that I would have shied away from this but as it turned out it was fairly easy to pick up. I suppose that was because I was paying proper attention when I was taught this time. Once I had picked it up I found I enjoyed it so much that I used to look forward to Joan's lunch hour so I could play switchboard operator. I don't mean this nastily but, it was even better if Joan was off sick because I was required to take over the switchboard the whole time. Because Rye Arc was a large firm with many departments, it had a Tannoy system installed. It made it easy just to page someone over the Tannoy and for that person to go to the nearest telephone extension to take the call that was on hold.

It had been busy that lunchtime and I made a few calls over the tannoy and after the last tannoy page it all quietened down. I picked up a book I had on hand to keep me occupied for when it was quiet. I have to tell you here that where the switchboard was situated it had an echo to it, and it could make even the worse singer sound good. I read a couple of pages of my book then I started belting out a song called 'My Mother's Eyes' at the top of my voice, when all of a sudden about twenty or more of the dolls' eyes dropped drown. I was in a total panic and I let out a few Effs and Bs. 'Okay, calm down here,' I said to myself, 'let's prioritise this; take the top manager's call first.' So I say, "Switchboard good afternoon." It was then that I heard him shout, "Turn that bloody tannoy off! We can hear you all over the building as well as in the yard." Dumbstruck I turned to look at the tannoy, sure enough the red light for the on switch was glowing brightly showing the microphone was still on air. My face turned as red a beetroot. I was so embarrassed. I answered more extensions, and everyone was pulling my leg and laughing at my singing. (I don't think I would have made it into the hit parade)

A few weeks before my twenty-first birthday, I went to see my nan. She knew that my birthday was drawing near. My nan never stood on ceremony and immediately asked me if I was going to have a party. "No! I wasn't." was my short answer. I had already asked Dad and he said I couldn't have one'. Hearing this my nan immediately set about making arrangements for 'A bit of a Do' at a suitable time and place as soon as she possible could. Meanwhile unbeknown to us all my dad had secretly been organising a twenty-first birthday party for me to be held in the Tidal Basin Tavern. All friends and relations were invited, which was great. Unfortunately for Dad, just before the day of the party my sister, Liz, had become ill. She was in dreadful pain, so much so that she was rushed by ambulance to Poplar hospital. After being examined it was recommended that she have an operation on her kidney immediately. Liz was under age and couldn't give consent for her operation, Dad was the only one who could do that. But he wouldn't give his consent. He wanted more time to think about it. He asked the doctors if for the moment could they make her comfortable by giving her some painkillers. Dad was in a dilemma as he knew there could be no party for Liz. But the surprise birthday party for his other daughter, Pat, should somehow go on. The doctors made Liz comfortable and the party went on. It was fabulous, I had a live group and they played all the latest songs. My Aunt Jinny, who had the café did all the food beautifully and my Aunt Iris and Uncles Frank and Alf were all there on hand to help. It was wonderful. Everybody did his or her utmost to make it a great night. The next day Dad went to the hospital and Liz felt a lot better. He decided to take her out of Poplar Hospital and get her into The Middlesex Teaching Hospital in Mortimer Street near Tottenham Court Road. After many tests over a long period of time, Liz finally did have an operation. It was in her neck. There was a need to remove a calcium gland. This was because the over production of calcium was causing a stone in one of her kidneys to turn and as it did so it was tearing the tissue causing her the pain and also causing her to pass blood.

Liz felt so much better and was released from hospital just in time to attend the twenty-first birthday treat my nan had arranged. The venue was at the Show Boat restaurant located in the Strand near Charing Cross Station. There was dinner, dancing and cabaret. Nan had also ordered a cake for me. All the family were there. It turned out to be a great night. Dave Allen the comedian was the host and was on top form.

Events of the 60s

The Vietnam War in full flow having started in 1959 and wouldn't end until 1975. Many young Americans dying supporting the South Vietnamese against the North

1960 The first episode of Coronation Street was aired on television

1961 An Israeli war crimes tribunal sentences Adolph Eichmann to die for his part in the Jewish holocaust

1961 John F Kennedy becomes the thirty-fifth president of the United States.

1962 Brian Epstein signs the Beatles, they sack Pete Best and take on Ringo Starr

1963 John F Kennedy assassinated in Dallas Texas

1964 Ali versus Liston: Cassius Clay beat Sonny Liston in Miami Beach, Florida, and was crowned the heavyweight champion of the world.

1965 The Mini Skirt designed by Mary Quant appears in London and will be the fashion statement of the 60s

1966 England Beat West Germany 4-2 in the FIFA World cup at Wembley

1966 The very first episode of Star Trek debuts on TV

1967 Donald Campbell dies as his jet-powered Bluebird K7 crashes during an attempt to break the water speed record.

1968 The Krays, Ronnie and Reggie, were convicted for the murders of Mcvitie, 'Jack the Hat', and George Cornell, George was murdered in the Blind Beggar pub in Whitechapel.

1969 Neil Armstrong becomes the first man to walk on the moon. What an exciting time that was seeing those pictures, who would have thought we would ever see that.

1969 The Concorde supersonic transport plane breaks the sound barrier for the first time.

Chapter 35

Having learned the switchboard at Rye Arc, I decided to go and get proper training to become a switchboard operator. I got a job with the General Post Office (GPO) in Holborn. It was the most modern exchange in London at that time. A GPO trained operator was highly prized in those days. You did your training on the job, under a supervisor. You had to do stints on the emergency 999 calls. I did about six months there but decided I wanted to be in charge of my own switchboard and looked around for a job. Whilst doing that I did temporary work for the 3Ts agency at St Paul's in the City of London where I landed a job on a construction site. Which turned out to be the site of the new London Wall project. It was winter and the site was a quagmire, I was up to my ears in muck to get to the portacabin where the switchboard was housed.

At that time the going rate for an operator was six shillings an hour, a trained shorthand typist/secretary was nine shillings an hour. I tell you this because after a day and a half on this massive filthy muddy building site, I decided I had had enough and went back to the agency, which was just around the corner. I told them I wanted off that job. The girl pleaded with me to stay, saying she would raise the rate to seven shillings an hour. So I went back that afternoon. By lunchtime the next day I thought this is not worth it, and went back to the agency, again they raised the rate to eight shillings an hour. This went on until I was up to eleven shillings and sixpence an hour. But in the end I said, "that's it, I'm done." All the money in the world wasn't going to be enough to keep me on that job.

I went on to work on other switchboards like 1A lamp signaling, and various positions ranging from a single switchboard up to a ten-position switchboard. I eventually found a permanent job with Greek Shipping Company, Capeside Steamship Ltd, at Tower Hill in Vincula House on the eleventh floor. There were probably about twenty people working there. It was a lovely modern office and my window overlooked Tower Bridge, the River Thames and the Tower of London. Now I was earning £23 per week.

This was a ship chartering company for mostly oil tankers, but they also chartered ships for dry cargo as well. The business was done through the Baltic Exchange in St Mary Axe. The exchange provided daily freight market prices and maritime shipping cost index's, which were used to settle freight futures. There used to be a trading floor similar to the Stock Exchange.

The Goulandris family owned the business. They were probably the third largest ship owners after Onassis and Niarchos. Peter John Goulandris headed up the London office, while his nephew of the same name was head of the New York office; there was also the office in Piraeus, Athens Greece.

They were an excellent company to work for. At Christmas I was shocked to learn that I got a £200 tax-free bonus. I had only been there ten months. They paid for our Christmas lunches at Wheelers Restaurant. We had days out down at Shell Haven with lunch on board one of the super tankers. That was an eye opener. Without the oil cargo, the ships were almost as high as a ten-storey block of flats. I thought because of the nature of their cargo, the ships would be filthy with oil. The only oil I saw was around the flanges where the black stuff was piped in and out. You could have eaten your dinner off the floor in the engine room. It was as clean as a whistle. Also I expected to see a large crew for such a large ship, but there were only about twelve people and that included the captain. The first time I had a meal on board, I ate every single thing on the plate that was put in front of me. What I didn't realize was we were having a seven course meal.

I had never had more than four courses anywhere before. I was stuffed.

Every week a lady came into the office to clean the telephones, she was from a company called Phonatas. All she would do was spray a little disinfectant and wipe around the receiver. I asked the company secretary how much they paid this company for this service; I can't remember what it was now. But I was always on the look out to earn more money. I said why don't you cancel the service and I will clean the phones for just a little extra in my pay packet. They took me up on my offer. So every Wednesday I would clean the telephones. I mention this because it leads me on to another story, which I will relate to you further on in my book.

The Goulandris families were into sport, which involved the football team Olympiacos. They also had a hand in Horse Racing. I used to take calls from various trainers such as Auriole Sinclair and Peter Walwyn. This interested me because at that time my family were still going to The Epsom Derby held on the first Wednesday in June, and a fortnight later to Gold Cup day at Royal Ascot held on a Thursday.

In 1969 I booked my day off to go to the Derby. I knew that Mr. Goulandris had a horse running in the Derby, so I was looking forward to being there for the race. As with most big races, office staff usually ran a sweep. This happened in our office. Mr Gouldandris had brought a TV into the office for the staff to watch the racing. Well, to cut a long story short, Mr. Goulandris's horse 'Shoemaker' almost won the Epsom Derby. Another horse called Blakeney crept up and snatched the title. What a wonderful thing for Mr. Goulandris if he had been the owner of the horse that had won the Derby. I felt gutted for Mr Goulandris. So close?

The next day I went to work, by midday I had to catch up and clean the telephones being as I wasn't there the day before to do it. I went into Mr Goulandris's room, not expecting him to be there, but there he was as large as life, head down mulling over paperwork. I only ever used to say good morning or good afternoon, I never got into any conversation with him.

But on this occasion I couldn't hold back I was busting to talk about the race. I said "Pity about Shoemaker wasn't it?" He asked if I had seen it on the TV, I told him, "No, I was there, that I go to the Derby every year and Royal Ascot too." He said, "Were you in the stands?" I said, "No, we always go in the middle of the course (on the Downs) at Epsom, but we go into Tattersalls at Ascot on Gold Cup Day." By this time he had pointed to the seat in front of his desk and we were chatting about horse racing, and all the time I had the telephone receiver in my hand still cleaning it. He told me that he had a horse running at Ascot on Gold Cup day, but not in that race, he said come to the parade ring and meet the horse. I said "Okay"

When it came to Gold Cup day and the race that his horse was in, I went to the parade ring, I saw Mr Goulandris there with some members of his family and his uncle. I thought to myself, I can't go over there, these are Greek shipping magnates, and I'm a switchboard operator. I didn't go. The next day I was at my switchboard and Mr Goulandris who was over six feet tall, came round to see me, he asked if I went to Ascot. I told him I did and that I did see his horse in the ring, but there was so many of his family I didn't think it was in keeping. He told me I was silly and that I been expected. You know, this family was so down to earth; there were no airs and graces with them.

I told you that they were up there with the Onassis's. At this same time Jackie Onassis was married to Aristotle. I got a call one day asking for Mr. Peter John; this was the nephew over from New York. I asked who's calling please and the female voice said, "Jackie Onassis." I said, "Oh yeah and I'm the queen," and pulled the plug out. A call came through again, same female voice and she said I think I was disconnected, I said, "Who's calling?" and she said, "Jackie Onassis." I thought I had better accept this and put her through. Turned out it was Jackie. Her stepdaughter, Christine Onassis called sometimes. She was almost engaged to Mr. Peter John; I think that merger was very sought after.

183

The business made and received calls all over the world, but mostly to the New York and Greek offices. Many calls were also made to and from Belgium and France. I don't speak French and the French didn't or refused to speak any English. It didn't present too much of a problem, if a conversation was required at switchboard level there were several people who could take the messages for me. I learned a couple of phrases to make myself understood,

Stay there, (don't quit) -Ne quittez pas, or, Mister Potter at lunch-Monsieur Potter, déjeuner.

Those little words got me by for years.

Chapter 36

Dialling thirteen digit international numbers you were bound to get the odd wrong number, which I did. When this happened with the New York calls I would say, "I'm sorry, I am calling from England I will try again." Sometimes this would prompt a conversation. One day when I had said again sorry, "I'm calling from England," a young man who was puzzled at my accent and phraseology said, "Whaddya you, some kind of nut?" I answered, "No" and that I really am calling from England trying get a number in the Bowling Green area. He apologised, and we started chatting.

He seemed a pleasant enough chap, and so I started calling him on a regular basis. His name was Lou Bronstein and he lived in Rockaway Beach on Long Island. He said he was coming to London for a holiday. So I booked a hotel for him just off Leicester Square and said I would meet up with him when he got here. And that is what I did. He was a nice feller, same age as myself, but you could definitely tell that even though we spoke the same language, the Yanks thought in a different way to us. Also because we got some American shows like *I Love Lucy* and others of that era, we got their sense of humour, but they did not get ours. The only show they saw from us was the *Benny Hill Show* and they thought that it was hilarious. Lou had a pleasant visit in London. I knew my way around the sights like the back of my hand and I was also able to show him places that were off the tourist track. He met my family and friends too.

Over time when I used to call Lou, sometimes his mother, Ruth, would answer the phone and we would chat a while. She used to ask all the time, "When are you coming to New York?" I told her, "One-day."

I was telling a friend, Maureen, about this constant invitation and she told me she had always wanted to visit New York, I said should we go then? We started to make plans for our journey to the Big Apple.

We had to book a charter flight three months in advance and that was with Freddie Laker's airline Skytrain; it cost £57 return.

October 1974 we were on our way to the Big Apple. Lou picked us up at the airport and we stayed with his family in Rockaway. Maureen and me did all the touristy stuff and went over to Ellis Island and the Statue of Liberty, and up the Empire State Building, Rockerfeller Plaza. Lou took us to a Halloween party in Brooklyn. We saw an Andy Williams Show on Broadway. We were there two weeks and crammed a hell of a lot in. I didn't much care for the New Yorkers; I thought they were rude and unhelpful. On the subway we asked the man (who sold the tokens for the subway) which train would we have to get for a certain destination and he said, 'Look lady, I'm here to sell tokens, not to give directions." We got this kind of response from a few people. We were even threatened because of our English accents. The area we stayed in with Lou's family was a predominately Jewish / Irish area. We went to a bar that was Irish and they heard our English accents. Things were pretty bad in Northern Ireland at the time. The bar tender became quite threatening and that included a cop who was drinking in the bar as well. We got out of there very fast. We went to another bar and this is where I made up my mind that the Americans were really nutty. There was a young man who looked like a copy of Tony Curtis the film actor, he chatted with us and asked where we came from, we told him, 'London'. He said he was Italian, I said, 'Oh, right, what part of Italy did you come from?' He said 'Nah, nah. My great grandparents came from Italy, I was born in NY,

186

and 'I said to him that therefore he was American.' But he wouldn't have it, he was Italian and that was that. I think Frank Sinatra also considered himself Italian even though he was born in New Jersey.

Quite a few things with America and the Americans surprised me. First thing was that, back home I was watching TV in colour while most the homes in NY we went into were still watching TV in black and white. I thought they were way ahead of us.

Also the naivety of the people we met and were introduced too had little knowledge about London and the geography of it. We were asked if we lived near Benny Hill and if so could we get his autograph for them. Also, we were asked if we had stores. I told them that we had stores called Harrods and Selfridges, that were comparable to their store's Macey's and Gimbels.

I went to meet the people at our New York office, Orion and Global. Maureen and I were taken out to lunch. I felt really honoured, just a lowly switchboard operator being taken out by head office managers.

I was so surprised how quickly the weather could change in NY and to what extreme. It was October. One lovely day Maureen and I were walking along the boardwalk in our shirtsleeves, the temperature was in the sixties. A day or so later and what looked like another glorious day was in fact an absolutely freezing day. I only had a thin Mac with me and Maureen's coat wasn't much thicker. We had to borrow a couple of fur coats to wear from Lou's mother.

At the end of our holiday, Lou took us to the airport. He asked that if he gave me an address of his friend Frank in Miami, would I send him a post card from London. I said okay. Apparently they had been in the US Navy together serving in Vietnam. When I got back to England I sent the post card. Several weeks later I got a post card from Frank who liked to be called 'Hop' Because Hopalong Cassidy the cowboy had been his hero as a kid and he told everyone to call him Hoppy and it stuck. That started a pen friendship that went on for over sixteen years, more about that later though.

Chapter 37

My friends had started to get married and have their babies; while others were engaged to be married. Diane married Mickey in 1966; the priest was my lovely Father Papworth. Diane looked beautiful, and it was a great wedding.

Barbara married Jimmy, I only went to the reception, and again Barbara looked absolutely lovely. This was a good match as Jimmy used to be in my class when were at school, so it was really two mates for me.

Theresa married Chris in 1968; this was a big wedding up the Canning Town Public Hall. Another great time.

Even my younger sister Liz was courting, at this time.

Diane and Barbara drifted away from me. Though we still stayed in touch over the years by sending birthday cards and Christmas cards. We would see each other from time to time down at the local market, Rathbone Street.

I still carried on my friendship with Theresa. Although she was married to Chris they weren't a couple that lived in each other's pockets. So to some extent we could still do things together as though she was still single.

At the same time I was at the Greek shipping company, Theresa was working on a switchboard at the firm of John Lenantons on the Isle of Dogs. We would be on the phone from 9 a.m. in the morning till 5 p.m. in the afternoon with an hour break for lunch.

As our voices were similar, she would say to me answer this call and push two keys forward on her switchboard, I'd say, 'Lenantons' with a good morning/afternoon and the caller would ask for an extension and Theresa would put the call through. So even though I was sitting in Tower Hill, I was talking to an incoming call on John Lenantons switchboard in Millwall. It was just a matter of pushing two keys forward and the connection was made. In effect it was a three-way conversation, but I was speaking for her or she spoke for me. Just for a bit of fun.

Theresa's husband Chris worked on the ships that came into the Royal Albert and King George V docks and when a ship arrived a GPO telephone was put on board for the sailors to use or business conducted. They were always the same telephone numbers. Over time Chris had given Theresa these numbers when he had called her up. Theresa mentioned these numbers so I persuaded her to call one of them and someone answered. The conversation was switched between the two of us. Theresa spoke first. Someone answered "*Rangitoto*" and Theresa said, "What's a Rangitoto?" they said, "It's a ship"'' and then Theresa said, "Where are you, at sea?" and so it would go on with me asking questions, they had no idea that they were talking to two people. By then the person had got curious about who was calling and would start asking questions, starting with wanting to know a name. Theresa would answer 'Mary Poppins' and they thought this was the truth.

The ships that came to the docks belonged to the New Zealand Shipping line. Calling the ships became a regular thing and over a lot of time and a lot of calls I started to make friendships. First by writing letters and then meeting up with some of the sailors who were returning to London after their voyage and going for a drink with them. There were four sailors that I formed friendships with. They were on the *Rangitoto*, the *Matara*, and the *Hurinui* and the *Dorset*. Mostly all the ships had Maori names, but New Zealand Shipping also had some ships names after English counties, Like the Dorset and the Essex.

This was of a period of time that I could hardly tell you what colour wallpaper we had up in our house. What with going out with friends, going round to Theresa and Chris's house and going out with my sailor boyfriends, it was hectic. I even had to start buying the Lloyds List paper to find out where each ship was and when it was due. I had to keep a file on what I had written and to whom I had written it to, so that I didn't get anything mixed up. The last thing I wanted was for a couple of these sailors to meet up in a port some time and start talking about the girlfriend they had in Canning Town.

There was one sailor in particular, his name was Ron Speakman, and he came from Cardiff in Wales. He was on a ship called the *Dorset*. He was a nice young man; he brought me lots of gifts back from New Zealand. One time when his ship was in port they had an open day and he invited his family down from Wales and also my family. We went on board and had a lovely meal and had a tour over the ship. It was an unforgettable day and experience.

Ron introduced me to one of his friends who he called Jackie, in fact Jackie was a homosexual man called Cecil. We called homosexuals 'queers' in those days. (Not a name to be used in these enlightened times) Being in a dock area there were a lot of (queers) around that frequented the local pubs. Whilst Ron and I were in our twenties, Jackie was into his late forty's so had a world of experience. Jackie was very flamboyant, and everything was over emphasised in a theatrical feminine and gay way. He was also extremely funny and quick witted. I loved Jackie.

On one occasion Ron had gone home to Cardiff to see his family and Jackie was at a loose end. I asked my Mum and Dad if I could bring Jackie for afternoon tea on the Sunday. Mum was horrified, "You'll get yourself murdered one of these days," she said. I pleaded and said please just keep an open mind, finally she agreed. My family has always had a fantastic sense of humour, and when Jackie found his feet with my Mum and Dad, they absolutely adored him. So much so, I came home from work one evening and there was a note left for me telling me that Jackie had called them and had taken them out to dinner.

Jackie took me to a party in Winchmore Hill, a very expensive part of London. You can imagine my face when I walked into the main room of the house and saw a grand piano and a bar all in the front room. Jackie introduced me to the host and hostess who were very, very posh, said 'hello dahhhhling' and kissed me on both cheeks. It was all very theatrical, but I was fascinated by it. I lost touch with both Ron and Jackie after a couple of years, but it was fun while it lasted.

Chapter 38

Theresa and I were talking one day and she said that we should try and hire a pleasure cruiser on the Thames and organise a DJ event and supply some food for a party. This was in the early 70s and all the cruise boats did then was take tourists up and down the river. So they nearly bit our hands off when we said we wanted to hire their boat. It was called the *Silver Dolphin*. It was going to be a party for fifty people. I got fifty tickets printed, and we sold them at £5 each. We struggled at first trying to sell these tickets. We couldn't give them away and we started to worry that we would have to lose a very large deposit. But finally the tickets sold. It was something new; no one as far as we knew had ever had a party on a Thames riverboat. It was a success.

Within weeks people were asking us to get another cruise up, so we hired a larger boat, I can't remember the name of this one. But it was for one hundred people. This time the tickets sold like hot cakes, we could have sold them twice over. Another success.

Again people said they would like another cruise set up so we hired and even larger boat called the *Vallula* this was for a hundred and fifty people. Theresa and I were quite blasé by it all by now. People were ordering tickets and paying us almost up to the night before. Yet again it was another success. Requests were made for more river trips

So again we did another cruise. This time we hired the largest boat on the river, which was based at Greenwich, and it was called the *Swanage Queen*. It held two hundred people. Again people were ordering tickets and telling us they would pay us close to the time of the cruise. Now it was the night of the cruise. We waited and waited at Tower pier for the people to turn up, time was knocking on for us to set sail. But no one turned up. Actually there were just twelve people and that included Theresa and I. It cost us a lot of money that night. Needless to say we didn't do that anymore. A couple of years later the riverboat cruises started advertising party cruises themselves. To think that only a few hundred people knew that Theresa and I were pioneers in starting Party Cruises on the River Thames.

Chapter 39

Dad was always thinking up something to do, he was always keen on a bit of photography. In the early 70s Dad bought a Canon Super 8 cine camera and he got us doing home movies. However did he managed to talk us into these things? I guess because we knew we were going to be crying with laughter before the time was out.

Dad loved magic tricks and he had taught himself how to do quite a few, even though in the early days he was a bit like Tommy Cooper and getting them wrong or they failed to work. He got me to do some filming of him doing some magic. We did trick photography. The idea was to make it look as though he was making Mum disappear. I would hold the camera on him and Mum while he did the abracadabra, then I had to stop filming whilst Mum got out of camera shot and Dad stayed frozen in the same position, once Mum had gone I would start the film again. Hey presto when you watched the film it looked as though mum had really disappeared. Then Dad got me doing a knife-throwing act; first he filmed me throwing a knife towards a target. Then stop the film; we would then stick the knife into the bull's eye of the target. When you ran the film back it looks as though I'm a crack shot knife thrower. Then we set it up as though I am going to throw and knife and split an apple on top of my Dad's head. So there is the piece of film of me throwing the knife, then the camera is stopped, it's cuts to my dad who has a plastic knife that looks like its cut his head in half, he has also bitten on a blood capsule and to all intents and purpose there is blood running from his mouth and he goes into a dying scene.

Each of these super 8 films only ran for five minutes, but to set these scenes and film them could take several hours. Of course we don't see the benefit of all this work until we get the film back from the processors, and play it through a projector onto a screen. We did loads of these little sketches, they were such fun to do and we had such laughs doing them. I was always wondering what Dad would get up to next.

Dad had a good rapport with the salesmen he dealt with over in Stratford Market. They were always joking around with each other and always trying to get one over on each other as well, so Dad was constantly thinking up little tricks to play.

A market salesman owed Dad some money, and Dad managed to get the salesman to pay him by cheque. A bit unusual as they all liked to deal in cash, but Dad needed the cheque. Anyway he got it. He then bought a tiny, extremely bouncy rubber ball. He sliced a bit off the ball and stuck on an old cheque, afterwards he said to the salesman, "''ere, that cheque you gave me, it bounced" The salesman replied, saying, "Whaddya mean it bounced?" Dad took out the ball with the cheque stuck to it and said, "'ere, I'll show ya," and with that he threw the cheque down on the floor really hard, and it promptly bounced right up again. The salesmen fell about laughing. And they called my dad mad?

On another occasion he bought some cucumbers. They were packed in a shallow cardboard box about 5" deep and 2'6" x 1' 6". He came home and took all the cucumbers out of the box, he made a hole through the one end of the cucumber box and put a fairy liquid bottle filled with water inside and just poking through the hole. He would be carrying the box on his head, held with one hand. The way they were usually carried in the market.

The next day Dad walked up to the salesman's office where he bought the cucumbers.

The salesman was cleaning the windows of the office, which were filthy due to the amount of dirt and dust in the market. "Ere," said Dad, "them cucumbers you sold me yesterday? They're watery, I brought em back." "Watery? Watery?" says the salesman. "Whaddya mean watery?' With that, Dad starts to squeeze the fairy liquid bottle and sprayed water all over the salesman. But on this occasion, Dad himself got caught out in his prank because he hadn't seen the bucket of water the salesman had been using to clean the filthy windows with. The salesman picked up his bucket of water and before Dad had time to run he tossed the whole lot over him. My Dad was absolutely soaked with filthy black water. When he got back to the shop and Mum saw the state of him she couldn't stop laughing.

With this water incident in mind Dad decided he could go a step further with yet another joke. He had a gun that looked authentic, it fired caps that were so loud it sounded real. Dad enlisted the help of one of the porters that worked for the salesman. The scenario was this. Dad and his Uncle Joe Watson were going to see this salesman and start an argument over the water incident. Dad would pretend to be really angry over the incident and pull the gun out on the salesman. The porter would appear to see what was going on? Dad would then point and fire the gun at the porter, but Dad had given a blood capsule to the porter and he was to act as though he was shot with blood appearing to foam from his mouth. This is more or less how it all should play out. After Dad and the porter had done the deed, the salesman went running through the market shouting that the "Jolly's have got a gun and have gone mad and shot the porter." When people came to see what was going on, they found Dad quietly going about his business buying some cabbages from another stand. The porter who had helped with the set up had cleaned himself up and was at his own stand carrying out his normal job. Someone called the salesman back and asked him what was going on. Dad and the porter denied everything that the salesman had said; everyone thought the salesman was having a brainstorm. After a while

Dad and the porter owned up to their dastardly deed. Later Dad realised that he had perhaps gone too far with this joke and that it could have all turned bad. Suppose someone had called the police? Dad could have ended up in a police station. After that he kept to his normal sleight of hand magic tricks.

Chapter 40

I must relate this story you about Christmas time in the shop.

Every Christmas Eve after the shop closed Mum and Dad would still be working; there were the Christmas orders to get deliver. These were the shopping lists of customer's fruit and veg that would carry them over the holidays. Unlike today EVERTHING closed down, no shop opened at all. If you had forgotten something, that was tough, you were just going to have to borrow it from a friend or neighbour or live without it.

So these orders were bigger than the usual shopping list of the customer, and because of this Dad offered the delivery service. It was a hard job and they didn't usually get done till 11. 00 p.m. It was a long day. Dad made up the orders and Mum would deliver them as they were completed. One year, things didn't go quite to plan.

The early orders were delivered no problem. Then by about 9 p.m. the orders started backing up because Mum was taking longer and longer getting back to the shop for the next delivery. Dad was getting worried after one delivery that Mum had not returned and asked me to go and find her, which I did. She was sitting comfortably having a drink with the customers she had delivered the last order to. I told my Mum she had to come back to the shop, she got up a little unsteadily, she was bloody drunk.

I had to help her home and take her straight up to the flat and let her sleep it off. I finished the orders that year with my dad.

The following year my Dad said to me, "Pat, I can't let your mother do the orders, can you help instead." I told him I was happy to help him, I was quite 'chuffed' that he asked me to do this important job with him.

So Christmas Eve came round and off I went with the first order. The customer asked where my Mum was and I told her that she was helping Dad prepare the orders. The customer invited me in for a drink, but I refused saying we were busy and I had to get back for the next order. This was how it went for about the first six or seven orders. Then I delivered an order to a customer who I knew more than the others, and she asked about Mum and I told her the same story of helping Dad 'cos they were busy with lots of orders. She asked me in and I didn't mind talking to this lady. She asked if I wanted and drink and I said 'no thanks' but this lady kept insisting. She gave me a tiny glass with a dark liquid in it. As the glass was so tiny I drank it. It was my first ever glass of sherry. I quite liked it and didn't refuse when she offered me another.

I went back to the shop and got the next order, I went through the same conversation with the customer about where my mum was. Then as usual she offered me a drink, I asked, 'Got any sherry' and when the answer was yes, I said, 'Well, I'll just have a small glass,' which turned into several. Half way through the orders I was as merry as anything after drinking all the sherry that I was now accepting from the customers. Needless to say I couldn't complete, by about 9.30 p.m. I was too drunk on sherry to deliver any more orders and Mum had to finish the task. I wasn't asked again and from then on Dad made up and delivered all the orders on Christmas eve. If you want a good job done 'do it yourself'.

Chapter 41

When 1972 came round, preparations began for my sister Liz's marriage to John Lacey, to be held in October 1972.

The first thing to get was a wedding dress. My sister had seen an advert for the sale of bridal dresses to be held in a hotel just off Oxford Street near Marble Arch. Basically you choose a dress and they take your measurements, return to Leeds to make it up and then send the dress and veil on to you.

Liz tried on a beautiful dress, edged with Guipure lace, which is a really good quality lace made by machine. She looked lovely in it. She would make a beautiful bride.

Then came the bombshell, she wanted me to be her maid of honour also known as chief bridesmaid. Not something I wanted to do, I said no at first but she kept insisting and was getting upset so I relented.

Now we both felt we should lose a few pounds so that we looked our best. So we joined Weight Watchers. I was about 25 Liz was 22 and we had never dieted in our lives before. Little did we know that this decision was going to send us on a road where our weight would be a problem for the rest of our lives.

Weight Watchers in those days was quite harsh. You had to eat at least five fish meals a week, plus one liver meal, and a certain amount of cheese. The weeks were just repetitive. But it was working and the weight was falling off. Liz was losing weight so fast that she had to stop. If she had carried on her wedding dress would not have fitted her.

The wedding was to take place on 2 October. She had now enlisted her best friend, Janice, to be a bridesmaid. We were to be dressed in pale lilac crepe with long sleeves, to defend us against the October chill. The bodices were a contrast of deep red and purple velvet and we would have lilac headdresses. There were three other bridesmaids, our cousins Lynda and Lisa, and John's young sister Jill. They varied in age from about 7 up to about 9. They were going to be dressed identical to me and Janice, except the main colour would be pink. I have to say we all looked very nice on the day.

The wedding was held in St Dunstan's church in Stepney, and the reception was held in Bromley by Bow Public Hall. All of Mum's family came from all over the country. Her dad and stepmother, her brother Ernie and his family and her brother Freddy and his family came down from Newcastle. Her sister Ethel and her family came from Warwickshire Her younger sister Lilla and her family came from Gloucestershire, and her young brother Eddy came from Wales. Half of this lot were going to be bedding down in our two bedroom flat. We did it and it wasn't a problem.

At that time John was in the wine game and the champagne he got was Bollingers, which was a bit of a step up then from Moet Chandon and Asti Spumanti, that we normally had.

The sit down meal was silver service provided by a man who used to work in the Savoy Hotel restaurant. There was a live band afterward, and it was a fabulous day all together.

That night Liz and John went back to a little flat they had found in Dagenham. I had been over there earlier and had secretly made an 'Apple Pie Bed'. When they would try to throw the covers back, they'd find that they had been tacked together, once they had got this undone, they'd find various bits of canteen of cutlery that I had hidden, and lots of other bits and pieces. It would either annoy them or make them laugh. Fortunately in this case it made them laugh and they gave us a good laugh telling us about it all.

We didn't have to wait long before Liz found herself pregnant. During this time Liz and John got themselves onto a scheme with Newham Council. The idea was to live in a block of high rise flats, pay rent and bit more on top. While doing this the council would build some houses, in this case they were in Stratford just off Vicarage Lane. Once the houses were built, the families would move in and carry on paying off to the council until they were all paid up. It was a good way to get on the property ladder then.

In 1974 Jane was born, Liz had her in Middlesex Hospital in Mortimer Street in London's west end At the same time John was pacing up and down waiting for his daughter to be born, there was another man doing the same thing. His name was Dec and he was one of the 'Bachelor's', who had hits such as '*Diane*' and '*I Believe*' to name just two of many.

At the same time Liz was in labour with Jane, we knew that our Mum's Dad was dying. So it was a sad and a happy time at the same time. Our granddad learned that he had become a great grandfather just before he died.

Jane was an absolute delight. Liz's pregnancy wasn't very good as she was sick all the way through it. It took a lot out of her, and quite a time to recover. Enter Auntie Pat, I would go round to Liz and John's flat most days to pick Jane up and fetch her back to the shop to Mum and Dad. This was wonderful. I loved this little girl like she was my own, but I didn't tell anyone that. I was able to see her first tooth came through, and when she laughed out loud for the very first time, and when she took a step for the first time. I felt very privileged to be there at that time. I used to sing her to sleep, with the 'Sing a Long a Max' medleys of songs by Max Bygraves.

Jane must have been around 18months when Liz and John moved into their new three bedroom house in Stratford. It was a lovely house that overlooked West Ham Park. I would go over regularly and babysit while Liz and John went out with their friends.

I would put Jane in bed with me for a while, till she fell asleep then transfer her to her cot. Jane by now had quite a large vocabulary, we were all constantly talking to her and repeating names of things. She could say cauliflower perfectly. She had also picked up a few other words we were not aware she had learned.

One night I took Jane to bed, she had been bathed and, with a clean nappy on, she smelled of Johnson's baby powder, and was wearing a bright yellow 'baby grow'. Jane was lying in bed facing me. I was taking in every contour of her beautiful face. She had pretty blond curly hair and the biggest blue eyes. I didn't speak to her because I wanted her to drift off to sleep. We lay with our heads on the pillow gazing at each other and then, without moving a muscle, Jane said, "F**k off Pat." I was shocked. I said, "What did you say?" Again, without moving she said, "F** k off Pat." I said, "You naughty girl you mustn't say that." With that, to show my disdain of her, I turned over on my side with my back to her. I had to stuff the corner of the cover in my mouth because I wanted to laugh so hard, the bed was shaking up and down where I was trying to stifle it. I lay there for quite some time, there was no movement behind me. So after a while I slowly turned back over and there she was still wide awake with those big blue eye looking at me. I didn't say anything to her, but then Jane said "F**k off Pat." That set me off again, in the finish I had to get up and hold her in my arms and sing a Max Bygraves medley to get her to sleep before putting her in her cot. When I told Liz and John the next day they couldn't stop laughing. The person who swore the most in our household was me, so Jane could only have picked it up from me. Naughty Auntie Pat.

Chapter 42

By May of 1976 my sister Liz had been married to John for four years and had two daughters, Jane at three years and Joanne four months.

As for me I had now left the Greek shipping company and had gone into several jobs as a switchboard operator that hadn't worked out, so I was signing on the dole. But the money wasn't enough to live on, I still had to find extra money so I went and found a job working in a mini cab office, which was Commercial Cars on the corner of Croydon Road and Barking Road, near the Abbey Arms, Plaistow E13.

To start with I just did a few days per week, then I started to do more days and some evenings, soon I was working weekends, day and night as well.

I hadn't been working there very long when I decided to buy myself a bike. It would save me waiting around for buses, and then a long walk once I got off the bus. There used to be a bicycle shop near the Greengate. I had my eye on a very well-known make, a 'Raleigh' it was the very latest fold up bike. For something so good you had to pay good money I paid nearly £200.

The day I went to get it, I had called up the governor of Commercial Cars, Brian, I told him a fib that I wasn't feeling too well. I had in fact gone to visit my sister Liz in Stratford. I told her about the bike and she said that she would take me in her car to pick it up. So that's what we did. We folded the bike up and put it in the boot of her car and went back to her house in Stratford. I had a bit of a play on it in a quite road behind her house, and then I told my sister that I was going to ride the bike home to Canning Town. Liz got really worried and said she didn't want me to do that, but I assured her I would be okay and after all what did I buy the bike for if not to get where I wanted to be. I decided to take the quietest roads, but the longest route as it was just about rush hour time and I wanted to avoid some of the trickier places. So off I went.

My route was from Vicarage Lane Stratford, past Plaistow Station straight on to Greengate, I carried on forward across Barking Road, down the first part of Prince Regent Lane, I then crossed the Beckton Road or A13 as it is known down the second half of Prince Regent Lane heading toward the Connaught and the Victoria Dock Road. It had been a bit hairy for me for the first part of the journey, not being used to riding the bike in so much traffic, but now I could relax and head straight down the Victoria Dock Road toward Tarling Road. A fine rain had been falling, so I had a scarf tied around my head, and the collar on my jacket was up. I was just passing Freemasons Road, when a white car overtook me. Not just any white car, it was Brian's car, my governor from the cab office. I thought 'Oh no', but maybe he won't recognise me, because he wouldn't expect to see me on a bike. But then his brake lights went on, so I slowed my pedalling, then the car speeded up, so I speeded up, then the brake lights went on again. We were just coming up to Tarling Road. I dare not turn right there as Brian would know it was me on the bike, so I sailed on past to the take the next turning that would take me to the back of our shop. Brian went past Tarling Road, and I thought I was in the clear, but then he turned into the road I was about to take and stopped, he had recognised me after all. I pedalled past him and he put his foot down and caught up with me as I stopped. I popped my head through the passenger window and said "'I won." He was laughing his head off at me, and saying, "'I thought you said you were ill?" I said "I was but I got better." Brian asked me if I was coming in the next day and I said, "I'll be there."

The next morning, I pedalled down to Croydon Road on my bike, and why was I not surprised to see all the drivers outside laughing their heads off at me. Brian had told them all what had happened. They all laughed at me, but they were begging me for a go on my bike.

I was working with so many blokes of all ages and from different backgrounds, there was always a laugh and a joke going on. Also there were quite a few affairs going on with the cab drivers. I had to learn quickly the names of the wives and the names of the girlfriends. I didn't like being part of the subterfuge, but it was accepted as part of the job. So be it.

The drivers had radios to stay in contact, but it got out of hand when a driver just took off for one of his clandestine meetings and I had his wife on one line and a job for him to go to on the other line. I became an expert juggler at times like this.

A lot of the drivers used to go shooting or fishing from time to time. The first time a bunch of them were going night fishing, one of them brought back a big bucket of maggots. They were wiggling and squirming. One of the drivers said to me, "I dare you to put your hand in there and hold it there for ten seconds." I hummed and ahhhed, because I knew something they didn't and that was I did a lot of fishing down on the River Medway where our caravan was. I started playing the scared female, then I said I'd do it if they had a money bet on it. They agreed, and a tenner (£10) was laid down. Well I put on an act that would have been worthy of an Oscar, the drivers were laughing and joking and egging me on, till finally I plunged my hand in and held it there for the ten seconds. I got the tenner. Then I stood there plunging both hands in and lifting handfuls of maggots just to let them drop back into the bucket. Then I told them, "I liked fishing too." They let me keep the tenner.

I sat in a tiny office that was within a larger office; it had a bolt on the inside of the door, which was for the controller's (me) safety sake, especially on a Saturday night. I had a cubbyhole on my left side to talk to customers, and a cubbyhole on the right where the drivers sat.

One afternoon, I'd just popped out to buy some milk, when I came back I made a cup of tea for me and a couple of drivers I then went into my inner office and bolted the door. While sitting there drinking my tea and chatting to the drivers, I felt something around my feet. The shop was very old and there could have been mice or rats that had got in. Nevertheless I jumped up and out of the way, but what I found wasn't a mouse or a rat, it was a bloody big yellow furry thing that I had never seen before. It was a ferret! My tea went up in the air. I couldn't get the bolt undone quick enough.

I was effing and blinding at the drivers to help me, they were crying with laughter and didn't lift a finger. Finally I got the bolt open and I shot out of the office like a bullet.

Chapter 43

My nan had always had a wish to go on a cruise holiday, I had heard it time and time again but no-one ever bothered to help her see it through. Then she mentioned it again one day and I decided that I was going to do something about it, so I sent to P & O Lines for a brochure. I took it over to her and we looked through it and I told her that if she really wanted this I would make all the arrangements. She said she did, so I spoke to my Mum and Dad and they said okay, they would go as well. I thought, well. If I am arranging this I may as well go along too. My two aunts Iris and Jinny would also have to go along because they already attended my nan's needs of washing her and dressing her, which my nan couldn't do because of her arthritis. So in January 1976 I booked two cabins on the Canberra for a two-week Mediterranean cruise in June. I had to save like hell to get the money together for my fare, they don't pay for things like that on the dole.

We were all getting excited, with just three weeks to go. Then a major shock! My nan suffered a stroke and was rushed to St Andrew's Hospital. The family was devastated. Over the next days she started to improve, but it was clear that she was not going to make the cruise. She was the glue that held our family together. As with a lot of bad stroke victims she held onto her old memories but lost the most recent memory. For instance as she lay in the hospital she kept talking about her husband Joe as though he was still around. She would ask how he was coping without her, or telling Iris or Jinny what to cook for his dinners. What do you do in that situation, do you tell them that the man she is talking about has been dead for the last seventeen years or so. Or do you play along with the world they are living in. They all chose to play along with the world she was living in.

On the second day my nan was spending in hospital, we got a phone call to say that my mum's uncle, Norman, had been rushed to hospital. Uncle Norman had come to London with the Jarrow Marchers. The Jarrow March was a protest in 1936 by a group of men as a protest against unemployment and the terrible poverty that was being suffered in the North East of England. There were over two hundred men who travelled from Jarrow to Westminster in London. They walked almost 300 miles. They had an MP Ellen Wilkinson also known as Red Ellen who walked with them, very little was done for them after all that effort. There was still no work for them. All they were given was £1 for their train fare home.

Uncle Norman decided to remain in London to look for work, he met a young lady called Sue, he courted her and then married her and settled down to married life in Belvedere, Kent.

Uncle Norman and his wife and daughter would often visit us. He was a lovely man. His daughter Hazel died in her 30s from leukaemia, and soon after his wife, Sue, died. We saw even more of him after that. So it was a shock to hear that he had suffered a heart attack.

When Mum took the phone call she was told that Uncle Norman was in the emergency unit. She told the person at the other end of the phone to tell her uncle that she would go and see him on the following day. When she got off the phone I persuaded her that she should really go that evening because it sounded quite serious to me. My Dad was visiting his own mum at the hospital and I was able to get a message to him on the ward that we were catching a cab to go to the hospital in South Woolwich. Dad rang us back and told us to hang on he was coming back home and would take us himself.

We got to the hospital and they said only one person at a time at Uncle Norman's bed. Mum went in first, then Dad had a few minutes, I popped in and give him a quick hello and goodbye kiss to give Mum more time to go in again to see him. He was very perky, and said it was all a lot of fuss about nothing. Everything seemed okay and we left the hospital after telling Uncle Norman we would be back the following day. All three of us were smokers and we sat in the dormobile van having a cigarette. Unbeknown to us while we were outside, Uncle Norman had another heart attack and died. We got this news when we arrived home. I am so pleased that I made Mum go that evening.

As for the cruise it was decided that rather than cancel the holiday, we would still go ahead and my sister and her husband and the two children took over what would have been my nan's cabin. My Uncle Joe came along and shared the cabin that me and my Mum and Dad were in. So that's how it was.

We sailed from Southampton late afternoon to a band playing on the quayside and people waving and streamers being thrown that dangled over the side, it was quite a sight and very exciting. We had a walk around the ship to get our bearings. We were all on 'A' deck, my sister's cabin was at the front of the ship and ours was in the middle. Being on 'A' deck meant that we didn't have to go up and down in lifts, or stairs to get out into the fresh air.

At 7.30 p.m. we met up for dinner. Our waiter was Francis, he was in his late fifties and he told us he came from Goa. We absolutely adored Francis and he liked us. By the end of the two weeks, Francis kept asking us to visit him and his family in Goa. We had a lovely meal, about six courses in all. After dinner we went for a stroll around the ship to see what the entertainment was like. We had a couple of drinks in different bars. Finally after a long day we decided to go to bed for a fresh start the next day.

Our cabin steward came in about 7.30 a.m. with a cup of tea and biscuit for us all. I didn't expect that at all. A great start to the day in my opinion. Then I got out of my bunk and went for a wash, that is when I started to feel the motion of the ship, and that's when I started to feel queasy. I got dressed and went along to my sister's cabin. The interior of their cabin was a bright green, and so was my sister, she too was feeling queasy. We decided to go out on deck to see if that made us feel any better, it didn't, it made us feel worse. We decided to go down to the doctor's cabin. I had read that you could get an injection for seasickness so we decided to find out if we could get one.

When we got to the surgery, who do you think was sitting there as large as life? Our Dad! He said, "I'm okay, it's just in case." Yeah right. He was as green as me and Liz. My turn to go in and I don't have to even open my mouth before the doctor said, "seasick?" I nodded. He told me to get on the bed and then he gave me an injection in my bum. He said, "Go back to your cabin you'll have a nice sleep and then you'll be awake in time for lunch." The way I felt? I wasn't going to be eating the rest of the trip. But I did as he said, and when I woke up I was fine. No more seasickness.

We realised that if we actually took all the meals that were given we wouldn't have much time for anything else. Tea and biscuits at 7.30 a.m., then it's breakfast followed by a short break and then it's elevenses, then lunch, a short break and then its afternoon tea. Later there was dinner, and finally supper. Then you started it all over again the next day. We decided to just have two meals a day; maybe we'd have afternoon tea if we felt peckish.

There were lots of organised activities on board like flower arranging, keep fit, and as there was going to be an evening of Race Night, you could make your own fancy Ascot hat. We started to learn some of the disco dances, the popular one was The Hustle. There were also some interesting talks and a library, also swimming pools and a cinema. There were all the deck games, including shuffleboard, and quoits. Didn't have a clue how to play them, but we had a go. Then there was the sunbathing; it was always a round 70 degrees, quite pleasant. Little did we know at the time that they were having an almighty heat wave back in London. We go away on our first summer holiday abroad for the weather, and we miss the 1976 hottest heat wave weather London has had for years!

After a couple of days at sea we eventually arrived in Madeira. Such a beautiful island but we were pestered for money everywhere we went. Also I have never seen so much wickerwork in all my life. And what did my Uncle Joe want to buy? Three big wicker baskets. He actually wanted to buy more but we talked him out of it.

We also visited Vigo, which is just inside Portugal, and Palma and Barcelona, though not necessarily in that order. I loved that holiday. I could buy a round of drinks and still have change out of a £1. At that time a martini and lemonade was 19p.

While on board I met a bloke who was a cabin steward, his name was John and when the cruise was over we said we would write to each other. We did and we also met up when Canberra was in port for any length of time.

Since about 1975 I'd been at loggerheads with my Mum, mostly over my boyfriends, we argued constantly. As a matter of fact we had constant run ins since I was about 15. Every now and then it would flare up and be out of control. On one occasion I had as much as I could take. For the second time in my life I tried to commit suicide, this time with sleeping pills. It didn't work because somehow my Dad realised that I was up to something and although he missed me taking the first four sleeping pills, he walked in on me when I was taking the rest and stopped the process. I tried to get the sleeping pills back off him and tried to get out of the house, but he got a kitchen chair and sat in front of the street door. I sat on the stairs waiting my opportunity to get out, but all that happened was I fell asleep with the pills I had already taken. I found myself in bed fully clothed, Dad had carried me upstairs. The place I wanted to get to was the mini cab office. I had it in my head that I wanted to be found by people who knew me after I had died, so knowing that the drivers came in early every morning I decided the mini cab office would be the perfect place.

I needed to leave and get a flat of my own, which I did. I rented a room in Crediton Road in Upton Park; it was just a place to lay my head at night. I was working all the hours God sent in the mini cab office. After about six weeks Mum persuaded me to go back home, I think her and Dad had a talk. She said that she would change her attitude. So I went back home, but I knew I couldn't live like this anymore.

I said this was the second attempt at suicide. My first attempt was when I was around 15 years old. I guess this was the start of the generation gap. I kept getting into altercations with my mum. It got me down. I went to the doctor and that was when I was first diagnosed with depression. After one of these arguments, I got it into my head that the family would be better off without me. So whilst Mum and Dad were working in the shop, I closed all the windows and turned on the gas, then I sat there and waited, and waited some more, It was a good hour I had been sitting there and then I got fed up waiting and turned off the gas taps. What I didn't realise was that we had just switched over to North Sea gas, and what I didn't know was that you couldn't gas yourself with it like you could with the gas we used to get. So only I knew of my failed attempt.

In later years I thought about it again. I was having a mental breakdown at the time and was taking medication for it. I was still working, work somehow kept me going. I would stand on the platform at Paddington Station some evenings waiting for my train to take me home. I would stand close to the platform edge and watch the tube train coming towards me. In my head was a voice-repeating JUMP NOW! Then the tube train would rush past me. I agree it is certainly a cry for help. More people are aware of mental illness now than back then. Since those last thoughts ran through my head all those years ago and with the medication I have been mentally fit ever since. They were dark days then, that's for sure.

Chapter 44

It was the Silver Jubilee year 1977 John the steward from the Canberra asked me to get married and I agreed. John was ten years older than me. He came from Birmingham, and he took me home to meet his family and friends. We wanted to get married quickly. I went and bought a dress and he went and bought a suit. We got a special licence to get married in St Luke's Church. One of the cab drivers who had a really nice car tied a few white ribbons on it and he became my chauffeur to the church. My sister laid on a cake and food for the guests. And so we tied the knot.

I knew I had made a mistake within weeks of getting married. John and I didn't have anything in common. None of my family liked him and I didn't even love him. If truth be known, my main reason for getting married was to get my Mum off my back. Being married meant I had become my own person. We lived with my Mum and Dad, but I knew more and more that marrying John had been a mistake. Six weeks later I told him so. I told him he had to go, I didn't want to be married to him anymore. He didn't challenge me on why I felt the way I did, so maybe he felt the same, I dunno. So we parted, no ifs no buts, that was it! However, having a married name now meant I could go to the council and apply for a flat. They didn't know that I no longer had a husband, but for the benefit of getting a place to live, I let them think I still had a husband. I told them that we were living with my Mum and Dad and that they no longer wanted us there blah! blah! blah! Within in about 6 months they offered me a flat on the fifteenth floor in

Dodson Point Maplin Road, Custom House. This block of flats was identical to another that stood close by. That block was called Ronan Point. It was the block of flats that in 1968 suffered an explosion in which five people died among them my Dad's cousin Tommy Murrell and his wife. The blast was on the fifteenth floor, one corner of the flats came tumbling down like a pack of cards.

Chapter 45

In 1978 my lovely nan died. She was in St Andrew's Hospital and was doing fairly okay after another stroke, until the hospital caught fire. All the elderly ladies had to be moved. It was a cold February day, and they sat in the cold for ages. Several days later she caught pneumonia and died.

It was about ten days later that she was to be buried. It's always the same for my family because of the tradition for them to be buried in lead lined coffins. The funeral homes don't normally keep lead on the premises, it has to be done specially.

It was a very big funeral. There must have been well over a hundred people there. There were eight cars following the hearse and every one of them had flower tributes on the roofs. Lizzy Jolley was a great, great lady, the mainstay of our family. After she died the family floundered a bit.

The family had always met up in the Poplar shop in my nan's kitchen. They would have a dinner there, have a glass of beer, just sit and chat. Where would they do that now? The answer to that question wasn't long in being answered. The family started meeting at my Uncle Johnny and Aunt Jesse's home in Barking. Not as cosy as nan's kitchen but a sight more comfortable than sitting on little kitchen chairs, and the family were together again.

Events of the 70s

1970 Greater London Council decide to build a Flood Barrier across the Thames

The Beatles break up

1971 Apollo 14 Lands on the moon. Third lunar landing

1972 Watergate Scandal

1973 US pull troops out of Vietnam. War ends

1974 President Richard Nixon resigns

1975 Arthur Ashe is first black man to win Wimbledon

1976 Concorde begins supersonic flight between London and New York

1977 Queen Elizabeth celebrates Silver Jubilee

Elvis Presley found dead aged 42

1978 First test tube baby born

1979 Margaret Thatcher first woman Prime Minister of Great Britain

Sony introduced the Walkman

Chapter 46

A few months before the offer of the flat, and at that time still living with my Mum and Dad, I applied for and was offered a job on one of the thirteen position switchboards at London Transport's Head Office above St James Park Station, 55 Broadway SW1.

I think there were about 14 of us including a supervisor. The switchboard in those days was manned twenty-four hours; men only did the night shifts. The girls did two shifts each week, earlys and lates. I started just at the end of September. After a few days I decided I was just going to work till after Christmas and then look for something else. There was a lot of cattiness among the girls, and I didn't want to be a part of it. On my very first day one girl was warning me about another girl, then someone else was talking to me about another girl and it wasn't very nice. I didn't want to be a part of this sort of thing. Gradually Christmas came upon us and I was receiving my first proper month's pay and so I went across the road to the Army and Navy Store to buy two beautiful teddy bears for my little nieces, Jane and Joanne. I wanted to get them something special. Suffice to say on Christmas day they were delighted.

London Transport had many offices all over the London area and each one had its own switchboard. As we were the head office we usually had to cover these other switchboards if there was sickness or holidays. I got called to cover a sickness at our Telstar House office in Paddington. I was quite impressed when I got there; the offices were modern in comparison to those at 55 Broadway. So too was the switchboard, I'd never seen anything like it. It was an IBM 3750 and you sat at it just like a desk and it had just a few buttons and a display screen that showed the numbers you were dialling. I really liked this place, but there was no point wanting what you can't have, I was only here to cover a sick leave, as soon as the other girl returned to work I would be back at 55 Broadway. And so it was. But a few days after my return to head office I was called into the supervisor's office and I was asked if I wanted to go and work in Telstar House permanently. I said I definitely would, so the following Monday I was working in Paddington with a supervisor called Pixie, and another girl who wasn't there very long and was soon replaced by another young girl called Kellie. We worked as a good team, Pixie was a very fair supervisor, she had been with London Transport since she was about 16 and by this time she was in her 40'.

I started to learn so much more about telephones, with this system we could swap telephones about with each other and between floors. It was fascinating. The fact that one of the departments that were housed in the building was the communications section made it interesting.

As I became more and more interested, I said to Pixie that I thought that there were telephones knocking around that we had no knowledge of and others that were obsolete, and so we should do a survey of all the telephones in the building to create a proper directory. We did this. I found working telephones in large plants' holders, and lodged in cupboards. And I also found that the young men in the communications section were to blame for this. I built up quite a good rapport with these engineers, for that was what these young men were. Pixie and I soon had a good directory and also we were able to identify telephones no longer in use and that could be disconnected. Basically we tidied up the system.

Here's a story showing my lack of geographical knowledge. Pixie knew a lot of people throughout the organisation, and some of them were directors. Including one called Mr Maxwell. He was very posh. Pixie and her husband Tommy had a holiday home in Majorca, Spain and would go there several times a year. On these occasions I took over the mantle of Supervisor. One day Mr Maxwell, called and asked for Pixie, I informed him she was on annual leave, He said, "Has she gone to the 'Balearics' again?" I said, "No, she's gone to Majorca." It went very quiet at the other end of the phone. Then I remembered, but too late as I had put the phone down that Majorca was one of the Balearic Islands. Mr Maxwell had gone, probably laughing his socks off at the dopey telephonist.

There was a pay structure for office workers. For us telephonists we were at the bottom of the ladder, CAs. Pixie was an HCA, a Higher Clerical Assistant, the switchboard operators were HCB. I thought that the work we put in wasn't appreciated not only within London Transport, but also throughout the commercial world. Well I couldn't do anything for the commercial world but maybe I could change something for us lowly switchboard operators in London Transport. I started asking the operators at the different locations what they felt about the pay scale, and they all said it could be better. I asked them if I put a letter together would they sign it along with me. A 'Round-Robin'. The term Round-Robin was originally used to describe a document signed by multiple parties in a circle to make it more difficult to determine the order in which it was signed. We didn't sign in a circle. All the operators were up for it, so we all duly signed. I sent it to our bosses, and it was refused as I expected it to be. But I had to go through the motions, because my next step was to enlist the help of my union. TSSA Transport and Salaried Staff Association. I started attending meetings, which I found very interesting. Show any kind of interest and the unions slowly starts to suck you in. Before I knew what was happening I was a union representative for all the switchboard operators and the HCB pay clerks.

I went to the meetings month after month. Wintertime was the worse cold and tired, arriving home late, and then having to get up for the early start the next morning. This went on for a year more or less. Then one day I got a call to say there was going to be a big meeting between the union boss and the hierarchy of London Transport at Head Office 55 Broadway. Off I went to the meeting. I didn't have to do anything just sit there and listen as the union boss put our case on the table. He asked me to fill in one or two details, but mostly he did the talking. After an hour I was asked to leave while they got down to business. It was lunchtime so I stopped to have something to eat and a coffee. Then I made my way back to Paddington.

I walked into the switchboard room and Kellie said, "We got it." "Got what," I said. We got the upgrade and a pay rise. The news had swept all around the switchboards and operators. I was the last one to know. A year of going all on my own to meetings, and the last one to know that we had been successful. Do you know? Not one of those telephonists rang me to say 'Thanks Pat'. My supervisor Pixie said thanks though because as we had moved up a grade, she was upgraded too. The knock on effect.

Photographs

Annie Murray · Iris Jolly · Jinny Jolly · Joey Jolly · Bette Jolly · Charlie · Billy Jolly · John Murray Jnr · Frank · Pam · John Murray Snr · Liz Jolley · Maud Murray

The Gunn Public House Pitsea, Essex

Jinny · Pat · Frank · Iris · Nan · Liz Jolly · Joey · Sea Knight

Wateringbury Kent

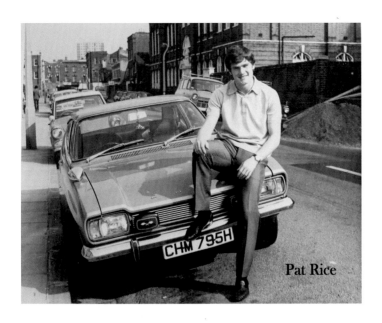

Pat Rice

Mum
Bette Jolly

Johnny Alf Bill Bill
Jesse
Joe Frank
Bette Iris
Liz
Jinny

Nan
Liz Jolley

The Showboat
in the Strand
Charing Cross

Pat Jolly

Pat at
Diane & Micks Wedding
above The Royal Oak
Canning Town
E16

Pat & Barbara

Pat   Jackie   Barbara   Diane   Kay   Denny

Billy Jinny Iris Johnny Joey

23 Tarling Road
Canning Town
E16

23 JOLLY'S 23

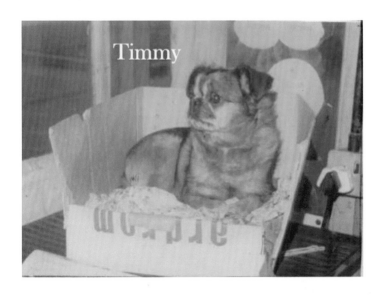

Timmy

Jolly's Greengrocers
23 Tarling Road
Canning Town
E16

A Jolly's
Christmas 'show'

My Nan
Liz Jolley

Pat & Theresa

Jane & Joanne
outside Shop in Tarling Rd

First Wedding
St Lukes
Church

Lenny & Pat
2nd Wedding

Frank & Pat
third Wedding

Site of Joe and Liz's
Shop 126 St Leonards Rd
Local residents named
it Jolly's Green

Poplar neighbourhood

JOLLY'S GREEN

95 new homes for local people

Mayflower Reunion

Pat

Barbara

Miss Finch

Theresa & Pat

Pat

Denny

Diane

Jackie

Kay

Barbara

Jo Liz Jane

Our Island
of Dreams

Billy & Bette

Chapter 47

It was now 1979. The flat in Dodson Point was lovely. But I was going to have to do it up to my taste.

Whilst I was working at Commercial Cars mini cab office I become friends with a couple who lived in Croydon Road, Elsie and Jimmy Collier. They were a nice couple with two children, a boy called Gary and a daughter called Susan. Jimmy was very handy and he offered to do the decorating for me. I was thrilled. It didn't take him long to get everything looking lovely.

My Mum got caught up in my excitement and offered to buy carpet for the whole flat. I got a lovely Axminster for the front room and passage, and a cheaper carpet for the bedroom and linoleum for the bathroom and kitchen. She got it on the Never Never and it took almost three years for her to pay it off. What a great Mum, she came up trumps in the end.

I didn't have any furniture; I sat on deck chairs for many months, until my sister offered me her three-piece suite. She had already given me a double bed and I was buying other bits and pieces from a second hand shop, or out of Freeman's catalogue. Mum and Dad gave me some bits and pieces, and soon my flat started to look like a proper home. I loved it. Those were very happy days for me. I had a good job, extra money in my pocket, a lovely home, and a social life with Elsie and Jimmy. I had a fantastic view from my fifteenth floor flat. In the immediate vicinity I overlooked my old school and Freemason's Road. Further away I could look all the way towards Beckton and from my bedroom window at the side I could look into the Royal Victoria Dock. And I could also just about see my mum's window of her flat above the shop, which was way over.

In the early days I didn't have a telephone, so after visiting my mum I would arrange that as soon as I got home I would switch my bedroom light on and off three times so that she would know I was home safe and sound. Then I would run to the window and she would do the same. It worked a treat.

One evening there was a knock at the door and it was a lady that I had never seen before. She introduced herself as Pat Newman and said that she lived on the twenty-second floor. She asked if I was aware that there were vacant room at the bottom of the block for the use of residents I said I wasn't aware. She went on to say that she would like to get a residents' association going and would I be interested. I said I would. High Rise living had already shown me in a short space of time that I didn't know any of my neighbours and wasn't likely to know any due to the hours I worked. I left for work each morning at 6.30 a.m. and didn't return home till 6 p.m. in the evening. I hardly saw a soul coming or going into the flats.

It turned out that Pat was a housing officer for Newham Council and she knew quite a few people on the council who could help get the room at the bottom of the block organised if we got the association going. Her husband, George, also worked for the council. There were a couple of meetings organised and much interest shown, so Pat approached the council and within a short period of time, the council had come down and repainted the room, put some tables and chairs in, put in a small kitchen and as an added touch, put some nice curtains up at the windows. It looked lovely.

The first thing we needed to do was raise some money and so we had a few jumble sales to begin with. We hired the hall out on certain occasions. Then we decided we would hold a dance. I was still into music and still collecting records. I had a great music centre. I told Pat and George that I would supply the music. We decided to ask friends and family, they could fetch their own food and drink. They would be charged £1 and residence would be charged 50p. Plus we would hold a raffle.

I invited my Mum and Dad and Elsie and Jimmy and other friends. Other residents did the same. And so we held our first dance, it was a great success. Everybody had a fantastic evening. So much so that we were asked to hold a monthly dance. We held a Christmas dance and New Year celebration dance. Over the next few years everybody got to know each other very well. After about eighteen months George bought some proper DJ equipment and speakers for the club out of his own pocket, but the club would pay him off over a period of time. That made my life a whole lot more exciting. I had played the part of DJ now for the second time, but here for the first time I had the right equipment.

Having the residents' association made a massive difference to our lives, we got to know more people in the tower block, for a while neighbours started to look out for neighbours again the way they used to when they lived side by side in streets. At least they did in our block Dodson Point. However, this didn't last long, and a certain factor of people started disrespecting other people and the property. One of the worse things was having to get into lifts where men would just have urinated. WHY would they do that? Of all the places that a man can relieve himself, why does he have to wait to get into a lift before emptying his bladder? It's beyond me.

There were five flats to a floor, three one-bedroom flats, and two three-bedroom flats. When I moved in it was understood that we each take a turn to clean the whole of the floor, including the lifts. So by rights if everyone did their turn, you would only clean once every five weeks and everything should have been spick and span. It worked at first but then the council had the brilliant idea of moving problem families into the tower blocks. It was okay at first, there wasn't much impact on our lives, but as most of the original occupiers were elderly, they started dying or having to go into a home or moving away all together, so there was a much bigger turnover. Then we really started to notice the difference. The idea was that all the nice families would raise the standards of the problem families. But it had the opposite effect and the problem families dragged the rest of us down with them. By this time I was the only one cleaning on my floor every week, nobody cared anymore. My neighbours would see me washing everything down, and let their kids throw sweet papers on the floor right in front of me. It really got me down.

One day after I had spent a long time cleaning my windows. I walked out of my bedroom into the kitchen. I couldn't have been gone more than seven or eight minutes. I walked back into the bedroom and noticed something on my window. I have to explain here that for me to clean the outside of my windows I had to completely spin the window over so that it was inside out, the windows were extremely heavy. I turned the window over to see what it was and then realised that it was shit. Now I had to clean the window all over again. But who the hell is throwing shit out of a tower block window. I found out later, that someone had thrown a baby's nappy out of the window and it had caught my window on the way down. This kind of thing started to gripe on my nerves. But for all that I could still cope.

Chapter 48

I mentioned Elsie and Jimmy earlier, Jimmy played drums in a band. When I first knew Elsie and Jimmy he played in the Anchor Public House in Star Lane. Later he was asked to join a Country and Western Group that met at St Cedd's once a week. We had some brilliant evenings. Everybody used to dress as cowboys or cowgirls or confederate or union soldiers some tried to look like their hero's. Wyatt Earp, or Doc Holiday. They all looked tough with their six guns. But when you got talking to them they did such mundane jobs. Elsie and I never ever put on any western garb; we wouldn't be seen dead in it. But we enjoyed the dancing and the music.

One evening a young man asked me to dance, he was dressed a bit different to the rest of the country and westerners. He wore a country and western suit, cowboy hat, string tie, he looked more like a country and western singer. Anyway we danced and chatted and he offered to walk me home and it was pleasant, he wasn't a bad kisser. He asked to meet me again and we arranged for the following Saturday. I got myself dressed up in my Saturday best and skipped out to meet the young man. As I am walking toward the place we arranged to meet I see that he has come out in the country and western outfit he had worn in the week. I was so embarrassed. I am well known in the area, I couldn't allow myself to be seen on the streets with someone pretending to be a cowboy. I rushed him into the nearest pub, called the Peacock in Freemason's Road. I had not been in this particular pub for years. It turns out it was 'Drag Night' with female impersonators. We got some drinks and sat down, he kept trying to hold my hand and I didn't want that, I kept pulling my hand away. Oh how I wanted this night to end. He was talking to me and I'm acting like I'm interested in what he's saying, but all I'm thinking about is how can I get out of this situation.

As I said he wore a cowboy hat and it made him a prime target for the drag queen that was 'doing a turn' at that point. He/she? came over and stole the cowboy hat. There have not been many times I have been lost for words, but this was one of them times. I was struck dumb in mid-sentence. The hat had gone and I am staring at the shiniest baldhead I have ever seen in a long time. It was shocking because I didn't expect such a young man to have a baldhead. At this point I wanted the earth to swallow me up. He got his hat back, we carried on talking, but now all I'm looking for is a way out. I found it, the ladies' toilet was in the next bar, that is where I said I was going, but instead I turned and ran out of the door all the way home. I never saw him again and he didn't go back to the weekly country and western dance where I met him originally. Phew.

Chapter 49

I would catch the 241 bus home from Plaistow Station to Freemason's Road. On one of these journey's home I was talking to a young girl I used to run into. As we were talking she said to me, "That bloke keeps looking at you." I turned to look and whom should it be, but my teenage sweetheart Lenny, from when we worked at W&C Tipple. I smiled and we started chatting, and catching up on old times.

Lenny got off at my stop, and we carried on chatting for a while. We were quite close to where I lived and so I asked him if he wanted to come up for a cup of tea so that we could carry on catching up. We talked and laughed about old times. I learnt that he had got married and had twin sons. I also learned that his marriage wasn't all that. Though I didn't take too much notice of that. So many years had gone by, I had heard that sob story from a few married men, and I'd steer well clear. After a few hours Lenny left. However, I started to see him regularly on the same bus and we would chat and sometimes he would come up to my flat for a cup of tea. I knew what was happening, and I let it happen, his being on my bus so often at that time wasn't coincidental. Lenny was still the charmer that I knew when we were younger. He had more maturity about him now. He still kept telling me about his 'on the rocks marriage'.

I learned that his Mum and Dad still lived in the same place, and I decided to go and see them to find out just how on the rocks this marriage was. Lenny's Mum Mary was really pleased to see me, as was his Dad, Bill. It turns out Lenny's marriage was all but over. So it wasn't too much of a surprise to anyone when Lenny decided to move in with me. We settled down to having a really good relationship, with two wages coming in our pooled resources gave us a pretty good life in the beginning. I hasten to add that Lenny still gave a good amount of money for his two boys, which I also contributed to as well. The boys would come round to the flat and we would take them out at weekends. They were good kids and needed the reassurance like any kids from a broken marriage that they hadn't lost their dad.

I had already put in for my divorce and at that time I had to wait three years. Lenny put in for his divorce and didn't have to wait so long. However, our decrees absolute both happened within weeks of each other. We had touched on the subject of marriage. Then one day we decided to go for it, why not, we were happy. Lenny's Mum and Dad were over the moon, it had finally happened, the marriage they wanted for us all those years ago. It was 1981. It wasn't anything spectacular. We married in a registry office in Stratford, and held our 'do' in the community hall where we lived. I did make a special invite to Miss Thom and her husband Reb, from my Tipples days. They always thought that me and Lenny would end up together. It was appropriate for them to be there and celebrate with us.

Chapter 50

End of an era for my part for the Jolly family. My Dad finally decided to sell his greengrocers shop in Tarling Road. He hadn't reached retirement age yet and would have to find work doing something else. And he did. Supermarkets had really taken off and businesses like my Dad's were finding it hard to compete.

By the end of September he was working for Viking Marine. It was a company that serviced life rafts. My Dad had been helping out there from time to time as a cleaner with my mum, but the governor decided that my dad would be able to do the job of servicing the rafts. However, he had to be certificated first. So they sent him to Denmark where the head office was, and Dad spent six weeks learning about life raft surveying. He was a fully-fledged surveyor when he returned.

There were only two greengrocers' shops now trading under the name of Jolly, one down Hermit Road, my Dad's Uncle Bill, and one in St Leonard's Road Poplar, Dad's brother Joe. Changes were beginning to happen and there was nothing that most people could do about it.

The London Docklands Development Corporation. (LDDC) 1981-1983 was a quango agency set up by Margaret Thatcher's Conservative Government in 1981 to regenerate the depressed docklands area of East London. During its eighteen-year existence it was responsible for regenerating an area of the London Boroughs of Newham, Tower Hamlets and Southwark. The LDDC helped to create Canary Wharf, Surrey

247

Quays shopping centre, London City Airport, ExCeL Exhibition Centre and the Docklands Light Railway, making the area highly sought after for housing.

I told you earlier that from the front window of our fifteenth floor flat, we could look towards Beckton. I had noticed a lot of activity going on down there. Piles being driven into the ground. This area was known as reclaimed marshland, being so close to the river Thames and the docks. There had been prefabs built in the area after the war to quickly house the bombed out homeless. Here we were in 1981 and they were just starting to re-house the people out of the prefabs to make way for this massive building regeneration project that included builders like Wimpey Homes, with Barratt Homes being the biggest.

By this time I had lived in Dodson Point for approx five years. It was beginning to get me down. I had come home one day to see our front door kicked in, narrowly missing the burglars by just a few minutes. They stole all of Lenny's jewellery but somehow missed mine. We'd had enough.

I persuaded Lenny to go down to Beckton to have a look to see what was going on. Some houses had been finished and they looked really nice. You could see what was trying to be achieved and it looked exciting. New Homes? How lovely. Not for us though. We didn't have any savings, and we would never get any money together in any short period of time.

We walked on and came to where the Barratt homes were being built. There was a big signboard. 100% mortgage! No deposit! Free carpets, curtains, fridges and washing machines. First year interest free! Maths wasn't my best subject at school, but this didn't take a lot of working out, could we do it? We decided to go into the show home and talk to the salesman. Within about thirty minutes we worked out that we could get one of these homes. Barratt's would arrange a mortgage broker. In fact Barratt's arranged EVERYTHING. We chose a two-bedroom house on Phase Two, purely from an artist's impression. The next few months were a blur of activity of meeting mortgage brokers, and signing this and signing that. It was daunting but the goal of getting on the first rung of the property ladder was intoxicating. My imagination was running away with me.

Then at some point we got some exciting news. Someone had dropped out of buying their two-bedroom house in Phase One. Did we want to take it? The only difference was that the one we chose was rendered on the outside the one being offered now was just brick. I couldn't care less, whether the house was rendered or not. I just wanted to get into our little two-bedroom house, little being the operative word. But I didn't care.

I asked my Mum and Dad to come and have a look at the new house. Dad wandered around looking here and there, opening this and shutting that. "Umm nice," he said. Mum was a little bit more vocal, coming up with a few ideas what I could do here and there. Later that day I rang my Mum, I said that Dad didn't have much to say did he? She said, "I asked him about that on our way home. He thinks you've bought a rabbit hutch there." She went on, "I told him that once you move in you will make it into a nice cosy home, wait and see."

Well he didn't have long to wait. We got the call to move in November 1983. Lenny and I had been married for about three years by now. It was one of the coldest days I could remember. The house wasn't exactly finished. There wasn't a letterbox on the door and it was blowing a gale through it. The house had only one gas fire hanging on the wall, which was all the heating it had. And we had stuff everywhere.

The first thing I did was to get the bed made up. The moment we had decided we had done enough sorting out and moving things around we could just jump into bed. It was so cold. Lenny and I went to bed that night dressed like a couple of Eskimos. We both wore hats and socks; Lenny kept his 'long johns' on. He was a scaffolder by trade and worked outside so they kept him warm under his jeans. I had a long house coat on top of a long nightie. Talk about passion killer, you won't be surprised to learn there wasn't going to be any

249

lovemaking that night. We were so cold we just cuddled up best we could for warmth.

Lenny had to go to work the next day; I had organised a few days off to get the house in some kind of order. When I had the time I went around and looked at some of the other things that needed to be done, and went round to the show home to get the chap there to get some workmen to my house to finish off the jobs. And that they did.

I was able to get a lot of other jobs done by different tradesmen on the cheap. Extra tiling in the kitchen and also in the bathroom. Getting a concrete path laid in the back garden, and getting turf laid; turf that had fallen off the back of a lorry so to speak.

Once I got everything shipshape, I invited my Mum and Dad back to see how it looked with all the furniture and knick knacks in place. Dad absolutely loved it. He really got caught up in it. He wanted to buy things for us, and he especially wanted to plant some fruit trees in the garden, which he did. A plum, a cherry, and an apple tree. Only the apple ever survived. A Spartan, lovely red apples.

When I went back to work, there was just one bus an hour. So I dare not miss it. It was quite lonely and I felt very vulnerable waiting at the bus stop at 6 a.m. in the morning. There were no occupied houses nearby. It was probably another six months before more people started using the same bus stop.

We had been living in Beckton for a couple of years by now. My sister and her husband and their two daughters, decided to move to a couple of streets away. They had been living in Stratford. House prices were reaching the most ridiculous limits. So many people were buying these houses and quickly selling them on at a profit. We bought our house for £32,000. After just a few months, houses like ours were changing hands for £40,000 and £50,000.

My sister's house was a four bedroom detached corner plot, it was like the Ponderosa compared to our little house. As a matter of fact when my sister's two girls came to see my house, they likened it to a Wendy house. It was nice having my sister close by.

It dawned on me that Lenny wasn't the brightest spark in the box. Maths he would lose you, basic logic, forget it. Here are a couple of stories about Lenny from those early days. We had been visiting my sister and her family after they had just moved in. Beckton was still a major building site. We were on our way back to our house, and we saw a lovely big ladder leaning up against an empty house. I told Lenny to nick it, he got it on his shoulder and we carried on walking. Lenny said to me, "What if the police come by and stop us." I told him "Just tell them you are a window cleaner coming home late." At the weekend we stood the ladder up against the house, it was way too long and needed to be shortened. We had found many tools lying around the site so we just picked them up and took them home, one was a saw. I told Lenny, "Cut about 6 rungs off." Then I walked into the kitchen, Lenny followed me in and said, "Which end shall I cut?" I thought am I hearing right? So I walked out into the garden with Lenny, and pointed to one end of the ladder and said, "I reckon you should cut that end because it's longer." And he did. I couldn't stop laughing.

The following year we had another cold winter with snow. Lenny said he was going out to clear the path at the front of the house. Off he went with a broom and shovel. After a while I got up and looked out of the window and saw a pile of black plastic bags. I went to the door and asked Lenny what was in the black bags. "Snow," he said. "The dustmen can take it away when they come." I said. "You are joking, they'll be taking bags of water, it's all going to melt. Why didn't you just pile it up and leave it." He said, "I didn't think." And that was exactly right he didn't think, Lenny was using my brain constantly and it was beginning to get me down.

I always knew that Lenny liked a bet, but I didn't know just how much. I was finding it a struggle to make ends meet. That lead to rows, I was getting so worried that I went and got a second job at the local Asda store working from 11 p.m. at

251

night to 2 a.m. stacking shelves, all for £30 a week. And still have to get up and catch the 6 a.m. bus to my day job the following day. But it kept the wolves away from the door, I was in control and it stopped me worrying.

There had been some more building going on at the top of our road, and I got chatting to a builder and found that they were building Warden Controlled Homes for the elderly on behalf of East London Housing Association. I mentioned this to my Mum and Dad and straight away Mum said let's try and get one. So I started bombarding Newham council to nominate my mum and dad to the housing association. It went on for months and months, but finally my persistence paid off, they were nominated, but there was a hiccup. They had to be over 65 to be offered one of these homes, I think they were about 63. It was touch and go, but finally they were given a firm offer of a flat. They moved in within a matter of weeks.

That was the beginning of another happy era. All the people that moved in were lovely people. The warden and her husband Pam and Dick were fantastic. They had their own community centre and it wasn't long before I offered my services as a DJ for their monthly get togethers.

I was still in contact with Pat and George from the tower block, they had also been moved to the Beckton area by the council, so I told them about the monthly get together, and it was just like old times. We had some fabulous times during those years.

I bought a little dog around this time Bobby a tri-colour King Charles Spaniel. He was my little pal. I was lucky now because Mum would go round to my house at lunch time to give Bobby a walk and his dinner and then he would be good till I got home in the early evening.

As time went by I started to notice Lenny was staying out more often and also later. On a Friday he was going to work a bit smarter than usual. It didn't take a lot of putting two and two together to know what was going on. I thought he was cheating on me. So I confronted him, and he denied anything was going on. I tried to follow him one time, but wasn't any good at it, so I decided to get a private detective at the cost of £200. Within a few days I had all the proof I needed. I confronted Lenny again, giving him ample opportunity to come clean and still he lied, so I showed him the paper the private detective had put together. It showed where he and she had been and what her name was, yet he still wanted to deny it. That was it, I told him he had to go, 'he wasn't going to have his cake and eat it.'

By the weekend he had all his stuff packed and was walking out the door. He stopped and turned to me and said, "If it don't work out after six weeks can I come back?" I said, "Six seconds after you walk out that door you can't come back." And that was that.

It was a worrying time. I thought the house would have to be sold and I would have to find somewhere else to live. I couldn't have that; I had worked too hard for this. Now I had to talk to the mortgage lenders and get the deeds changed over to my name. Not that easy, they worked out that on my London Transport money I couldn't afford the mortgage. I told them I had other jobs. They informed me that they don't count. Then my Dad's younger brother, Johnny, stepped in and said that he would stand guarantor for me, I told him that it would be for the next twenty-five years and he said that is all right. I told him I would never let him down. And I didn't

Chapter 51

There had been some changes at London Transport. Pixie, my supervisor had a nervous breakdown and was medically retired.

Technology had moved on and whereas we used to have lots of different operators working at different offices we now had two main switchboards. One was located in Head Office at St James Park and now we had one in Baker Street. All the operators were condensed into these two sites. I wasn't happy at Baker Street, the supervisor we had was a waste of space, she never had the knowledge of the organisation that I had and she favoured the girls that she had brought with her. All of whom were some of the laziest people I ever come across. But for now that was the least of my worries I had to earn extra money.

The first part-time job I got was cleaning offices down near the Tower of London. £3 per hour, two hours every evening for five nights a week. I hated it, but it was money coming in.

I kept looking for something better, and very soon after I found another job working for, wait for it, Phonatas. This is the company I did out of a contract all those years ago when I took over the cleaning of the telephones. Now they not only cleaned telephones they also cleaned computers. A lot of the work was in financial dealers offices in the city. These people were filthy. The keyboards on the computers were as 'Black as

Newgate's Knocker'. But what satisfaction I got when I had cleaned them up and they looked almost new. I would love to have seen the faces of the users when they walked in the next day to see the clean keyboards. I liked the job. I had to work on a Saturday as well, so I didn't have a lot of free time for myself.

One day, a young man called Alan Cattell from the Telecomms department in the offices I used to work in at Paddington came over to fix something on my switchboard in Baker Street. We got talking and I told him how unhappy I was and what was happening with me having to work two jobs. He told me that there was a job going in his office. It was a job that the other telephone engineers were all able to do. But I wasn't a telephone engineer. Alan said, "I know you could do the job." There was a new head of his department, Mark Plato. I had known Mark when he joined telecomms as an apprentice. Now here he was head of that department. I said to Alan that surely I must need some sort of qualifications, but Alan insisted I didn't and he was going to have a word with Mark.

Mark created a job application for me. It had to be advertised throughout the organisation and many people applied, but they were never going to get job, it was there for me. Within in a matter of weeks I was back at Telstar House, Paddington, the only girl in an office full of young men. A girl's dream, not for me though, they were all either married or too young, but they were all great fun.

As it was a male dominated office there was a few Eff's and B's followed by apologies to me. I thought I got to put these boys out of their misery. I said, "Look here, you can Eff and Blind all you like, it ain't going to be a patch on what you are going to hear coming out of my mouth, and I ain't gonna be apologising to you." I was now one of the boys, or an honorary bloke as they called me.

I picked up the work quicker than they expected me to, and had more of an understanding than they expected me to have. Basically if someone wanted a new phone installed, it was my job to choose a number and add it on via a computer package to a piece of equipment in one of the twenty-two London Transport exchanges. Then send an engineer off to actually fit it. That is it in the most simplistic terms.

One problem was that I never ever had enough equipment to fulfil the request for new telephone lines. So using my knowledge from my telephonist days in Telstar House when I did a survey and found lots of telephones hidden and not being used. I decided to put the idea to Alan to see if we could reclaim some of this telephone equipment back. I needed his expertise on how to do this. One exchange could serve many stations and offices and it was crucial that I didn't disconnect any station numbers. Alan gave me an idea how I could do it and I set about it. Unbeknown to me someone was listening to my idea. His name was Andrew; he was a bit of a computer geek.

I carried on in my own way and did reclamation of one exchange. I was able to get back over £40,000 worth of unused telephone equipment. I was on a roll. I started on the next exchange. This job was going to take me the best part of two years to complete. The spin off from this was I was able to make a new and comprehensive telephone directory. We now knew who owned the telephone and exactly where it was located. Bearing in mind some cases there could be a telephone up a tube tunnel that had been forgotten about for years.

I still had my part time job with Phonatas. But that was soon to come to an end. They wanted to give their permanent staff more overtime, and they weren't able to because of all the casual labourer such as me. So very soon I was out of a job and needed to find another one quickly. I saw a job advertised for a part-time switchboard operator in a hotel. I called the number and got myself an interview. This wasn't just any old run of the mill hotel. This was Claridges. I had my interview and I was taken on. My hours were 5. 30 p.m. to 10 p.m. every night and alternate three shifts on a Saturday and Sunday. I was now working all the hours god sent. Seven days a week and at least five nights a week. But it was work and those wolves were still not knocking on my door. I had already been working part-time for about two years by now. Surprisingly I was enjoying the whole thing, the adrenalin was flowing like water. I was on a constant high.

It didn't take me long to pick up the hotel way of life and it is a way of life. One hotel's personnel will know many people at another hotel; they are of a certain breed of people that move within the hotel business.

One of the first things I had to learn was how to address people. The people I was about to deal with were film stars, rock stars, royalty, presidents, and people who thought they were somebody but were in fact nobody and these were the worst kind.

The rudest couple we ever had to deal with were a Baron and Baroness from America. The way they spoke to people was uncalled for, and unnecessary. They had the housekeepers running all over the place. Then if it was noisy they had the managers running round trying to stop the noise, every little thing that they could find to complain about they did. More money than sense in my opinion. They were always at Claridges for the 'season' and we dreaded them.

Then you had class, the Royalty. We had the King and Queen of Spain, such nice people to talk to. My favourite was King Constantine of Greece. What a gentleman. He called from the ballroom telephone one evening and asked for a number. I dialled it but it was engaged. I asked his highness, "Sir, would you like me to page you when I have the call?" He said, "No, he would wait on the line." So I tried again, and again and again, I kept apologising for the delay and informing his highness that the line was till busy and that I was still trying the connect him. I offered time and time again to have him paged when I had the call, and each time he said, "No he would hold on." I don't know how long it took, but it was an extremely long time before I got the call. Finally I said, "There you are, Sir, your number is ringing." He thanked me and I left him connected. What a lovely patient man.

Another nice person was Henry Winkler and also his wife Stacey. He was really funny. He would often joke around with us. We would try to do our job without being familiar and he would get chatting so that in the end you felt like you were chatting to a friend. A lovely couple.

Here is a list of some of the people I had the pleasure of talking to during my time at Claridges. King Constantine of Greece, The King and Queen of Spain, Princess Elizabeth of Yugoslavia (her daughter was Catherine Oxenburg in Dynasty) Leslie Bricus -songwriter, Brian Forbes - film director, Douglas Fairbanks Jnr-actor, Audrey Hepburn-actor, Lord Churchill, Lord Snowden, Joan Collins, Princess Irene of Hellenes, Princess Lala Hasna of Morocco, Duke of Luxembourg, Harry Dean Stanton-actor, Julie Andrews and Blake Edwards, Duke and Duchess of Bedford, Richard Dreyfus-actor, George Bush senior when he was just a vice president. Henry Kissinger, Christina Onassis, and Sammy Cahn-songwriter, and Peter John Gouldandris who I worked for all those years before. All these people were very nice to talk to. When I was getting a call for Mr Peter John I mentioned that I used to work for him at Capeside Steamship, and after a few exchanges of questions and answers he actually remembered me. Class, that's what I say.

There was an actress that lived in Claridges, her name was Elaine Stritch. I had to go up to the first floor waiter's room to get some milk and I could hear the rasping voice of Miss Stritch. I stood by the open door and waited until she was through and then I would get the milk. She spotted me standing there and called me in. She came over to me and touched the jumper I was wearing and said, "Gee, I like your sweater." I said, "Thank you, Miss Stritch." She carried on, "Where did you get it?" I said, "I got it out of Freeman's Catalogue Miss Stritch." Then she spotted a little plastic pendant I was wearing, She said, "I bet you didn't get that in Freeman's' catalogue did you?" I said, "No, Miss Stritch, my mum bought this for me in 1957 on a day trip to Calais." Down to earth that's me. She asked what I did in the hotel. I told her I was one of the team who worked on the switchboard. The faceless ones. The next day Miss Stritch came down with one of the flunkey's, his arms full of boxes of chocolates for all the team. How kind was that.

During my time at Claridges I met a young man called Gavin who was to become a good friend.

I didn't know at the time that Gavin's Dad worked for Henry Cecil the racehorse trainer. Once Gavin knew that my Dad was into horse racing he told his parents and they invited my dad down to have a look round Warren Place. It was a fantastic day seeing all the thoroughbred horses just being themselves; you forget they have their own personalities. You just tend to think of them as racing machines that you see on TV. As a souvenir Gavin's parents gave my Dad a beautiful pencil drawing of a horse called Reference Point. We were at the Epsom Derby the year Reference Point won it. So it was very special for my Dad. I had the drawing framed for Christmas that year as his present. He was thrilled. Our families met on several more occasions after that when Gavin's parents came to my home for dinner.

I've digressed. I was doing so well at my job in the communication department, that Mark decided I was due for an upgrade and a raise; in fact I went up two grades. I was now earning enough money so I didn't need any part time jobs. So I gave my job up with Claridges and the first thing that happened to me was I got sick. It seemed the whole time my adrenalin was flowing I couldn't allow myself to be ill. No work, no money. Now that I was able to relax it seemed it all caught up with me. Strange.

I was still reclaiming equipment around the exchanges the cost of which was getting very high. I was really proud of my work.

One Friday Andrew, the computer geek, asked if I was going for a drink with the rest of the boys, I told him no I didn't have enough money. Andrew said he would pay, I said no; I don't want to get into debt. Andrew said you don't have to pay it back. I thought this is strange, Andrew was as 'tight as a drum' with money, and this generosity was unusual. I saw Alan and couldn't wait to tell him about Andrew. But Alan said to me, "I've got something to tell you and you are not going to like it." I said, "Go on then, what's the matter?" Alan said, "You know all this reclamation you have been doing? Well Andrew comes in on the train with Brian Mellet, a senior director of London Underground." I said, "So what's that got to do with my reclamation scheme?" Alan said Andrew has told Brian Mellet it was his idea and he had been awarded 5% of the overall reclamation total. I had accumulated approx £250,000 in equipment. I went ballistic. I called Andrew all the names under the sun, I effed him uphill and down dale. I left him not knowing what day of the week it was. "You stole my idea you f**king moron." I had struggled all that time with two jobs and this f**ker takes what was rightfully mine away from me. All he was going to do was buy me a couple of poxy drinks.

There was nothing anyone could do. All the boys in the office had a go at him, but it was like water off a duck's back. All I had to my name was the fact that everyone knew that the reclamation was my idea.

Chapter 52

Frank (Hop) Wilson had been in my life since my visit to New York in 1974. Hundreds of letters had flown across the Atlantic between us. I had told him my innermost secrets, hopes and dreams and he had told me his. He sent me beautiful presents, and I sent him gifts too. It was like a secret love affair. Even when I married John who I met on the cruise, I couldn't stop writing to Hop.

Hop had girlfriends and sent me photos, I was still having boyfriends and sending him photos. I always felt a little jealous when I read about his girlfriends. Around the time that I met up with Lenny again, Hop had met a woman and he married her. Not long after that I married Lenny. Hop and I still continued to write to each other, right up until Lenny and I moved to our house in Beckton. But Lenny was jealous of my letters, so reluctantly I explained to Hop about the situation and that maybe we should stop corresponding. That was it! I really missed those letters dropping on the mat from America.

Then as I have already told you Lenny and I divorced. Unbeknown to me Hop's marriage was also on the rocks. Imagine my surprise when one evening after I came home from my stint at Claridges I found a letter from America waiting for me. I was so excited. I tore it open. It was lovely to read the words Hop had put down on paper. He had got a divorce. I couldn't wait to write to tell him that I too had divorced.

Pretty soon our letters were flying back and forth once more. Then one day my phone rang and there was this man with an American accent talking to me. It was Hop. This was the first time I had ever heard his voice. He sounded so sweet and gentle on the phone. After that there were many phone calls. I would make a few calls from work. (Let London Transport pay) I would even call from Claridges switchboard for a quick chat. I put the calls down to wrong numbers.

It was a Sunday and a sunny summer's day in 1989 when my phone rang, it was Hop. We chatted as usual. Then he said I've got something to ask you. So I waited, and he said, "Will you marry me?" I asked, "What, me come to America or you come here?" He said. "I'll come there." I said, "Okay, if you turn up, you got yourself a wedding." Now this news was going to come as a complete surprise to my family. I didn't feel that I could just drop the bombshell of news. I felt I would have to drop subtle hints here and there.

Soon after large boxes of Hop's personal stuff started arriving. Some of the stuff was t-shirts to be given to my dad and other members of the family. The frequency of the arrival of the boxes increased. My mother was aware of this, and one day she said, "He's not going to be following them is he?" Very sharp my Mum. I told her yes that is what is going to happen. My Mum and Dad weren't pleased. But it was my life and I could do as I pleased.

Events of the 80s

1980 Ronald Regan becomes President

John Lennon shot and killed in New York

1981 Aids virus first Identified,

1982 Argentina invade the Falkland Islands, England at war again.

Princess Grace dies in car crash

1983 Space Shuttle makes maiden voyage and carried the first woman astronaut into space.

1984 Indira Gandhi assassinated

1985 Titanic wreck found.

Milchail Gorbachev becomes leader of USSR – bringing two new words to the West, Glasnot and Perestroika.

1986 Space shuttle Challenger explodes killing all seven people on board.

Chernobyl nuclear accident

USSR launch Mir space station

1987 DNA first used to convict criminals

Maggie Thatcher wins a rare third term as prime minister

1988 Terrorist bomb on Pan Am 747 explodes over Lockerbie, 259 killed.

1989   Berlin Wall falls and opens up to the West, Communism breaking down

Students rally for democracy in China,   Tiananmen Square. Many killed.

There were a couple of other events that happened during the eighties.

There was a miner's strike that went on for about nine months led by Arthur Scargill.

It was a very bad time for the miners trying to survive. There was much picketing and many fights between the miners themselves. Miners getting beaten up because they wanted to work; their families were threatened too.

Also there was a terrible famine going on in Ethiopia. Bob Geldof and Midge Ure got a band together of the star singers of the day and created a one off band called Band Aid. They sang a song called 'Do They Know It's Christmas' it was a massive hit.

By 1985 Bob Geldof, who was himself once in a group called the Boom Town Rats organised a live show called LIVE AID. There was one held in Wembley and one held at the same time in America at the JFK stadium. They had all the top singers and groups to help raise money for the famine relief. At that time it raised over £50 million pounds. Bob Geldof was later knighted for his efforts.

Also around November 1985 everybody was talking about Halley's Comet. I mention this because the thing only comes around once every seventy-six years, and here it was in my lifetime. It appeared on or around 2 December that year.

Chapter 53

1990-1 It all happened very quickly after that, Hop arrived at Gatwick Airport on 3 October 1990, which was our very first meeting, and by 12 October we were married. Another registry office wedding in Stratford. I was getting married there so often by now I thought about getting a season ticket. The next thing we did was to apply to the Home Office for the paperwork to let him stay in the UK. It was all very strange at first doing your courting and getting used to being married at the same time, but we got along all right. Hop got a job working as a night security guard. They particularly like people who have been in the military. Hop did two tours during the Vietnam War. So they looked on him like he was John Wayne.

It wasn't an ideal way to start married life. We didn't see each other much at first, as I was leaving for work I would see Hop coming home from a night shift on the opposite platform at Plaistow Station. Then when I got home in the evening he would be gone again. We carried on like this for almost a year, but every night at work Hop would scan the newspapers, in particular the local Newham Recorder for something better. His diligence paid off and he got a job as a street cleaner, it doesn't sound much but I was proud of him. His actual trade was a painter. Hop had worked for many years for the City of Miami, in Florida. At that time the building trade wasn't up to much and there wasn't any work around for trades. Hop enjoyed the work he did. He was getting good pay, with the prospect of a pension and weekends off, unless he wanted overtime which he did when it suited us.

On the family front, my Mum and Dad and the rest of the family weren't so keen on me marrying again to what they perceived to be a total stranger. Hop was just a stranger to them. They didn't know him like I did through his letters. I felt they would come to love him as much as I did.

1992 Hop's Mum sent us $10,000 and we decided to use it to go over to Florida so that I could meet his family. We asked my parents if they wanted to come along. My Dad declined, but my Mum was up for it. We decided to fly out Economy and come back Upper Class, with Virgin Atlantic. Having come back from New York in 1974, it was so uncomfortable travelling through the night and arriving early morning. I didn't get any sleep at all. I wanted my Mum to be comfortable. Liz and John drove us to the airport and saw us off. This was Mum's first time on a plane.

We arrived in Miami and were picked up by Hop's old supervisor and friend Vernon and taken back to his house to meet his wife, Arlene. Vernon and Arlene were a nice couple, a little younger than me and Hop. They had a lovely home, the garden was full of palm trees and orange trees and 'pot'. I am not talking about a pot plant I am talking about a cannabis plant. Vernon and Arlene it seemed liked to chill out smoking a little pot. It didn't bother us at all, each to his own, me and mum would stick to Benson and Hedges. Vernon and Arlene cooked dinner for us, barbeque steaks. One would have been enough for three people, or at least two people, and here we had one each. I think this was a sign of things to come.

After dinner I heard Hop talking to Vernon and asking for his 'dictionary'. I wondered, why does Hop want a dictionary, we all speak English, though we still didn't necessarily understand each other. Then with everything else going on I forgot all about it.

Later we went over to visit Hop's Parents, they were a nice. Though I noticed that these Floridian's all seemed to look older and act older than their actual years. My Mum was just a couple of years younger than Hop's parents yet my Mum looked like a teenager by comparison. And Mum assured me that I looked younger than Vernon and Arlene, who were much younger than me.

We had booked ourselves into the Marco Polo hotel on Collins Avenue, right along the beach. We were high up and had a terrific view. The first thing my Mum wanted to do was call home to talk to my Dad. They had hardly ever been separated since they were married and now an ocean separated them. She was very tearful when she got off the phone.

The next day we went to pick up the car that we were going to travel around in. It was a white Plymouth, very nice. Hop drove us around Miami to see some of the sights and to do some shopping. We saw where Mohammed Ali used to train. We went to a restaurant called Wolfie's which is very famous in Miami because of its gangster connections during the 40s and 50s. The walls were plastered with autographed photos of singers and film stars who had been there. I loved it.

We were having such a good time. Then while we were sitting at some traffic lights, a car came from our right and slammed right into the side of us, causing the air bags to explode. We were all stunned for a few minutes, then I made my Mum get out of the car and we went and sat on a bench till the cops arrived. As luck would have it, Hop knew the cops who turned up to the scene. It appeared the other driver was a Puerto Rican and didn't have a driving licence, so he was hauled away. We, on the other hand had to take our banged up car back to the people we hired it from. Hop went and did all the explaining and showed them the police paperwork, etc.

While he was doing that me and Mum were emptying the car of the purchases we had made. Mum noticed something under the front passenger seat and told me to get it out. I looked and saw a brown paper bag, but I didn't think it could be ours as all the stuff we had bought was in the boot of the car. But Mum insisted, so I pulled the bag out, it was heavy and had grease marks on it. I said, "I think someone has left

267

dog bones in here." It was one brown bag wrapped inside another so you couldn't see what was inside. I pulled one bag off and I was left holding the butt of a handgun. I dropped it like a hot potato and called Hop to come over, but he waved me away as he was dealing with the person who was going to exchange the car. But I insisted he come over and so he did. I said, "Hop, me and Mum have found a gun under the front seat." And Hop said, "Yeah, I know it's my dictionary." I said, "Whaddya mean it's your dictionary?" Hop said, "Well, it's speaks any language, put it in your purse." So I did. We got the new car and drove back to the hotel.

The gun was a Magnum and I didn't like the idea of having it, but Hop said if we are going travelling then we need to have it. I thought what a holiday this is gonna be. We referred to it from then on as 'Chocolate Fudge'. More or less for the rest of the holiday I walked around with a camcorder on one shoulder, a 35mm camera on my other shoulder, and a Magnum in my handbag (it was a large handbag). I felt like a pack horse.

The next day we had an early breakfast and got on the road heading for Georgia, but we were going to make an overnight stop on the way in Ocala to see a couple of friends of Hop's, Floyd and his wife Dotty. We booked into a motel and then set off to find where Floyd and Dotty lived, we got lost a couple of times but we finally got there. They seemed like nice people and it was a nice visit. Mum noticed lots of grey stuff hanging from a large tree in the garden. It turned out to be moss. Floyd got some large handfuls of the stuff down for my mum and put it in a bag for her. She said she was going to put it around her pot plants when she got home. Apparently it is an offence to remove the moss from the trees, which was lucky Floyd told us otherwise she'd have been stripping every tree that had it on.

The next morning we set off for Georgia, we were going to do a bit of sightseeing around Atlanta, but we got lost again and it was very dark by the time we arrived and found a hotel to stay in. It was a place called Dunwoody, we were that tired, I said they should call it Dunroamin. We had to forgo our sightseeing in Atlanta as it would have put us behind schedule. So we left Atlanta heading for Tennessee and the first place we came to was Chattanooga which is more or less on the border of Georgia and Tennessee. We saw a sign for the Choo Choo and went to check it out. If you are a reader that was born in the 20s or 30s you would have been old enough to hear a song called Chattanooga Choo Choo played by Glen Miller and sung by Tex Beneke. It was still being played after the war and I knew it.

The song was written by the team of Mack Gordon and Harry Warren while travelling on the Southern Railway's 'Birmingham Special' train. The song tells the story of travelling from New York City to Chattanooga. The inspiration for the song was a small, wood-burning steam locomotive which belonged to the Cincinnati Southern Railway, The 'Choo Choo' train is now a museum artefact.

We left Chattanooga and headed on to Nashville. We booked into the Ramada Hotel. We did a couple of tours around the country and western stars homes, stopped off at Twitty City, Home of Conway Twitty. There was a small theatre there and a country and western show was put on for us.

The next day we went to the Ryman Theatre which was the original home of the Grand Old Oprey. We took a tour and that was really interesting. We were all ushered onto the stage of the Grand Old Oprey and the tour guide started to get us all to clap and join in the song 'You are my Sunshine' When we had finished he said you can now go home and boast that you sang on the stage of the Grand Old Oprey. We did a few other tours, Including the Country Music Hall of Fame. When you see the clothes that the people wear they look so small. I really liked Nashville.

The next day we were heading off to Mississippi. Our first overnight stop was in Jackson the capital, before we headed on to Memphis. We went to a diner for breakfast, and we sat at the counter and ordered something. Mum was still struggling with the portions, Hop was happy eating his 'Grits'. A bloke must have heard our accents and started up a conversation with us, it wasn't long before it was established that he like Hop had served in the Vietnam War. He went on to explain that the military teaches you how to kill, but they don't rehabilitate you when you get back. He then started to tell us about an incident some years before where he was walking alone and someone attempted to mug him. He went on that he pulled his knife out, stuck it in the bloke's belly and slit him upward, dropped him and left him there. It was in the papers the next day about a murdered black man. I said to Hop, "I think I would like to get out of here as quick as possible. We don't need to be around this type of person." We left. Scary!

When we got to Memphis we did the whole Elvis thing, visiting Gracelands and going around the gardens to see Elvis's grave along with the rest of the Presley family. Mum was never particularly an Elvis fan but she loved this visit. It was an odd feeling to be walking around the house that Elvis lived in, seeing his 'things'.

Then we were on the road again to Louisiana and New Orleans. Hop was driving 150 to 250 miles a day from one state to another. We would stop along the way and take photos or video film. I wanted to see a cotton field, you hear about them in so many southern songs. At every state line there is a Welcome Centre that also incorporates rest room facilities, from what I saw they were mostly manned during the day for people travelling that route. They were especially good for tourists as you could pick up information leaflets. I really did experience the Southern hospitality that people have spoken about.

So far we had booked our hotels ahead of our arrival, for some reason we didn't do it for our visit to New Orleans. Consequently when we got there the hotels were fully booked. There was a cardiologists' convention being held. We made our way to Charles Street (where the street car named Desire travels - if you know the film with Marlon Brando) and also where there are lots of hotels. We tried about three hotels and it was the same answer every time, no rooms available. I went into one hotel, and there was the receptionist on the phone, and another lady standing by. But from a room I could hear a weird noise of exhalation. I had stood there for several minutes and then I asked the lady standing there. "What's going on in there?" She said a man was having a heart attack and her husband was giving CPR. Then the receptionist came off the phone, I asked about room vacancies and she said there weren't any. I felt like asking, "Can I wait to see how that gentleman gets on, maybe we could have his room?" but I didn't. I was getting desperate by now.

My next hotel I went into was the Ramada and they said they didn't have a room for that night but could fit us in the following night. So now if we could just get a room for one night we'd be okay. We eventually went down to the French Quarter to try our luck there, and found a place that had a small hotel and also an apartment in a historical plantation house. The rooms in the hotel were full but the apartment was available. We grabbed it.

It was a beautiful house, the architecture was wonderful. It stood just on the edge of the French Quarter. It had a plaque outside explaining that it had been a plantation house, it gave dates, etc. Here we were, about to stay in a remarkable historic building. It was a change to be catering for ourselves. There were basic groceries in the fridge, some dry goods, milk, coffee. We would be able to have breakfast without going out shopping for anything. I was impressed. There was a large living room with open plan kitchen. It had a bed settee. Then there was a massive bedroom. The bathroom was called a 'Jack and Jill' you could access it either from the bedroom, or the living room. You would have to ensure that you locked both doors. I thought it was a good idea. We explored the garden which was beautiful. There, just below the house, was a small jail. Obviously, the plantation house would have had slaves, and I guess if one of the workers did something the owner didn't like, this was a way of punishment.

We could have stayed in the plantation house for the duration of our stay. But Mum had enjoyed the luxury and

271

security of staying in hotels. To give my Mum peace of mind we booked the following night at the Ramada.

We had a good look around New Orleans, especially the French Quarter, I loved the architecture. I could just imagine what it was like back in the day with those southern belles and gentlemen. We took a ride on a streetcar along Front Street. We also booked a trip on board a Mississippi river boat called the Natches. Before the boat sails they play a steam organ on top of the boat. It certainly got your feet tapping, as did the jazz music that emanated from all the bars along Bourbon Street. Everywhere you go there is music. The French Market was a source of so many exotic smells. I would love to go back to New Orleans.

We had a few meals in the French Quarter. I remember our last morning we went to have breakfast. Mum decided that she was just going to have a waffle. She had been struggling with all the meals since we had landed in America. The portions were just too large for her. I guess in my Mum's head she was thinking about the silly little waffles you get in the freezers in the UK. When the waffle she had ordered came up, it was so large and piled so high with cream it was difficult to see my Mum behind it. My Mum looked at it and then looked and me and said, "I dunno, the less you ask for the more you f**king get." Well, me and Hop just went into fits of laughter.

We started to head back to Florida, taking a different route. This time we passed into Alabama, before entering Florida again. We were going to stop off either in Pensacola where there is a large naval base and where Hop was once stationed, or Tallahassee which is the state capital. But Hop was feeling good on the drive and we sailed right past both of them. We started to head down the Gulf of Mexico side of Florida to a place called Naples where there was another friend that Hop used to work with. His name was Walter and his wife was called Ginger.

My Mum had developed a cough about a week after we left Florida, it had got a little worse as the days went by and we got cough mixture from pharmacies although it hadn't helped much. We had stopped for lunch on the drive down to Naples and just before we were served Mum burst into tears. This wasn't like her so I knew I had to get her to a hospital to get her checked out. We booked into a lovely motel in Naples. I asked the owners where the nearest hospital was and they gave us directions to it. Once we arrived the doctors gave Mum a good examination and x-rays and said she needed antibiotics. So we sat and waited while they made up the prescription. We noticed that many doctors and nurses kept walking by and having a look in at Mum. We were quite bemused by it. When the doctor came back into the room, we mentioned about the people that seemed to be staring at Mum. He apologized about it and said they just can't believe that she is 69 years old. She looks very young for her age. That cheered Mum up no end.

Later we met up with Walter and Ginger at their home. They had dogs running all over the place, and they were all scratching, a sure sign they were flea ridden. Walter and Ginger didn't look the cleanest of people to me either. They asked us to stay for a meal. There was no way of getting out of it so we accepted. It consisted of pasta and something else I could not describe to you. Suffice to say it was awful, I tried to eat something but kept gagging. It didn't help that I found a hair in my food. The house smelled of cats and dogs and something dead. I looked at Hop and tried to make a face to him that we wanted to leave as soon as possible. And then we did.

We left Naples and were now heading down toward the Florida Keys. We drove through the everglades on the Tamiami Trail, it was a nice road to travel, we stopped off at an Indian cabin and bought some Indian craft work. Then we went on through Homestead where we saw the destruction and devastation that Hurricane Andrew had caused only a few months earlier. I saw steel twisted into such shapes I never thought possible unless blown up by a bomb.

We made our way to Key Largo, We booked into the Hilton Hotel which had a balcony with a view over one of the waterways. Just along by our hotel was a replica boat of the

African Queen with a dummy of Humphrey Bogart (Charlie Allnut) sitting in it. The area was beautiful. Hop went off somewhere and came back with some tickets to take a trip on the African Princess, a glass bottom boat (that should have been a clue).

We went to board the boat at the allotted time and off we went. The waterway was very pretty. Then, we came out of the waterway and started to head out to sea. The waves were coming over the front of the boat and all three of us got soaking wet, but we were having fun so we didn't much care. Then when we had gone quite some way, they cut the engine just enough to still have control of the rudder. They asked everybody to go below to look at the coral reef. I didn't want to look at any coral reef. I was remembering my time on the Canberra and how seasick I felt. The boat was now bobbing about like a cork, and the feeling of sea sickness was soon upon me. I couldn't wait till they all got fed up looking at the coral. How long does it take to look at a bit of coral anyway?

Keep your eyes on the horizon that's what they say, so I kept my eyes on the horizon and I still felt as sick as a dog. I was keeping my eyes on the horizon when my Mum's head popped up as she came up the stairway. She said she was starting to feel queasy as well, two minutes later Hop came up as well. Mum said she thought the glass on the bottom was cracked. Hop assured her it was a piece of algae. Oh and if that wasn't bad enough we were sitting right inside the Bermuda Triangle.

Mum kept trying to talk to me and I was too ill to talk and got annoyed with her and told her to shut up, using more colourful language. I kept saying to my mum and Hop, when are they going to turn this f **king boat round and head back home. FINALLY, they said they were going to head back as the waves were getting too high; I could have told them that. Mum and me were so glad to get on firm ground. It didn't bother Hop he had been a sailor, what did he care.

Over the next couple of days we explored the rest of the Florida Keys and did more touristy stuff. They are truly beautiful Islands. Key West is lovely. We went to the bar where Hemmingway drank, if that floats your boat.

Soon it was time to head back to Miami for our last day or so and to say goodbye to Hop's family and Vernon and Arlene. This time we met Hop's brother, Charles. He was a little worse the wear for drink, but he was happy go lucky. He tried to flirt with my Mum, and she didn't like that at all.

I am glad I had the forethought to book Upper Class for the journey home, it was much more comfortable and a lot quieter too. Mum was comfortable, that was the main thing and we were all able to get some sleep. It's certainly a better way to travel.

Liz and John picked us up from the airport and brought us back to Beckton. Ah, to see Mum and Dad meet up again was wonderful. They both had tears in their eyes as they kissed and cuddled each other. True love. Dad had been looking after my dog Bobby. When I left Bobby he looked like a dog, but by the time we came home he looked like a black and white ball and could hardly walk, it was hard to tell his head from his bum. Dad had been feeding him a little too well I think. I was just pleased that he had been in safe hands, and they were company for each other for the three weeks we were gone.

Over the next few years me and Hop travelled back to Miami for other holidays including Thanksgiving and Christmas. And I have to say the Americans have got it made for themselves. Vernon and Arlene invited us for a Christmas get together one year I offered to help prepare the food and they said, "No, they'd be fine" I knew there was going to be at least fifteen people there, so I figured they had some big job to do. But when we arrived, they were as cool as cucumbers. The food was all laid out, turkey, ham, and vegetable and also an eleven layered chocolate cake. I asked them how come they were able to manage so well, and then they told me the secret. You go to 'Publix' which is their supermarket and order it over the counter. That's the way to do it.

1994. For the second time Mum and Dad were going to be apart. Dad had never wanted to go up in an aeroplane. If he had he would have accompanied us on the Florida trip. But in the summer of '94 his young brother, Johnny, more or less ordered him to go to Spain with him and his wife, Jesse, and his cousin John and his wife Mary.

Dad was really quite nervous about flying and really didn't want to leave my mum for so long. Mum said, "Look at the journey I did, it was nine hours on a plane you're only going to be on a plane for about three and a half hours. I could spit that far." Mum had a way with words. It didn't make Dad feel any better though.

Finally the day came and Johnny arrived to pick Dad up. Me and Mum waved him goodbye. Johnny told us the story of what happened later. They were in the departure lounge and Dad said he wanted to go and ring Bette, my Mum He wanted to say another goodbye to her. Johnny waited for him close by, then the call for the passengers to go to their flight was called and Johnny told my dad to hurry up as they had to go. Johnny told us when Dad turned round he had tears rolling down his cheeks.

Dad was apprehensive when he boarded the plane but once they had taken off he realised the flight wasn't that bad after all. He then went on to enjoy two lovely weeks on the Costa del Sol where Johnny and Jesse had a large three bedroom rooftop apartment. Johnny was like a lamb with two tails showing his big brother the sights and sounds of Marbella and many other places. He particularly enjoyed introducing my dad to food that my dad wouldn't have dreamed of trying before.

Dad, being the keen photographer he was, took some great pictures to show us when he arrived home. His cousin John videoed the whole holiday for my dad as a keepsake. Knowing Dad I knew he couldn't wait to get back to show his family all the images he took.

1995. A Golden Wedding Anniversary!

I knew this milestone golden anniversary was coming up on 24 January for my mum and dad and I wanted to do something special to mark the occasion. I had begun saving a year before, and had provisionally booked the public hall at East Ham. I had also booked a band called The String of Pearls. They played a lot of Glen Miller Music and other big band stuff as well as having a male and female singer as the big bands used to have back in the 40s. Somehow my Mum and Dad found out my plans and told me in no uncertain terms that they didn't want any fuss on that scale. I had to cancel it all and lost quite large deposits. But I was determined not to let the event go by without a celebration.

The complex that Mum and Dad lived in had a very nice community room. It had a kitchen, ladies' and gents' toilets, and it would certainly hold all of our my family and friends of the family. I enlisted the help of my sister to help prepare food and run a few errands, and help decorate the hall. We had good fun doing that. Because I had done DJ work for many years I was able to supply the music. I had a large cake made with a picture of Mum's and Dad's greengrocers shop on it. How we got this all organised without my Mum and Dad finding out this time was a miracle as the flat they lived in overlooked the community hall. The ruse to get them over the community hall and more importantly to get them dressed up for going out, was that the warden of the complex had put on a little party for them and had invited some of the other residents. When Mum and Dad walked in they couldn't believe their eyes seeing all their relations and friends. Some of Mum's nieces had travelled all the way from Gloucester, Somerset and Warwickshire, which is testimony to how highly thought of both Mum and Dad were.

As I had been saving for their party for over a year I had saved over £2,000. It cost about a £1,000 for all the food and drink etc., leaving me with the balance of another £1,000. So I bought one of those large cheques that people use when donating to charities, and made it payable to Mum and Dad then presented it to them half way through the party. To say they were shocked was an understatement. However, by the next day, Dad had worked out how it was to be spent. He'd been in touch with his brother Johnny and asked if he could go to his apartment in Spain sometime in the summer and take all the females in the family, Mum, me, my sister Liz and my two nieces Jane and Joanne for a couple of weeks. Johnny agreed, and in June that year dad paid for all our return flights from the £1,000.

This is the man who didn't like flying now he wanted to do it all over again. The pleasure it brought him to show us all the things that Johnny had shown him the previous year. He took us to Mijaz, Marbella, and Porta Buenous, and Fuengerola. He made me laugh when we went to Fuengerola, he said I'm going to take you to a lovely restaurant. I was expecting something Spanish, on the beach maybe. But no, we turned a corner and he said, "Here it is, they do lovely fish and chips here." I couldn't stop laughing.

1996. This was a special year for my eldest niece and indeed all the family. Jane had been attending Queen Elizabeth College and was getting her degree and had invited us all along to see her receive it. It was special in that she was the first person in the family to get such a good education and receive such high honours. A Bachelor of Arts, for English and Drama. At last we had some brains in the family.

I also celebrated my fiftieth birthday this year. Half a century, I didn't feel 50. And so onto the next half century.

1998 Things had not been going well back home in America, Hop's mother and father were really becoming infirm and Hop's brother, Charles, who had been caring for them, along with his wife, had decided to move two hundred miles away to North Florida. Hop's parents were not going to have anyone on hand to help them when they needed it which was most days of the week. They were pretty elderly, so Hop and I decided that he would go back to America to care for his parents and then when they had popped their clogs he would come back. We figured with all their ailments it wouldn't be more than a couple of years. We had survived sixteen years as

278

pen friends so another couple of years wouldn't hurt. So Hop flew back to the States, and I carried on by myself. A couple of years went by and Hop's parents were still going strong, so much so Hop decided he had to get a job to keep himself solvent. Gradually Hop took up his old life again.

Hop's mother died, and Hop carried on caring for his father who was getting very cantankerous to deal with, so Hop enlisted the help of his niece to help out from time to time. Unbeknown to Hop she took her grandfather to an attorney and got him to sign a will leaving everything to her. Hop's mother had come from a wealthy family, Hop and I had a copy of the original will where she was leaving everything divided between her sons. So eventually when Hop's dad passed away, he found he didn't have a roof over his head anymore and no inheritance.

As everything had taken longer than we thought. It was decided that Hop should remain in Miami because he couldn't keep chopping and changing countries. We decided that we would leave our getting back together until we both retired.

More letters across the Atlantic.

Events of the 90s

1990 Nelson Mandela is released from prison after twenty-seven years

1991 Gulf War – Operation Desert Storm

1992 Official End of Cold War

1993 Inauguration of Bill Clinton/Use of Internet grows rapidly

1994 Rwandan genocide/ Channel Tunnel opens/Mandela becomes President of South Africa

1995 War in Bosnia

1996 Mad cows disease/ Two Royal Divorces

1997 Princess Diana dies in car crash in Paris/Hong Kong handed back to Chinese

1998 Clinton sex scandal/India and Pakistan test nuclear weapons

1999 Single currency The Euro introduced in Europe.

1999-2000

New Year's Eve, a New Century

There had been a row brewing all year over the construction of the Millennium Dome. It was built in Greenwich but it could be clearly seen from many points in Canning Town. I had been fortunate to visit 'The Dome' site whilst it was under construction by invitation from one of the departments in London Transport. I was then fortunate in two pre-opening visits. Once with my friend. Gavin, who lives in Greenwich, and then again with my friend, Theresa, who supplied catering facilities to the workmen and office staff prior to the construction of The Dome during clearing of the site and then while the dome was being built. For her service Theresa was nominated and awarded the MBE, quite an honour.

The Dome drew a lot of controversy when it was opened. I have to say I loved it, many did not. Strange a lot of those that didn't like it had never even been for a visit. The Dome has now been renamed the O2 and has proved quite a success as an arena for large concerts. On the eve of the new century it was excitement all round. There was much celebrating and firework displays going off all over the country. People were chatting and laughing, singing together. Celebrations were going on all over the world. It was a wonderful time to see in a new century and be a part of it.

The joy of a new century didn't last long for our little family. We lost three much loved pets in that first year. First little Timmy, he was a tiny Yorkshire Terrier aged 16 years old and belonged to Liz and John, He started fitting and so had to be put to sleep. We were all devastated. Then in the April I had to have my dog Bobby put down because of old age. He was 14 years old. I was worried about another tumour that had developed. He had had several cut off in the past and I thought the same could be done again. But the vet who had known Bobby since he was a pup said that Bobby was tired now and it was time to let him go before he started to get pain. It was just before the Easter weekend. I said that I would bring Bobby back on the Tuesday, after the Easter Monday.

My Dad suggested we take Bobby over to Greenwich Park as a last family outing together with him. This is how soft we were about our animals. Bobby couldn't walk too far so we got an old push chair that had belonged to one of my nieces when they were younger. I found a cardboard box to fit in it and inside that I laid a couple of cushions. We got the video camera, and a still camera, we filled a flask with tea and off we went. Bobby would have a little walk then he would look at one of us, and we would know he'd had enough and want a little ride in the box. Then when he had been pushed enough, he would show us that he wanted to walk again. It amused a lot of young children to see a dog being pushed around in a cardboard box.

On the Tuesday my Mum, my sister and I took Bobby back to the vet where Bobby was put to sleep. The three of us balled our eyes out. I brought Bobby home and laid him out in my parents' bedroom till my Dad came home and could see him. Dad cried hard too. Then I took Bobby to have him cremated so that I could keep his ashes. I think my Dad is very astute at these things. Because of his suggestion I have a lot of lovely pictures of Bobby and a lovely video to watch of his last day out. Then one evening in August, Rowley, the half-brother to Timmy escaped from the garden. We searched for him everywhere. It wasn't until the next morning that a further search found his little body covered by a shirt of some sort. He had been killed by a car. Hard for some people to realise that for people like us it is like losing a very dear member of your family. Heartbreaking.

I couldn't bear the lifelessness in my home so I went a bought a budgie, and called him Billy. We had a budgie when I was a kid and he had the same name. I felt sorry for the little budgie being on his own all day whilst I was at work. So I went and bought another budgie. Another boy, or so I thought. I would come home in the evening and see from the pile of poo in one place showing that Billy had not moved at all. I noticed the other budgie whom I called Joey would sit with one of it's feet on top of Billy's. I thought the new budgie was getting comfort from Billy. But soon after I noticed a deterioration in Billy, so I took him to the vet and it seemed he was past help and I had to have the little bird put to sleep. I never knew I could feel as much for a little bird that I only had for about nine months as I could for a dog that I had for fourteen years. Now I was left with a little budgie being on his own again. I decided enough was enough and it wasn't fair. A few doors along from me lived a family who had a lot of birds. African Greys, a Cockatoo, Cockatiels, and other exotically coloured birds. I asked the family would they take on the little budgie, and they agreed. They already knew what had happened to Billy.

I found out a few weeks later that Joey was not a boy. What happened was they decided to put Joey in with another budgie that they had been given, and a similar pattern of behaviour was happening again that was making the other little bird depressed. So the birds were separated. That's when I was told that Joey, now renamed Smithy was a girl, a hen, and hence the expression of an overpowering women over her husband being labeled as 'Henpecked'. That's what Joey/Smithy had been doing, she was being overpowering and henpecking the other little birds. You live and learn.

2001. Not much of note went on in my life this year. But historically it is worth mentioning about the terrorist attacks on the two towers of The World Trade Centre in New York. Islamists had tried bombing it several years earlier. This time however, they made sure of their target. Three aeroplanes were hijacked. One was supposed to head for the Pentagon, but that was brought down by the passengers on board themselves. How brave they were giving up their own lives. To save their country from terrorism.

The other two planes hit their targets, one in the North Tower and one in the South Tower. The NY fire department raced to the scene to rescue people stranded on the floors above the flames. The whole world watched the scenes unfold on the newsreels. People jumping from windows, rather than be burnt alive, but were never going to survive the drop. Suddenly one of the towers just collapsed like a pack of cards. No Steven Spielberg film could ever dream up enough special effects to show a disaster that was unfolding in front of our eyes. Then just as suddenly the second tower collapsed in the same way. Unbelievable, what a tragedy. The brave firemen and the policemen that were killed trying to save others. The area became known as Ground Zero and has become a monument to all those who lost their lives on that tragic day.

On a lighter note, this was also the year that Concord flew for the last time and landed at Heathrow, after thirty years of supersonic flight. Apart from one crash caused by debris on a runway it was unblemished. It was a magnificent plane to see in the sky. I saw it three times over London, and it never failed to take my breath away.

2002 Liz and John's youngest daughter, Joanne, had been living with Chris for sometime over in East Finchley. The family learned that Chris was going to propose to her. He had gone to John and asked his permission to marry Joanne. He was determined to do things the right way.

Chris is Scottish and so he decided that he would hire a piper. Apparently it went something like this. Joanne was on the phone to her mum when she heard a knock at the door and then someone started playing bagpipes. She called out to Chris but he insisted that she open the door. She told her Mum she was looking at someone playing the bagpipes and although Liz knew what it was all about she played dumb. Chris said to invite the piper in. Joanne told her Mum she would call her back. The piper came in and when they were in the front room Chris got down on one knee and proposed with a beautiful diamond ring. Joanne said 'yes'. This all happened a year before in 2001 and it was now 2002 and the wedding was arranged. It was to be held at Marylebone registry office in London. All the men had to wear kilts including Joanne's Dad who didn't have the best legs in the world.

Joanne had hunted high a low for the material and style she wanted for her wedding dress. She found it and had it made. It was stunning. Her sister Jane was dressed in a beautiful blue gown which complimented the wedding dress.

Joanne has always been a bit of a comedienne, she has a good sense of humour and can laugh at most anything. Chris too had a similar sense of humour. And because of this we more or less laughed the whole way through the ceremony. It all began when they were led in by the same piper that Chris had hired when they got engaged, on the engagement evening, to stand in front of the registrar. There were smiley faces all round and little jokes and quips going on and when they were pronounced wed we all clapped. The registrar commented that it was the happiest wedding he had ever conducted.

The reception was held close by in a building where people practiced folk dancing. In fact there was a practice going on in another hall at the beginning of the reception. I believe they were Rumanian, and they were actually practising a wedding dance for a bride and groom and invited Joanne and Chris to join them. It was a very unusual day and a very happy one at that.

2003. I had been living in Beckton for about twenty-three years by now and in that time had a very conservatory built on the back of the house. I already explained earlier that this area was reclaimed marshland. Towards the end of the winter in 2003 we had a bad rainstorm. I noticed that water was getting in through my conservatory. What was actually happening was that the garden was gradually sinking and pulling the conservatory away from the back wall. This was no 'lean to' type of structure, I had paid £11,000 for it 1992. So I had to think carefully about what to do about this.

There had been talk of subsidence in other areas around and about the Beckton area, fortunately the problem I was having didn't affect the house itself. There wasn't any subsidence and it was solid as a rock. My problem was the garden itself that was sinking. I started wondering what to do. Do I throw good money after bad and keep propping up the conservatory. Or should I cut my losses and run. The Beckton area was becoming quite run down. In the twenty-three years I had been there people had been buying up the properties to let them out. The people who were renting weren't bothered about the upkeep of the properties, and the people who were letting weren't bothered either because they didn't have to live there. It didn't take long to make my mind up. I was going to move, but where to?

2003

House Hunting?

It's time to start scouring the online estate agents in and around the London area but nothing was catching my eye. My dream since the early 60s was to have a little cottage in the country, with room for a dog, a donkey, a goat and some chickens. I dreamily started looking at the place where we still had our caravan, Wateringbury. Wouldn't it be nice if I could move there. I don't drive, but there is a station and two buses run right through the village. They both began and ended between Maidstone and Tunbridge Wells, one going via Paddock Wood and the other via Tonbridge. It would be lovely, IF I could afford it. I found a couple of flats and a three bedroom house. A friend offered to drive me down to have a look, I passed straightaway on the flats they weren't for me. But the little three bedroom house looked promising. It was actually smaller than my two bedroom house that I was selling, but as there was only me I didn't think it would be a problem, so I put an offer in and it was accepted. My house sold within a week, then I waited and waited for the chap whose house I was buying to get a move on himself. It turned out that he was waiting to purchase a 'Project'. Well I decided I couldn't wait for him and his project so I pulled out and set to on finding something else. Then I saw a little two bedroom semi-detached bungalow.

My friend drove me down again for a look. It belonged to an elderly gentleman, who was selling up to move in with his son. He was a canny Scotsman and wouldn't budge on my low offer, but then he finally gave way a little bit.

Armed with my photograph of the bungalow, I took it round to my Mum and Dad's to let them see. Dad said, "You know Pat, you are going to bury yourself in that village, especially in the winter time." I told him it would be fine. I could still easily commute up to London for my job. And wouldn't it be nice for them to come and stay at weekends. Part of my little dream was coming true.

Then the people who were buying my house decided they wanted to move into my house before the Christmas. It was the end of November. I asked Mum and Dad 'if I put my stuff in storage could I move in with them.' They were very reluctant, which surprised me. It looked as though I was going to have to book into a local hotel. I was really upset that they weren't helping me. My Dad said, "It will be too much for your mother." I said, "But I will be at work all day, I'll only becoming home to lay me head down at night." There was a bit of a row and a few tears shed. Then Mum hit me with the real reason, Dad had been diagnosed with lung cancer, he was to have radiotherapy.

It all went back to June when a lump appeared on Dad's chest about the size of a 10p piece. Within a short period of time it had grown to the size and shape of a saucer. During this time the doctor had been treating him for a chest infection. On the next visit to the doctor's, my Mum demanded that they send my dad for a chest x-ray. That's when they discovered it was cancer.

Now we were into late November, Dad waited and waited for the appointment for the radiotherapy. My sister, who had moved to Lincolnshire with her family in 2002 wanted to invite Mum, Dad and me up for the Christmas holidays. But Dad was afraid to leave his home in case the appointment came. He was becoming weaker as the days passed. My sister Liz, rang the chest clinic and asked what was happening about the radiotherapy appointment. The person she spoke to said, "You all have a nice Christmas together." My sister gathered from that, that Dad didn't have long.

Even though I had moved out of my house, I told my buyers and the seller that I couldn't complete till the New Year and the reason for it. They were okay about it and were willing to wait. My Dad is not a silly person and knew that his time was coming to an end on this earth. And he decided he wanted to have a 'sort out'. Dad was a bit of a hoarder of 'this that and the other'. Paper cuttings, horse racing papers and books lots of 'bits and bob's.' Just loads and loads of 'stuff', but it was his 'stuff'.

I would get his 'stuff' papers etc., and he would go through them and mostly throw it all in a black bin liner. I took a few bits and pieces that were interesting to me. And that's how it went. Then a good friend of mine gave me a slide projector. What a gift. Dad had been a prolific photographer throughout his life, and had accumulated hundreds of slides. He did have a projector, but it was old and you had to push the slides through manually. This new projector took more slides on a carousel and it was operated just by the press of a button. Dad's eyes lit up when I brought it into him. He immediately made me go and get the screen to set it up. Then I had to load all the slides into about five carousels. I put the first carousel on the projector and Dad had the lead with the button on it, so he was in charge. Mum and me settled down to reminisce over the pictures that appeared before us. Every so often Dad would say "get rid of that one." Dad had become more critical of his photos and wanted to get rid of those that were out of focus, or where someone's head had been cut off, or ones that were overexposed or under exposed. In the old days we kept all the photo's whether they were good or bad, because they were such a novelty to look at. My dad couldn't have been a bad photographer because we whittled them down to about four carousels. Considering that each carousel held about a 100 slides.

The whole point of this exercise was so that he could take the whole 'kit and caboodle' up to Lincolnshire to show Jane and Joanne and their respective partners photos they had never seen before, and for Liz and John who hadn't seen the photos for many years. The best part was that although Dad was ill and weak this projector put him in charge. I was his lackey, putting the screen up and setting up the projector and changing the carousels. But it was Dad who held the button and could give a talk on the pictures and what was going on at that time. He was in control, which was good for him.

The next day he decided that as Joanne was now earning her living as a photographer, and as my dad had been her inspiration to take up photography in the first place, she should have all the slides and equipment to keep. And why not, what a keepsake given by her granddad.

I have to go back to the day we went up to Lincolnshire. Liz drove down to pick us all up and take us home with her. We put Dad in the back seat sitting on pillows because his bum had become so sore, and made him comfortable. This was going to be his first time out in many weeks as the news of his cancer had set him into a depression. Dad liked music and I made a tape of all the music he liked so that we could have a bit of a sing a long on the journey. That's what we did, and it was a pleasant journey.

We arrived at Liz's and John's house and all piled out. Mum and Dad went straight into the conservatory to have a cigarette. Well why not, no point giving up smoking now, 'what was done, was done'. Liz and I got the cases out of the car, and then the next important thing was to put the kettle on for a cup of tea. I went into the conservatory, Mum had gone upstairs by this time, and Liz followed in after me. She said something to my Dad like, "I'm so pleased you are here, dad." and with that he burst into tears. I was choked. Liz cuddled him and he composed himself and said, "I don't know where that came from. Don't tell your mother, will you." We didn't tell.

We were having a lovely time, eating, drinking, talking, and laughing. Watching TV as well as watching the photographic slide show. On Christmas Eve Dad got quite tired and said he wanted to go to bed, Mum said she would go up with him and off they went. I stayed up a little while longer with Liz and John, then Liz and I decided we'd had enough were going to bed. We went up the stairs together and noticed through the crack in the door that the light was still on in the room Mum and Dad occupied. So we called and asked if we could come in. "Yes, come in," Dad called. There they both were sitting up in bed giggling and laughing like two naughty children, and then I noticed that they had hung Dad's socks on the bottom of the bed for Father Christmas to fill them with present. I pointed this out to Liz and we burst out laughing. It was so funny. Dad's sense of humour was still intact.

We enjoyed Christmas Day with Jane and Jason, Joanne and Chris, myself and Mum and Dad and Liz and John. We exchanged lovely presents, we ate a fabulous dinner and drank expensive wines. God bless us one and all.

2004. Back in Beckton It was New Year's Eve. We invited Pat, Mum's neighbour and best friend over for a drink and to see in 2004. It was just the four of us. As the clock struck twelve we stood and joined hands and sang Auld Lang Syne, then we kissed each other and wished each other a Happy New Year. We were all choked up with tears because we all knew that it wasn't going to be a happy new year. Dad's time was coming to an end quite quickly.

I contacted my office, they already knew that my Dad had cancer. But now he and Mum needed more help. I called my office at London Transport and told them that I was taking time off to see this through to the end. I had moved in with them by now. I asked if I could do that without pay. They said I could do that and I would still be paid. So that was a result.

We now made contact with the Macmillan nurses, and Social Services. In case we needed anything from them. The only people that came into see my dad was a physiotherapist who gave him a few exercises to do. We were coping okay. If

Dad wanted to go to the toilet he would lean on me or Mum to get there. Luckily they lived in a flat that was all on one level, no stairs to deal with. I would wash him every day, and once a week give him a good bath. Fortunately, in my family we weren't prudish about our bodies, so it never bothered me or my dad for me to see him naked. When his bum became sore with bed sores, I changed all the dressings. I knew my Dad would prefer me to do all this than a complete stranger.

Finally, Dad got his appointment for his radiotherapy, he was so happy, it seemed to give him some hope. That same day I was going to my solicitor to sign the contracts for the sale of my house. I had to go to Ilford.

Dad was waiting for the ambulance to take him to Bart's hospital and as had happened on previous hospital visits in the past a 'carer' goes with the patient, that would be my Mum. On this occasion the ambulance driver told my Mum she couldn't go as there wasn't enough room because of the amount of other patients he had to collect. So off my Dad went in the ambulance, leaving Mum in a right panic. I had done my business with the solicitor and was walking back toward Ilford Station when my mobile phone rang. (Thank God for that little invention.) It was Mum explaining what had happened. I told her go and get a bus to Stratford bus station and wait there, I would catch a train from Ilford and meet her there. I arrived just a few minutes before she did. We went to the underground and caught a train to St Pauls.

When we got out of the station there was a kiosk. I went in and bought some sandwiches, other nibbles, fruit and water, not knowing how long this was all going to take, one of them might get a bit peckish. We went straight to Barts and thinking we had made good time, which we had, we thought we may just get there before Dad arrived there himself. I walked up to the reception and started to ask about the ambulance and patient Jolly, when I heard my Dad calling me. He looked terrible. He said he had felt sick on the journey with all the stopping and starting. He was sweating. I helped him take off a layer of clothing. I told him I had some food and water, and he said he wanted a sandwich. I found a coffee machine by this time and brought us all a cup each. After about ten minutes the colour started to return to my dad's face. I could see how grateful he was that we were there. Then his name was called and I helped take him down to the radiotherapy room. I waited outside till he was done and then brought him back to my mum. Dad said to me, "Pat, I can't go back in that ambulance again." I told him I wasn't going to let him go back in the ambulance, I was ordering a mini cab, and that is how we got home.

Within a matter of a days the large saucer like shape lump had shrivelled, but the radiotherapy had taken its toll on my dad and he was becoming even weaker. It was a good decision that I had made to stay and help care for my Dad. He was 5ft 10 inches tall and my mum was just about 5 foot. She wouldn't have been able to cope with his weight and size.

Dad got weaker and couldn't get himself out of the chair to go to the toilet or anywhere else in the flat. Luckily we had my grandmother's wheelchair which had been stored at the bottom of the flats under the stairs for many years. I brought the wheelchair up to Mum's and Dad's flat. Between us, me and Dad devised a 1,2,3, swing back and forth action for the momentum to lift him out of his chair and then turn him to sit in the wheelchair. Then I could wheel him to the toilet or bedroom or kitchen wherever he needed to go. If it hadn't been for that wheelchair, I don't know where we would have been. It was a godsend.

We didn't have many visitors come to see Dad. He didn't want anybody there He only wanted me and Mum and Liz around. Liz would travel down several times a week, and the rest of the time keep in touch by phone. Dad couldn't stand people who had the doom and gloom attitude. He liked Pat popping over to see him as she was always positive and upbeat. He particularly loved talking to his cousin Annie. She would call once or twice a week and they would talk about the old days, Annie had a good memory and would bring back stories that Dad had forgotten, a lot of which made him laugh. He looked forward to her phone calls.

Dad got to the point where because he wanted to go to the toilet so often, it would be better to be in bed and have a catheter inserted, and he wouldn't have to worry. On 9 February the male nurse arrived and that afternoon he inserted the catheter. I then decided that if he was going to have to be in bed, it would be better to move his into the front room then any medical attention he needed from the doctor or nurses would be easier as they could access him from both side of the bed. Mum and Dad had twin beds so this would be an easy option.

I asked my friend Martin if he would come over and help me move the bed, and early that evening he did just that. Martin stayed for dinner and then left. We got Dad into bed and made him comfortable.

Mum and Dad had become very friendly with the family that ran the local chemist and post office, The Patels, they seemed to like my parents very much. They knew of Dad's deterioration and asked if they could come and visit him. They arrived just after 8 p.m. after they had closed the shop for the night. It was a lovely visit. Mrs Patel was standing close to the radiator at one point and my Dad told her to be careful in case she burnt herself. They stayed about twenty minutes and then left saying they would visit again.

By about 10. 30 p.m. Mum was very tired and I told her to go to bed, I said that I was going to sit with Dad in the front room that night because he seemed to be getting agitated about the catheter and wanting to pull it out, as well as trying to get out of bed saying he wanted to do a wee. I knew he couldn't walk so he'd have probably fallen, then we would have been in trouble. I went into the kitchen to get a jug of water, and other bits and pieces that I may need to make Dad more comfortable. He had been given mouth swabs to refresh him when he couldn't actually drink. As the minutes ticked by he got more and more agitated and I was beginning to struggle to keep him calm and in bed. By now he didn't seem that he could actually talk, he was slurring his words and mumbling. I went and sat on the side of the bed and started soothing his brow and telling him to conjure up a vision of being down the caravan in Wateringbury Waking up, it's a beautiful sunny morning, the mist is rolling down the river Medway. It's still chilly in the caravan. Mum and me have woken up and he is making us a lovely cup of tea for us. Then he goes out and collects his fishing rod and bait and goes down to the river where the boat is moored. He puts everything in it and starts the engine. He turns the boat around and starts heading in the direction of Yalding, along the way he spots a nice place to moor up. He puts a maggot on the hook and casts out. The sun is getting higher and warmer, there are a few ripples on the water where the fish rise to feed. All that can be heard is the rustle of the leaves on the trees and the birds singing. In the distance he can hear the 'pop pop' of men either shooting rabbits or pheasants. His float disappears and as he reels in he sees he has caught a lovely Bream, he unhooks it and sets it free again. Then he looks at his watch and see's he has been fishing for about an hour and a half, it's time to head back to the caravan as breakfast will soon be on the table. I see the boat as it rounds the corner and tell Mummy, "Daddy's on his way back." Then you moor the boat up and you can smell the bacon and eggs wafting on the air. You'd roll up and there is your breakfast. Bacon, eggs, tomatoes, baked beans, fried bread and a lovely cup of hot tea.

All the time I related this story Dad was calm, but then I couldn't go anywhere else with the story and I dried up, and he started becoming agitated again trying to get out of bed. I asked him if he wanted something to drink, and he nodded his head, yes. I walked round to the other side of the bed and poured some water into a beaker, I was about to put a straw in it for him to sip from and I turned to look at him. He was holding an invisible glass to his lips and sipping from it. I said, "I haven't given you the water yet, Dad." Then he looked up to his right, I was standing on his left. He held out his hand to no-one there, and whispered in a clear voice, "Hello, how are you?" At the same time he was holding his hand out and giving a handshake. I asked him who it was that had come to see him. I felt then that Dad wasn't going to last the night. Then Dad started to get agitated again and making it clear he wanted my Mum. I went into the bedroom and told Mum about his agitation and that he wanted her, in the meantime I called the night nurses to come, in the hope they could give him a sedative to calm him down.

Mum went and sat on the bed with Dad and he calmed down almost straightaway and shortly after seemed to go into a doze. Mum went into the kitchen to have a cigarette, and then the night nurses arrived. They were two black women. I explained what had happened, they tried to wake my Dad but he didn't come round, then I noticed my dad's breathing had changed, I went into my Mum and I said, 'Mum, I think daddy is going." She came into the front room and started talking to my Dad as I stood by with the two nurses. The nurses said we could call for an ambulance, but they will pull your Dad around and it would be distressing, or, you can just leave it, he is not in any pain. So we left it. Then with one last breath Dad was gone.

One of the nurses went outside the front door and shortly afterward came back inside as she was wiping her eyes with a tissue. She said, "I have never seen anyone go like that before." I misunderstood her and said 'What, you have never seen anyone die before'. She said, "No, I have never seen anyone go that peacefully." The other nurse asked for a towel, I went and got one and she rolled it up and wedged it under my dad's chin to hold his mouth closed. I would never have thought of that. They were so kind and helpful. I told the nurses that I think God sent us two lovely black angels to help me and my Mum. They smiled said, "God bless you," and left. It was the early hours of the 10 February 2004, and Dad was 82 years old.

The first thing me and Mum did then was go and light a cigarette. Big deal for me as I had given up smoking for a year, but I just lit up like that year never happened. I called Liz and gave her the sad news and they got dressed and drove down from Lincolnshire straight away. I slept on the settee in the front room, next to my dad, John and Liz sat and slept the best they could in the two armchairs and Mum went to bed. The next morning we called the doctor who wrote the death certificate. We called the undertaker but we asked him not to come until the late afternoon. We wanted to keep my Dad so that we could tell his young sister Iris who we knew would want to see him before being taken away. Mum, Liz and I would keep popping into the front room to touch and kiss my Dad. I was amazed that his chest was still warm hours after he had died.

Iris finally arrived with my Uncle Alf, she had taken the trouble to make a large pot of stew. You think to yourself that you can't be bothered to eat anything. But later that evening we relished it.

Dad had more or less arranged his own funeral. A couple of events had happened the previous year. Adam Faith died and Dad saw part of his funeral on the news. He saw that Adam Faith's coffin was a wicker casket. Dad commented that he would like a wicker casket for his funeral too. Later that same year one of his neighbours died and his funeral was being conducted by the local funeral directors T Cribb. Dad had known the undertakers all his life, they had buried many of his own family. The governor of the business was Stan Cribb. But this wasn't Stan conducting the funeral, neither was it Stan's son, Graham. It was another young man, and for the life of me right now I can't remember his name. Anyway, Dad thought the young man was carrying out his job very well and called him over, he asked his name and told him how well he thought the young man was doing, to which the young man replied that he was taught by Stan himself. Dad said, "I can see that, I would like you to do my funeral one day." The young man said he would be happy to oblige.

As a family we had many chats over time about dying and funerals. It was the custom in Dad's family to be buried in lead lined coffins. I remember my granddad and grandmother having lead lined coffins and when Dad's elder brother Joey died he was also buried in a lead lined coffin. Joey was the last one to be buried and he was in a four person grave over East London Cemetery, Hermit Road. So there was room for three more people.

Dad's original instructions were that whoever died first between him and Mum, would be cremated, then when the other one died the ashes of the first person were to be placed in the lead lined coffin. So we followed the instructions and got a wicker casket We also found the young man that dad had spoken to and he conducted the funeral.

It was a fairly large funeral with a hearse and six black cars following, plus private cars following on after that. Normally a costermonger would have horses but Dad had already stated at some time that he didn't want horses for his funeral. I wrote the eulogy for the priest to read with help from Mum, Liz and Jane and Joanne, and between us we chose some of Dad's favourite tunes to be played, with a nod to his catholic upbringing having Andrea Bocelli singing '*Ave Maria*', and in the middle of the service we had Tony Bennett singing '*On a Clear Day*', The service ended with Joe Brown singing '*I'll See You in My Dreams*'. It was a very soft funeral befitting my dad. I never met a person who didn't like him. And still to this day he is spoken of in the nicest kindest way.

Mum was understandably lost without Dad, it was hard for her to come to terms with the fact that he wasn't around anymore. They had hardly been apart all their married life. When people say they have been married fifty years. You could double that for my Mum and Dad because they worked side by side every day, all their married life. I got on and started dealing with all the things that you need to do after someone dies, winding up their affairs. It was during this time that I decided that now might be the time to retire from work. After watching Dad die, I thought to myself you're a long time dead. It can't all be about money. I got in touch with the pension department in London Transport and they gave me some options to consider. I decided that I could go with one of the options, and after speaking to my own office it could also be arranged that with annual holidays to be taken I wouldn't have to return to work. Perfect. Me and Mum needed each other at this time.

There was another saving grace. The bungalow I bought needed a new kitchen and bathroom and redecorating, so it wasn't ready for me to move into. It would give Mum some time to adjust to being a widow, but without being totally alone to deal with her grief. And I wanted to be close to my Mum while I dealt with my grief too. It suited us both.

We got Dad's ashes back and made a little grotto in a cabinet along with a photo of him, and there he stayed and we still talked to him. It was very comforting.

Life went on. I travelled to Wateringbury quite a few times to ensure that everything was on track. Mum came with me a couple of times and we stayed in the caravan, just like old times. The bungalow was taking shape and looking good. By the beginning of May it was already for me to move into. My friend Martin helped with the move. He hired a van and had to make a couple of journeys over a couple of days. Then came the big job of sorting everything out. I didn't have a bed, but had one on order, though I did have a mattress. I didn't have any settees or chairs, they were also on order. Mum said she would come down with me and give me a hand with everything. We did well working as a team and got quite a lot done and sorted out. I didn't have a bed, but I had a double blow up bed. I inflated that and then put the mattress on top, it was almost like a proper bed, in height as well, and very comfortable. Mum stayed a few days and then it was time for her to go back home, to begin living on her own, and for me to begin again living on my own. We did it.

Life now was a lot different for me, I now had to get used to living on my own in a place where I didn't know anybody. Luckily I knew my way around so got myself out and about to start getting some sort of routine. I realised soon enough that I had hit the jackpot with my neighbours on either side of me. They were so helpful right from the start. In the first few months I kept locking myself out, so it seemed easier for me to give both neighbours a set of keys, since doing that I have never locked myself out since.

Me and Mum would talk to each other three times a day on the phone and every two weeks I would go up to London and stay for the weekend, help with her shopping and do her housework, hoover, clean the windows, change the beds and just be company for each other. Also I could meet up with my lifelong friend Theresa. It became a nice routine for us to look forward to.

One day whilst I was on a visit Martin turned up with a computer. My Mum asked what and who it was for and he told her that it was for her and it was to keep in touch via webcam with me in Kent. I have to say my Mum will give anything a go, and very soon she was able to do some typing and have some understanding about the computer. I got her broadband installed, and pretty soon she was emailing me, talking on the webcam and also sending messages on Instant Messaging. She was a real goer my Mum. She used to get a real kick on the webcam talking to and seeing each other, it really made her laugh. I would be sitting there watching the TV and I'd hear 'ping' I'd look at my computer and there would be an Instant Message 'Are you there, Pat?' Then we would be typing messages to each other for a while. She was amazing, I was so proud of her.

Molly. My birthday was on the first of May. I was 58 years old by now. I had made a promise to myself that I would get another dog at sometime and now seemed as good a time as any. Martin egged me on to look into it and finally I found a place in Yalding where I could buy a little Yorkshire Terrier. Martin drove me there where we saw two little Yorkies in a cage. I don't think I had my sensible head on that day as I did everything wrong. The first thing was I didn't like the woman's attitude, the way she was talking to me, then I didn't ask to see the parents of the Yorkies. I was just falling in love with the little bundles of fluff in front of me. Which one to choose? I wanted a really small female Yorkie. I picked the first one up, it was tiny. But there at the back of the cage was another little bundle of fluff and I asked to have a hold of that one as well. This second Yorkie had such a shy look in her eyes she melted my heart away. Decision made, I wanted this one. I got my cheque book out and then Martin surprised me by giving half the money towards her purchase price for my birthday. As we were getting the money together for payment the women took a call on her mobile phone. Her half of the conversation went like this. "Yes, I have Yorkies, Shih tzus, Labradors." I looked at Martin, but he didn't seem to get it. This woman was selling dogs from puppy farms. What do I do, do I leave this little creature or carry on and give her a good life with me? Go with your instincts every time, mine was to take this little ball of fluff home with me.

Like an expectant mother I had a name already picked out for her and she was to be called Molly. It suited her even more as the woman I bought her from told me she had come from Ireland. Martin then took me to Pets at Home animal store and I bought everything I needed for Molly.

The next day I rang the vet as I wanted them to give her the once over, more importantly, check that she was healthy. It turned out that she had lice eggs, but he told me her heart was sound. I said, "Well as long as the engine runs we can fix everything else." And so I got down to the job of teaching this little girl manners. She was a quick learner, and wanted to please. I noticed though that she hated seeing black plastic bags, and any loud noise freaked her out, nor would she go under a table or anything that was above her head. This was a nervy little animal. Gradually over many months she gained confidence. She still whimpers a bit when she sees me changing the black bin liners, and she still doesn't like of loud noises, but she has gained so much more confidence.

I continued to go up to London every two weeks, with my knapsack on my back and little Molly. Mum fell in love with her right away. My Mum loved to be nosey looking out of her front room window and so did Molly and they would both be there side by side seeing what was going on.

2005. In July 2005 Jane and Jason decided to get married after having lived together for about twelve years. Besides, Jane was pregnant and they both wanted to do the right thing for themselves. It was a lovely wedding and even though Jane had a big bump in front of her she still made a beautiful bride. Dad's younger brother Johnny and my cousin Lynda and her husband Doug travelled up from Essex to Lincolnshire and another cousin travelled up from Exmouth in Devon to help celebrate. It was a great day. Missed my Dad on these family occasions, he would have been proud.

And just in time as baby Grace emerged into the world on 9 September I was now a great aunty. Me and Mum went back up to Lincolnshire just for a day to see the new baby who was a few weeks old by this time, and then later we were invited up to Liz and John's for Christmas when we were able to spend more time getting to know the little sweetheart.

Another thing that happened in 2005, a milestone for me, was that I would try to give up smoking again. I had already given up for a year prior to losing my Dad, and I liked being a non-smoker. So I vowed that before the anniversary of his death I would do that. And I did. By January I was a non-smoker again.

Life was good for the next few years.

2006. This year was the start of myself and friends celebrating our sixtieth birthdays and for retirements.

My friend Diane was 60 on 1 January and was retiring in the February. She decided to have a big party and invited all her friends from work and her friends from her youth club days, which was myself, Barbara, Denny, Jackie, and Kay. It was so nice all being together again that we promised we would meet up for a lunch in the not too distant future. And so we did in the April, we had a really good time and so much enjoyed being together that we decided that we would make more of an effort to stay in touch. Which we did I started to see more of Barbara and Jimmy as they only lived forty minutes

302

away from me in Lamberhurst. Diane came down to Wateringbury for a visit as well.

Also in this year my best friend, Theresa, decided to buy a café in Yalding, Her daughter, Maria, and her partner, Lee, bought a dormer bungalow adjoining the café for their family. Her youngest daughter, Sarah, bought a house further in the village for her family. The idea was that Theresa would travel down every Friday till Sunday to help with the busy weekends, but for the rest of the week she would have someone working for her. My life was becoming richer by the day.

2007. This year was a good year and a bad year. The good part was when my friend Gavin whom I had met and became friends with from my days at Claridges had met and been living with a chap called Peter and they had decided to enter a civil marriage. Gavin had come out to me many years before, but found it hard to open up to his parents, especially his dad. It was a difficult time. I had met Gavin's family and I couldn't see why they couldn't get past this.

Gavin had several relationships that both ended badly I was hoping that this one with Peter didn't end the same way. Gavin wanted me to meet Peter and we went for lunch, I liked him right away. I hoped that this would last for both of them. As time went on you could see that it was a real match, so when Gavin told me that I was invited to the ceremony I was thrilled. It was a lovely day the ceremony and the reception was held in the same building so you didn't have to go from one venue to another. It was one of the best days ever, and I loved it.

Chapter 54

It was a Friday night toward the end of September 2007. I was standing in the kitchen washing up the plates from our evening meal. Mum called me, I turned to walk towards her. She told me she had very bad pain in her chest. I told her, "You can tell me how bad the pain is by answering one of these options. Do you want me to call a doctor or an ambulance?" She answered 'ambulance'. Within ten minutes the ambulance was there, and the paramedics started their assessment of her in the flat and then continued in the ambulance until we reached Newham General Hospital. After hours of waiting, at about 2 a.m. With a few tests and x-rays in between, they finally gave Mum the all clear to go home. It turned out that it was a touch of Pleurisy, which I understand is very painful. After that things went back to our usual routine.

Iris and Alf. One late morning I got a call from my Aunt Iris saying that her husband, my uncle, Alf, had a fallen in their flat. She went on to tell me that he had been unwell for almost three weeks and wasn't getting any better. I told Iris that a doctor would have to be called, which wasn't what she wanted to hear as she had an absolute fear of doctors, nurses, hospitals, just about anything to do with the medical profession. She had never been to a dentist or an optician in her life for fear they might find something. She associated hospitals only with death. Her mother, and elder brother had both passed away in hospital. I felt that after all that she had told me Alf needed to

304

see a doctor. So I got in touch with their GP who called in to see Alf, and after a quick examination it was decided that Alf needed to go into hospital right away. Iris couldn't think straight, and knowing this I decided to drop everything and pack a bag, grab the dog, and get myself up to London. I called my Mum to explain what was happening so she was expecting me. I was very lucky that all my train connections were on time. So within a couple of hours I was walking into my Mum's flat. After a quick cup of tea, I called a cab to take me to the hospital. I found both Iris and Alf still in the emergency department. You could see the relief on Iris's face when I got there.

Alf was a nice man, he had a terrific dry sense of humour which I loved. He would have me crying with laughter at times. And even now as ill as he was he was still making jokes. We were told he was being admitted and was going to Cambridge Ward, he said to me, "Did you hear that, Pat, I'm being sent up to Cambridge?" I got his humour right away and that started me laughing.

Knowing Iris as I do, I knew that she would want to stay with Alf for whatever the duration was going to be. She would find a chair to sit in and sleep there, so that she was on hand if needs be. I had to get back home as my Mum was caring for my little dog Molly, and I knew that she would have cooked me a dinner too. I left Iris and told her I would be back the next day.

When I arrived home, sure enough there was a lovely dinner waiting for me. I explained what was going on with Alf and that I was going to stay in London for whatever time it took to get Alf sorted out. My cousin Lynda was always a great help to Iris, but at this time she was having her own problems with illness, so Iris and Alf had no-one else to help them. Iris was told that she couldn't stay at the hospital, so every day I got a cab to her flat to pick her up and off we would go to the hospital.

Alf had been in the hospital two or three days, and I noticed that no-one had bothered to shave him. So I found a

305

male nurse and told him that they need to shave him and brighten him up a bit. After this it seemed that I had to be behind the nurses all the time to keep up some sort of standard. I would walk into the ward and find a full urine bottle sitting on the table next to some food that had been left. Then a patient opposite told us that two nurses had dropped my uncle, no-one had told Iris or me about that episode. So I asked about it, and it was confirmed. They gave my uncle constipation tablets that weren't even required as my uncle's bowel movement was fine. But this propagated an incident whereby my uncle was calling for assistance and none was forthcoming, so he tried to manage getting to a toilet by himself and ended up pooing all the way up the ward to the toilet. The nurses were furious that someone was going to have to clean up after him. Iris asked for a mop and bucket, AND WAS GIVEN THEM to clean the mess up herself. I decided to type a two page letter on A4 paper, outlining all the failures that were happening to my uncle. I made two copies and showed one to the ward sister first and told her to read it. I told her that if things did not improve, I was sending the original letter to someone senior in the hospital. After that things did improve somewhat. However, my uncle was not improving, he wasn't eating anything that the hospital made. I took an egg and cress sandwich in one day and he loved it. Iris started to make food and bring it in, but mostly Alf couldn't eat it. One day I had to go straight to the hospital and Iris was making her own way there. I arrived first, and was having a nice chat to Alf. Then he said to me, I wonder what concoction Iris is going to bring today to tempt me. About ten minutes later, Iris arrived pulling a shopping trolley behind her. She stood at the end of Alf's bed, dove down into the shopping trolley and pulled out a flask which she held up like a winning trophy and said, "I brought you some nice soup Alf" Me and Alf looked at each other and laughed. Then we let Iris in on the joke.

I got a call from the hospital to tell me that Alf had suffered a fit and had gone into a coma and was having lots of other little fits. I was told that all they could do now was make him comfortable and that it was going to be just a matter of time. They moved Alf to a lovely modern ward, it was a pity that he couldn't appreciate it. Me and Iris continued to be there every day. Every day I would have to leave the hospital just before lunchtime to go all the way back to Beckton and take my dog for a long walk, then I would make my way back to the Royal London Hospital in Whitechapel, I did all this by public transport. I couldn't leave it all to my Mum it would be too much. By early evening I would leave and come home for the night. Iris would stay as long as they would allow before getting a cab home to her flat.

Iris didn't like leaving Alf. So unbeknown to me she asked for him to be moved to a private room. When we went the next day we found Alf had been moved back to the oldest part of the hospital. It was awful. The place looked like it could do with a good scrub, and that is what we proceeded to do. I ran across the road to Sainsbury's supermarket and got a load of cleaning materials. I also bought some pretty cards to stick up on the wall as well as some potted plants to make the room cheerful. There was a curtain up at a window which was hanging off its runners, which I put back properly. The room began to look a lot better with all our effort. It now meant that Iris could stay all day and all night now, which is what she wanted. Alf was still fitting and deteriorating rapidly. It wasn't going to be long now.

I told Iris if anything happened during the night to call me right away. And a few nights later, about 2 a.m. in the morning, I got the call I was dreading. I got myself ready, called a cab and got up to the hospital, I found Iris deeply distressed. My aunt had some funny ways with her and I knew quite a few of them. I knew she would love to lay on the bed and cuddle her husband. So I told her to do it and she did. I left her like that while I went and called her twin brother, Johnny, who lived in Essex and asked him to come and collect us, which he did. We went back to Iris's flat in Poplar and all just sat in silence drinking tea as the sun started to come up over Canary Wharf. Alf had been in the hospital for three weeks.

The problem had been that a 'bug' had got into his bloodstream and because of the delay in the beginning of getting a doctor involved, the 'bug' had reach Alf's heart and that was to be his demise. Iris in her own way of trying to make Alf better over the three weeks and not calling a doctor because of her fears, had in fact helped him to die earlier than he probably would have.

Johnny drove me back to Beckton and I got into bed for a few hours. When I got up I went back to the hospital to get the paperwork needed to register Alf's death. Once this was done we could proceed to organise Alf's funeral.

I rang all the family and let them know about Alf's passing, and started to organise Iris's paperwork, as she didn't have a clue about anything. I knew what had to be done as I had dealt with a few deaths including my Dad's just a few years before. The funeral was going to be an ordeal for Iris. I knew that I would have to handle her with kid gloves and steer her the best way I could.

Our family had always used T Cribbs undertakers since the 1900s. But I knew that Iris was going to need some special handling. My dad and I had read a couple of books by a funeral director from Bermondsey called Barry Dyer, The Undertakers was called Albin's. Barry had also had a documentary on the TV called 'Don't drop the coffin'. He was the same director that had conducted Jade Goody's funeral. I knew that he had taken over a funeral parlour along Barking Road at the Abbey Arms, called Hitchcock's.

I explained to Iris all that I knew about this funeral director and that maybe we should pop along there first, and if they weren't to her taste we could always go back the funeral director that the family has always used. Iris was happy to go along with that. And what a good decision that turned out to be. The person that dealt with making the funeral arrangements was a young lady called Debbie, and the way she handled Iris was amazing. But the thing that made Iris want these people to carry out Alf's funeral was the motto of this funeral home. 'Whatever the question, the answer is yes'. And they were true to their word. Every request that Iris made was granted, nothing was too much trouble. Even to when Alf was laid out in the funeral home. There were flowers surrounding him in the cubicle. They were yellow. Iris mentioned that Alf liked pink flowers and so the next time Iris went to sit with Alf in the funeral home, they had put pink flowers out for him.

Being as we are a catholic family, Iris wanted a Catholic priest to take the service. But no one had been to church in many a year so it was left to Debbie to suggest a Catholic priest who also came from the other side of the water, Plumstead.

Iris and I needed to meet with him to give him the format of the funeral that Iris wanted and the words that were to be said. The priest's name was Father Michael Branch and we arranged to meet him at the Trafalgar Pub in Greenwich. I was expecting a stern looking priest in his middle age. But the person we met was a young 30 something happy go lucky young man with a terrific sense of humour. We ordered some drinks and began going through the service. As I said before, I have assisted in a number of funerals and knew what is required. So before Iris and I went to meet Father Michael we already had our part of the service typed out ready to give to the young priest. Father Michael went over what he would say and the type of prayers he would say and that part of the meeting was more or less over in about twenty minutes. The rest of the hour we spent chatting and surprisingly, laughing our socks off, to the point Iris and I were almost in tears with laughter. Iris couldn't believe how just how much she was laughing, and seemed to feel a bit of guilt. I explained to her it is form of release and relief. However, over the next week and even on the day of the funeral we were still laughing our socks off.

Iris purchased a double grave plot in Pitsea Cemetery in Essex. The family still had ties with the area. The funeral cortege was to leave from my Mum's flat. On the day of the funeral Iris had a mini cab fetch her over to my Mum's flat. And we watched out of the front window as the hearse and one black car came into the forecourt. Barry and Father Michael came and had a quick cup of tea with the three of us, me and Mum and Iris. My Mum took an immediate liking to the young priest, and got his sense of humour straight away. Shortly, we set off from Beckton to Pitsea Cemetery where the rest of the family would be waiting.

We invited Father Michael to ride along with us in the car. Barry conducted the hearse and car out of the complex where Mum lived and he was magnificent in the way he did it. Soon we were speeding along the A13. All four of us were chatting; it was hard to believe we were on our way to a burial. Father Michael I think, had he not been a priest he certainly would have been on the stage in some way shape or form. He told us of one of his favourites chants and then broke into song. It was all in Latin. The young priest closed his eye as he reverently sang. It was lovely. He asked if Iris wanted him to sing it during the service and my Mum piped up. "Yeah, chuck that in." That quip set us all off laughing again. We were all beginning to feel quite guilty for laughing so much, then Father Michael started to sing another chant in Latin, but this time I almost started to laugh, but held it in till he'd finished. I said, 'Do you know Father Mike? I wanted to laugh when you started that one, because I thought you were going to sing this,". Then I started to sing the Boy Scout song 'Ging gang goolie goolie goolie goolie watcha, Ging gang goo, ging gang goo'. That set all four of us off laughing again. Thankfully we started to compose ourselves by the time we got to the cemetery. The service went as good as expected, Father Michael did his chant as promised and when he finished looked in our direction and gave a little wink. Alf was duly laid to rest, and it was pleasant to see so many family members had made the effort to attend.

Iris's twin brother Johnny had his home about ten minutes away so everybody drifted back there for refreshments. I on the other hand had to get back to Beckton for my little dog, Molly. So I rode back with Father Michael. Iris and I often spoke about what a happy/sad day it was and how Alf would have enjoyed it.

After that Iris was lost, she found it difficult to cope. Once I had finished sorting out all the paperwork and give her some idea how she was going to live from then on, it was time for me to go back home to Kent where life went on pretty much as usual. I would ring Iris every few days to see how she was coping and I also went to visit her when I popped up to see my Mum. I had never seen a woman grieve as much as she was grieving.

Chapter 55

I was home in Wateringbury when one lunchtime I got a phone call from my Mum's GP, Dr Goose, she told me that my mother had called for her to come to the flat because she was finding it difficult to breath. Dr Goose told me that she couldn't wait for an ambulance and so had taken my Mum to the hospital in her own car. I wasn't surprised at this as my Mum and Dr Goose had an exceptional relationship, they both genuinely liked each other. So here I was once again packing my bags and taking the dog up to London.

I dropped my bags and the dog at my Mum's flat, called my sister in Lincolnshire and went straight to the hospital. It was decided that they were going to admit my Mum that evening.

The next day my sister arrived and we went to the hospital together. Mum was comfortable and they were going to do a battery of tests on her including x-rays. Finally they told us that they were going to perform a small procedure. They wanted to make a hole in her back and insert a tube into her lung to remove some fluid. As it was a small operation they could do at her bedside. This I wasn't happy about, as we had just learned that there was MRSA on the ward. I told the doctors that I wouldn't allow the operation on that ward. If they wanted to perform the op they would have to move my mother. This they did, and it was a much nicer ward. Aside from the MRSA on the previous ward, the woman in the next bed was an alcoholic and all her drinking buddies would turn up, there would often be as many as six around her bed, they were loud and rude. So it was a good move all round.

It was very tiring being at the hospital practically all day. I would have to come home two or three times to let the dog out for comfort breaks and then it would be right back to the hospital. It was okay when my sister was there as I got a lift, other times I did it by bus back and forth. Also we were preparing meals and flasks of tea for Mum. She didn't much care for hospital food. Who does?

It came time to do the procedure, it was late in the evening. There was a senior doctor and two 'learners', a young man and young woman. The senior doctor was going to oversee the young lady doing the procedure. They came breezing in and immediately told me and my sister to leave and swished the curtains around the bed. I noticed the young man was making some preparations to my mum, however I had not seen him either wash his hands or use any of the antibacterial gel. I pointed this out to him; he said he hadn't started yet. I told him when you do make sure you clean yourself up.

I kept a constant eye on the comings and goings of these three people and when they were all out of sight behind the curtain, I would pop my head through to keep an eye on them all. They gave my Mum an injection, which once it took affect gave the impression my Mum was drunk. They placed her with her legs dangling over the side of the bed, and laid a pillow across a table for her to lean on, but I noticed she kept slipping, and I pointed this out to them. The doctor asked me if I wanted to come in and hold her. I told him, "Yes I would."

The young girl got a sterile package out and proceeded to cut a small hole in my Mum's back, after which a tube was to be inserted. This was proving difficult for her. All the time my Mum was chatting away. At one point she looked up and me and said, "I love you Pat." And I said to her, "I love you too Mum."

I know these doctors have to learn their trade and they have to learn on people such as my Mum. But after quite some time, the sedative was beginning to wear off and I noticed my mum was flinching, so she was obviously beginning to feel pain and discomfort. I told the senior doctor, I'm gonna let your girl have one more go and if she doesn't do it, then I want you to take over and finish the procedure. That must have gee'd the young lady up as she did complete the procedure. A tube was inserted and it had a tap on it and then the tube continued into a large bottle. They said it would soon fill up with fluid. After making Mum comfortable me and my sister left.

About 7.30 a.m. the next morning Mum called me on her mobile. I asked how she was and she was quite upset, as she had hardly had any sleep because her back was leaking. It had soaked all the bedclothes and her nightgown and she was now sitting in the chair beside the bed. Right away my sister and me got washed and dressed and armed with a clean nightie and knickers, and a fresh flask of tea, we made our way back to the hospital. I fully expected them to bar us from entering the ward at such an early hour. Not that it would have made a difference to me I was going to sort my Mum out regardless.

We took my Mum and got her washed up and dressed. I got the nurse to put a clean dressing on the wound in her back then we put her in a clean nightie and a warm house coat, gave her a cup of tea and then I went in search of the nurses who should have sorted all this out. I gave them all a good tongue lashing and told them I want my Mum's bed changed immediately and get me a doctor down here right away as the bottle that should have had fluid in it was completely empty. They did as I asked, except for getting the doctor as she was on her rounds and I would have to wait. Finally, a couple of hours later, the woman doctor breezed in with a load of students in tow. They did a quick chat and an assessment and were about to move on, when I stopped the doctor and told her that my mum had had a procedure that should have released fluid into a bottle but the bottle was empty and Mum had been soaked all night in a wet bed and nightie. She tried to palm me off with some explanation that sometimes it took a while for the liquid to come through. I came right back at her, the liquid was coming through but not through the tube as it should. Someone needs to take another look at this situation. I was told the doctor and student that did the procedure would be sent down to check. Another hour went by and finally they turned up. They were also going to palm me off with an excuse. To which I replied take the tube out because it is not doing what it is supposed to do. The senior doctor had another look. He made a slight twist on the tap on the tube, and out flowed the fluid like Niagara Falls. That was all it was, they forgot to turn the tap on. I understand now how these elderly people who have no one to fight for them get neglected in these hospitals.

My sister and I started to suspect something was wrong when certain individuals started turning up at Mum's bedside to make themselves known to us. We were finally called into a room to see a doctor. And our hearts sunk. It was the same man that diagnosed my Dad with lung cancer. He was now telling my sister and me that Mum also had it. We asked about her future, and we were told her future wouldn't go beyond three months.

Impossible. Mum was bright and perky, she had been in good physical condition apart from her legs aching when she walked to the supermarket. Getting her a mobility scooter had solved this. No, he'd got it wrong this time. I could see Mum being here a lot longer than the three months he'd given her. Mum had always been a very astute woman and she knew when we came out what was coming though we couldn't actually say it to her. My sister Liz's eldest daughter, Jane, was pregnant with her second child and due in March, this was November. Mum just looked at our faces and said, "Will I be here when the baby is born." We said, "Yes." What else could we say?

I kept in touch with all our family and friends by email and informed them of the news and after that gave them regular updates on Mum's condition.

When Mum came home it was clear that her breathing was not what it should be, but we decided that she would get on her scooter and we would go to the park where she could start to walk to see if we could get the strength back into her lungs. We measured her progress by lampposts. On the first day she could only walk from one lamp post to the next. Over the course of ten days she could walk five lamp posts so she was making progress. The weather was against us though. Being wintertime we couldn't always get out and so all her efforts started to be for nothing.

Mum was asked if she wanted to go on a trial for a cancer drug. It was one of those where she could actually get the drug or it could be a placebo. It was worth taking a chance. My sister would come down from Lincolnshire to take us all to St Bartholomew's (St Bart's) Hospital in the City of London, for her check and to collect the prescriptions each time.

Mum was going to need someone with her constantly now. There had been some acrimony between my sister and me as to which one of us would care for our Mum. My sister lived in Lincolnshire and had a husband and a job as well as a daughter living close by with a daughter of her own. She had another daughter that worked away from home. I on the other hand had no ties whatsoever. My sister thought that I was taking over everything and leaving her out. But try as I might I couldn't make her understand that I was not trying to take things over. I just thought it was the most practical solution.

After several bad arguments my sister's youngest daughter came up with the idea of each of us doing a week each. I agreed to this with some reservations. Having seen how my father's illness had taken hold, I learned quickly that routine was the order of the day, along with discipline, and we must pay particular attention to medicines and timings. I'm not saying my sister couldn't do this. But I knew that as we passed over to each other at the end of each week we would have to have the correct information for each other to carry on caring for our Mum.

I did the first two weeks as my sister had a prior arrangement to take her granddaughter on a day out. So I had those two weeks to set the routine. Certain pills had to be taken at certain times. Some pills couldn't be taken with other pills. Some pills were reduced and others increased. This all had to be written down. And so it went on. Then came the time for my sister to take over. I came home and left her to it.

It was soon realised by my Mum and my sister that it would probably be the best option to have just one person doing the caring. My sister agreed later that she was a lot softer with our Mum, when a more rigid approach was required. So I came back to London to take over fully the care of our Mum. It was the right decision. This enabled my sister to carry on working and helping out with her daughter and grandchild and allowed her to come to London to visit without upsetting her own family life too much.

Mum started to show the same signs of decline and poorer health over roughly the same period of time as our dad did. I felt really sorry for my Mum. With our Dad, what was happened to him through his last three months was new to him and new to me and of the rest of the family. None of us knew what to expect or what would happen next. Now with Mum, the identical things started to happen to her so she could measure her own decline against that of my Dad. Getting out of a chair for example became difficult through lack of strength. When this happened to Dad, I would put my arms around him and ask him to start rocking back and forth one, two, three, then a big push from him and big pull from me got him into a standing position. This began to happen with Mum, though we didn't mention it to each other. I believe she was aware of these same things happening to her at the same time they happened to my Dad.

Christmas was very poignant, knowing it would be her last. But we made the most of it. We had many visitors, and lots of presents, and we had our own version of a Christmas dinner. A chicken leg, roast potatoes, peas, Yorkshire pudding parsnips and brussel sprouts. In Mum's case it just about filled a large tea plate. She was beginning to lose her appetite.

As a family we had never been afraid to talk about death. And Mum decided she wanted to arrange her own funeral. She

317

said could you do the same for me as you did for Daddy. We told her we could but we would make it more feminine. I showed her some pretty white wicker caskets, which she liked and chose the interior to be blue. She chose her own music. Which was '*Amazing Grace*', '*Danny Boy*', because this was her own mother's favourite tune. Lastly because she always did a take off of Tina Turner we chose '*Simply the Best*'. She also asked if she could be buried in a turquoise nightie and the bed jacket that Liz had bought for her at Christmas. We told her we would do that for her. It seemed so strange discussing our Mum's funeral with her and knowing that it would be just a couple of months away. When I was alone, thinking about this conversation later that evening, I had a lump in my throat and tears stinging my eyes, knowing that this was truly the end for her.

Having said that, during her illness there were times that she would be a bit belligerent and not want to take a pill or not want any food, or wouldn't take a meal replacement, I would find myself arguing with her. I would have to stop myself quickly and remember that there is no point to this, why it is I am arguing with a dying woman?

We had the Macmillan nurses come in from St Joseph's hospice. They were very helpful. They asked Mum if she wanted to go into their hospice, but Mum was able to say that she was being well cared for and wanted to remain at home. Mum's lovely Dr Goose was also there to support us. After that it became a routine for Dr Goose to pop in every day to see how Mum was doing and just visit as a friend.

We needed quite a bit of help from Social Services. Mum had started to develop bedsores and so they gave us an airbed that did a ripple motion. This helped enormously. We also got a backrest that could be electronically raised and lowered. This was a great piece of equipment. Mum could raise herself up or down as she wished, just like they do in the hospital.

Mum used to wear a little blue knitted hat when she went shopping and she had asked me a few times to wash it knowing that it would reduce in size. Constant wear had stretched it a bit. Finally I did wash it and dried it and put it on her head, and she said it now fitted perfectly. At the same time Cilla Black was on the radio singing '*Anyone who had a Heart*', one of Mum's favourite songs. I brought the radio into the bedroom and she began singing along. I noticed that she couldn't get her breath properly to sing and at some point she lapsed into unconsciousness for a minute or so, then she came back to again and carried on singing. I was so choked up to see that happen, but I had to hide my feelings and emotions from her. Still she was happy about her hat.

Then came further decline in her health, first they put the catheter in. Then they started Mum on the morphine; she wore the canula for oxygen constantly by now to help her breath. Then mum became unconscious and we were told the end would probably come within hours. But it didn't, Mum was still fighting on. In fact she fought on for two more days. My sister and I made a rota to sit with her through the night and we changed over every four hours, to give the other one a rest. They were long nights I can tell you. Mum's friend Pat came and gave both Liz and me a rest, by sitting by her bedside.

Mid-morning on the 13 February 2008 Dr Goose came as usual with the district nurse. The nurse was doing all her usual checks, but I noticed that there was a change in Mum's breathing. Then I knew that the end really was close. My sister was in the kitchen and I told her to come as Mum looked like she was going to leave us. I noticed a tear in the corner of Mum's eye and went and got a tissue and caught it. I pushed my arms under my Mum and cuddled her, and whispered in her ear to go and find Dad, now you can let go. Then I told my sister to have a cuddle too and she whispered that Mum should go now. And so Mum took her last breath. It was so peaceful, so sad.

The next thing that happened was that Dr Goose, the district nurse, my sister and myself stood and held hands in a circle and we were all crying. What a beautiful ending.

The Funeral. We decided to engage Albin's again for Mum's funeral, they knew Mum from when we had them for

Alf's funeral and she had made quite an impression on Barry Dyer, the governor. Later that evening Albin's came and removed our mum.

Three days later they brought Mum home to be laid out in her own front room, Wearing her new turquoise nightie and a new bed jacket identical to the one Liz bought at Christmas. She was laid in her white wicker casket with the blue interior. The florist who occupied premises opposite Albin's funeral home were asked to put a garland of greenery with white flowers around the casket which looked beautiful. Barry Dyer, the governor of Albin's, came himself when they brought Mum home and brought with him a large wooden cross, and two up lights and a lectern with a memorial card that anyone could sign. They made it look so lovely, and we didn't even request these extras. When I mentioned this he said, "Well, it's for Mum isn't it" How kind of him.

Over the next few days many people came to see Mum and pay their respects. I particularly was grateful for this, as I was alone in the flat at this time. Just Mum, me, and the dog. And that's a strange thing; they say how animals sense things. My little dog Molly never ever jumped up on my Mum's chair. She would get on the settee, or on the chair where I normally sat or lie on the bed that I slept in, but never ever on my Mum's chair. Now she was either lying on my Mum's chair or lying underneath the casket. Molly wouldn't move unless I called her to go for her comfort breaks in the garden or I took her for her walks or for her meals. It was the first time I had witnessed such a thing.

Finally the day came for the funeral. Father Michael was going to do the service in the cremation chapel at East London Cemetery. Mum had made such an impression on Fr Mike and he was so pleased to be asked.

I can't praise Albin's enough for the way they conducted Mum's funeral. It was military precision. When all the mourners entered the cars, there were six of them; there was no slamming of one door then another as each car was filled up.

320

No! Once all the mourners were in the cars a nod was given and all the doors were closed simultaneously. How about that?

Further, when we got to the crematorium, something else happened I had never encountered before. Barry Dyer the funeral director stood in front of the mourners and gave his own little speech about my mum. Amazing. Then the service carried on as usual with Fr Mike.

It was a moving service as most funerals are until we came to the end of the service, the last piece of music to be played was '*Simply the Best*' and one by one we all started to clap in time with the music. Mum was a very happy-go-lucky person and this suited her to a T. I looked around and people were smiling, then I caught sight of a person I didn't expect to be there. Dear Dr Goose, she had taken time to come as well. She genuinely liked my mum. It was a perfectly happy ending for my dear mum.